Arab Public Library
20030601

OCT 1 - 1993

53101

346.73 20030601
Cha   Chambers, Carole A.
        Child Support

ARAB PUBLIC LIBRARY

346.7301

CHILD SUPPORT

HOW TO GET WHAT YOUR
CHILD NEEDS AND DESERVES

Carole A. Chambers

SUMMMIT BOOKS
New York   London   Toronto   Sydney   Tokyo   Singapore

SUMMIT BOOKS
Simon & Schuster Building
Rockefeller Center
1230 Avenue of the Americas
New York, New York, 10020

Copyright © 1991 by Carole A. Chambers

All rights reserved
including the right of reproduction
in whole or in part in any form.

SUMMIT BOOKS and colophon are trademarks
of Simon & Schuster Inc.

Designed by Irving Perkins Associates
Manufactured in the United States of America

10 9 8 7 6 5 4 3 2 1

Library of Congress Cataloging-in-Publication Data

Chambers, Carole A.
   Child support : how to get what your child needs and deserves / Carole A. Chambers.
      p.   cm.
   Includes bibliographical references and index.
   1. Child support—Law and legislation—United States—Popular works.   I. Title.
KF549.Z9C45 1991
346.7301′72—dc20
[347.306172]
                                                91-25708
                                                    CIP

ISBN: 0-671-73449-0

Acknowledgments

MY DEEPEST thanks to my agent, Dan Green; my editor, Robert Asahina; and his assistant, Sarah Bayliss. My appreciation to Robert Spelger for his researching capabilities despite a heavy law school curriculum. Special thanks to the following individuals for their assistance: George Rosato, Richard McCrory, Esq., Gordon H. Lester, U.S. Bureau of the Census; Carol Mentel, L.A. County District Attorneys Office; Representative Linda Lea M. Viken, Malcolm Ellis, Esq., and Roger Rowin, State of Wisconsin Department of Health and Social Services.

*To Robert, James, Sean, Tristina, and Christopher
for all their loving support and encouragement*

Contents

Foreword   13
Introduction   17

PART ONE: *The Preparation*   25

1. The Starting Point   27
2. Taking Inventory   30
3. Your Child's Expenses   37
4. Evaluating Special Needs   50
5. Inflation and the Future   59
6. Insurance   64
7. The Education Trust   69
8. Evaluating Your Spouse   76

PART TWO: *The Proceeding and the Aftermath*   81

9. Selecting an Attorney   83
10. The Attorney-Client Relationship   93
11. Your Day in Court   107
12. Maintaining a Diary   114
13. Post-Hearing Evaluation   119
14. Intimidation and Rationalization   121
15. Visitation   125

PART THREE: *Your Remedies*   131

16. Contempt Proceedings   133
17. Child Support Enforcement Agency   152

18. Parent Locator Service 159
19. Uniform Reciprocal Enforcement of Support Act 160
20. Wage Deduction 165
21. Alternative Collection Devices 172
22. Bankruptcy and Support Enforcement 177

PART FOUR: *In the Future* 189

23. Modification 191
24. Your Self-Esteem 198

APPENDIXES

A. Obtaining Forms and Records 201
B. Child Support Advocacy Groups and State-Funded Groups 203
C. State Child Support Enforcement Offices 211
D. Helpful Studies and Reports 222
E. Forms 224
F. Delaware and Wisconsin Formulas 244

Notes 267
Index 275

"The duty of parents to provide shelter and sustenance to their dependents according to their capability is an obligation which is perhaps the most fundamental and necessitous known to society, both animal and human. It is axiomatic that civilization would be driven to extinction [if the dependent were not cared for]. . . . That the capable support the incapable was a law of nature long before it was a law of man, and until our return to the paradise that was the Garden of Eden, this will continue to be man's burden to bear. . . . [T]he power must abide in the state to compel its able members to support their dependents."

—Judge Richard D. Huttner
New York State Supreme Court

Foreword

SHORT OF THE DEATH of a parent, there are few more devastating events in the life of a child than divorce, the death of a family. Demographers predict that by the end of this century, half of all children under eighteen in the United States will experience divorce in their immediate families. Children frequently experience the emotional pain of separation and tension between their parents in an acutely personal way. But increasingly, emotional stresses are just the beginning. Economic deprivation follows.

Children in intact families can benefit from the attention of two parents devoted to their welfare—which includes dedicating financial resources to the family enterprise. However, an overwhelming number of children of divorce lose not only attention and care but also the dedication of family financial resources to their needs. In her landmark study of the economic impact of divorce on women and children, Lenore Weitzman concludes:

> These economic changes have drastic psychosocial effects on the children of divorce. The sharp decline in mothers' standard of living forces residential moves with resulting changes of schools, teachers, neighbors, and friends. Mothers pressured to earn money have little time and energy to devote to their children just when the children need them most. Moreover, when the discrepancy in standard of living between children and father is great, children feel angry and rejected and are likely to share their mother's feelings of resentment.[1]

This book reveals how a parent contemplating and experiencing divorce can minimize some of these losses. Here, Carole A. Chambers offers the traditional economic "victims" of divorce—women and their children—the information, step-by-step instructions, and valuable tools needed to prevent financial and emotional victimization. This book is about taking charge of the painful process: understanding the risks for children and being assertive in protecting their interests. It recognizes the emotional disabilities common to divorce and offers reasonable responses to the often disorienting, demoralizing encounters that accompany the divorce process.

Many people experience the legal system for the first time when their families are coming apart. This books explains how the legal process for determining child support awards works. The sections on electing an attorney, preparing for court, evaluating one's spouse, and assessing expenses are pragmatic, de-mystifying, and extremely helpful.

In my thirteen years as a trial and appellate judge, nothing has distressed me more than observing the "shell shock" experienced by divorce litigants who are entirely unprepared for the economic fallout from the divorce process. The historic inadequacy of child support awards and enforcement, leading to record numbers of American children growing up in poverty, is a national disgrace. New federally mandated support guidelines and increased efforts to educate the state judiciaries about the problem are beginning to have an impact. These efforts are supported by such organizations as the National Association of Women Judges, of which I was president. Individual women, however, cannot afford to wait passively for the system to reform itself to protect them. My experience convinces me that women must learn how to use the system to protect themselves.

I would like to make this guide mandatory reading for every mother—and father—in the dissolution process. In fact, it should be required reading for many divorce lawyers I know. A surprising number of divorce lawyers don't themselves understand the complexities of documenting and demonstrating the actual costs of child-raising in court. They don't know how to assess the cost of future education requirements commensurate with what children could have expected had the family remained intact. Until more lawyers become more prepared, women can help themselves by reading this book.

This book is also extremely useful for those assessing the economic implication of a decision to divorce. Divorce is of course frequently unavoidable and often absolutely necessary. But no one should divorce without clearly understanding what she will have to do to protect the well-being and future of her children.

Knowledge is power, and the power imparted by these chapters will empower women negotiating the threatening and foreign processes by which we manage divorce and child support in this country. Lenore Weitzman calls for institutional change to "protect women and children for the economic devastations of divorce," and to "follow through on the road to fairness, equity, and equality in the legal process. . . ."[2] Systems change slowly. In the meantime, Carole A. Chambers offers women the means to fight their own battles for fairness and equity in practical, effective ways.

Christine M. Durham
Justice, Utah Supreme Court
Past President, National Association of Women Judges and Women
  Judges' Fund for Justice

Introduction

THIS BOOK addresses all aspects of child support—from structuring the original support agreement through methods for collecting unpaid child support. You may be seriously contemplating a divorce, you may be in the middle of settlement negotiations, or you may be experiencing the problems of collecting support long overdue. Regardless of where you are in the process, this book is for you. There is an abundance of information you should know in order to ensure your own well-being and the well-being of your children. There are agencies that can assist you and attorneys that can help you, but after you have read this book, you will understand that in every case you are the catalyst. For something to happen, *you* must make it happen.

Failure to pay child support is the largest single crime in the United States. Child support defaults exceeded $4 billion annually in 1984. That same year, Congress reviewed Title IV-D of the Social Security Act, the federal program for child support establishment and enforcement, and determined that "obligors were still ignoring support orders in epidemic proportions, and nearly half of all custodial parents did not even have a support order."[1] In a 1984 *Arizona Bar Journal* article, "The Child Support Problem: Credible Threat and Use of Incarceration Works," the Honorable Robert L. Gottsfield wrote that "depending on which source you cite, 75 to 87 percent of all children in single-parent households who are entitled to receive child support receive no support from absent parents."[2]

The federal government has mandated that all states adopt child support guidelines to help remedy this situation. In 1987, however, the aggregate amount of child support due was estimated to be $14.6 billion, and the aggregate child support deficit was estimated at $4.6 billion.[3] For the same year the Census Bureau reported that one-half or more of the custodial mothers with child support awards received partial payments or no payments at all.[4]

Of the many people I have met while preparing this book, not one judge, attorney, or court officer was surprised by these statistics. Contrary to popular belief, most men not making child support payments can afford to pay something. One study found that fathers earning $30,000 to $50,000 a year were just as likely not to pay child support as fathers making less than $10,000 a year and two-thirds of the men involved in the study paid *more in monthly car payments than for child support*.[5] While there may be some consolation in knowing that you are not alone if you fall into the category of a nonreceiver, this knowledge does not help heat your home or put braces on your children's teeth. Inflation continues, and your children don't stop growing until you can afford larger clothing.

Statistics certify that a woman's standard of living typically suffers tremendously from a divorce, and her children are inevitably affected. Whether you are going after big dollars or small amounts, guaranteed child support payments will be an essential ingredient of your family's economic well-being. Your husband may be a CEO capable of paying $3,000 a month or a mailroom employee who can pay $300; whatever the circumstances, your child deserves to be supported in the best manner possible.

Most of you have probably confronted these prospects before now, but many of you might not have been exposed to the legal system before. People who are involved in the legal system on a regular basis—lawyers, judges, employees of child support enforcement agencies—approach matters of a legal nature rationally. As you read this book, you will understand why you must also learn to approach your tasks rationally, not emotionally, in order to be effective. You will learn how to *think* about child support in a practical way, and you will learn why you have to ask for things for your child *now* in order to modify them later. You will learn what is in your power to change and what is not.

Perhaps most important, you'll learn how to bolster yourself emotionally for the long-term process of child support negotiations. Everyone agrees that divorce is a traumatic experience, but not everyone realizes how traumatic the aftermath of divorce can be if you must rely on child support payments that are not being made. Your strength may be diminished just at the time when you need it the most, just as your funds are expended, just when it is time to seek enforcement in the future. But now you must lay the groundwork for the rest of your child's minor years.

At the time of your divorce you may believe that your relationship with your husband is coming to an end, but it is not. It is going through a metamorphosis. What will evolve is a redefinition of your relationship—a reestablishment of terms with your spouse. The true constant in both your lives, however, is your child. As the guardian of your child's future, you have a major responsibility that requires mature and rational thoughts and actions on your part. What you do or fail to do at this time will have a tremendous effect on your future.

The information you'll find in this book applies to all custodial parents, male and female. The fact that I've written with the mother as the custodial parent is not meant to be sexist. There are fathers who are the custodial parents and mothers who fail to make child support payments. As Joseph I. Lieberman points out in *Child Support in America*, the vast majority of custodial parents who are not receiving child support are women.[6] Although the U. S. Census Bureau has not yet prepared a study for 1989, their figures for that year indicate that out of 15.5 million children under eighteen living with a single parent, 13.7 million or 88 percent, lived with their mother. While other sources estimate a higher percentage of female custodial parents, there is no question that the majority of custodial parents are women.

While many legislators and some members of the judiciary are continually looking for ways to improve the enforcement of support orders, the fact that so many fathers fail to pay child support is still an enigma. To quote the Honorable Robert L. Gottsfield: "One of the most disturbing social patterns of the last half of the twentieth century is that large numbers of otherwise law-abiding men do not pay child support *voluntarily*. It is not unfair to single out men because it is estimated that fathers represent 95 percent of the parents who fall behind on child support. More startling, perhaps, is the finding that there is little relationship between income and the father's failure to comply with court-ordered child support."[7]

Regardless of your sex, age, or financial status, preparation is the key to prevailing in any lawsuit. And regardless of your attorney's expertise, you must provide him with a great deal of preliminary information. This preparation will take time. The information you supply will impact on not only the child support award but your property settlement and spousal support award as well. The step-by-step outline I've given for obtaining information about your ex-husband's assets is designed to facilitate this task while maximizing the results of your efforts. In addition to the financial data, there are other areas in this book where divorce and child support issues coincide, such as the chapters on finding an attorney and maintaining a professional attorney-client relationship, evaluating your husband's patterns and assessing his willingness to abide by his agreement or court orders, and becoming familiar with courtroom procedures.

This book is structured in a chronological format: First you are led through the process of obtaining an equitable child support order, and then you learn the various options available for the enforcement or modification of that order. If you are in the initial stage of a divorce, then I strongly urge you to start at the beginning of this book to understand how the process unfolds. On the other hand, perhaps you were divorced some time ago and are attempting to seek *enforcement* of your child support order. The various methods for collection and options available to seek enforcement are contained in Part Three. The following overview is designed to help you locate the information that will assist you in whatever stage you are currently experiencing:

The Starting Point How to take stock of your emotions and prepare yourself psychologically so that you will be able to proceed with your child's best interests in mind. How to avoid the pitfall of making an irreversible mistake for the wrong reason.

Taking Inventory How to prepare the information you must provide your attorney regarding your husband's assets and net worth. This information is crucial to lay the groundwork for your property settlement and/or spousal support as well as child support. How to be your own investigative agent.

Your Child's Expenses This is not the time to underestimate expenses. How to analyze and calculate the actual costs incurred in raising your child. Learning which expenses the courts will con-

Introduction 21

sider and how miscellaneous expenses mount up. These are the figures your attorney and the court will require.

Evaluating Special Needs Focusing on your child: his or her special needs, talents, and education. Learning that you are the only one who can ensure a safe future by preparing *now* because there's a good chance you can't go back later. Understanding the advantages of structuring a child support agreement with your husband *before* going to court.

Inflation and the Future Exploring options that are available to offset the negative impact of inflation. A realistic look at the effects of inflation and what you can expect in the future. How much does it *really* cost to raise a child?

Insurance Making sure that your child's health insurance is covered. How some states are making sure that children's medical expenses are covered. How not to be fooled into believing your husband's life insurance will help support your child in the event of his death.

The Education Trust Providing a way for your child to obtain a college education. A guide to realistic tuition rates based on historic increases. Investment vehicles for you and your husband to explore.

Evaluating Your Spouse Taking a good, hard look at your husband's behavior patterns to assist in strategic planning for enforcement and anticipatory requests from the court. Precautionary measures you may want to put into place before the problems arise.

Selecting an Attorney Exploring the various ways to find a qualified family law attorney. Understanding attorneys' fee structures and billing procedures. What to look for in your first meeting with an attorney and what questions to ask. Making sure that the attorney you meet with will be the one who ultimately represents you. How to switch attorneys in the event you've made a mistake.

The Attorney-Client Relationship Maintaining a professional relationship with your lawyer. What you have the right to expect from the relationship and what you shouldn't tolerate. Finding out if this attorney will still represent you if your husband doesn't make his child support payments. Avoiding the pitfalls, including attorney-client sexual relationships, that can destroy open, professional interaction.

Your Day in Court An overview of courtroom procedure. Avoiding a confrontation with either your husband or his attorney. How to dress appropriately and prepare yourself psychologically. What you can anticipate happening, including emotions you may experience.

Maintaining a Diary How to understand why keeping a diary of payments, events, and information is crucial. How to organize your diary and record child support payment information. Using your diary for enforcement and modification hearings.

Post-hearing Evaluation Evaluating your husband's compliance or noncompliance with the court order. Recognizing the danger signs that signal a need for you to go on the offensive.

Intimidation and Rationalization Exploring the reasoning that some obligors use to justify not making child support payments. What to do if your husband attempts to intimidate you. Why you must avoid confrontations and why you shouldn't be the instigator.

Visitation Understanding the distinction between child support payments and visitation rights. Why it is destructive to your child to deny him the love of his father. Letting your child be a child—not a messenger or vehicle of communication between you and his father.

Contempt Proceedings Examining the procedure for a motion for contempt. Who *really* has the burden of proof and how to obtain it. What results you can expect from the hearing. Determining who is going to represent you at contempt hearings and who pays your attorney's fees.

Child Support Enforcement Agency Understanding the mechanics of this government agency that even has the power to intercept IRS tax refunds due to a payment-evading obligor. What you can expect from the district attorney's office. Services available to all custodial parents—those receiving Aid to Families with Dependent Children assistance as well as nonwelfare recipients.

Parent Locator Service How this service assists in locating your husband if he has left the city or the state.

Uniform Reciprocal Enforcement of Support Act Understanding URESA and how enforcement proceedings can be brought against your ex-husband for nonpayment of support even if he is living in another state. A realistic look at the length of time it may take and the results you can expect.

Wage Deduction Using one of the most powerful enforcement tools to ensure payment of child support. States that allow wage garnishment and income withholding and the states that require this enforcement method be written into the original court order.

Federal Employees Special provisions the government makes for enforcing child support collection from their employees.

Alternative Collection Devices Understanding a debtor's examination. The pros and cons of using a collection agency attorney. Learning how a judgment can become useless if you wait too long. Using your ex-husband's credit rating as leverage.

Bankruptcy and Support Enforcement Ensuring that you will receive child support and spousal support *even* if your ex-husband declares bankruptcy. How the bankruptcy laws protect you if you know what to do. Finding an attorney with the expertise to represent you.

Modification Preparing your case to request an increase in child support payments. Understanding what "a change in circumstances" means. Why the courts expect modification requests. How your husband can potentially obtain a decrease in the amount of child support he was ordered to pay.

Throughout this book you will find samples of forms used in various proceedings in regard to child support. These are provided primarily as examples since court forms vary from state to state. These forms are *not* to be mistaken for the national standard.

I have referred to judges and attorneys as "he" throughout this book. The use of sex-specific language is in no way meant to be sexist. Many of the country's finest attorneys and judges are female—and many (but only 12 percent) of custodial parents are male.

The law is not an absolute science. Throughout this book you will find a generous use of terms such as "generally," "in some jurisdictions," "in some cases," and so forth. If there were simple answers to every question, there would be little need for the number of practicing attorneys throughout the United States (128,000[8] in California alone).

Each state has its own laws (statutes) that govern its jurisdictions, and the decisions within each jurisdiction vary. A 1979 study of child support orders in the Denver district court showed that orders for the support of one child varied from 6 to 33.3 percent of obligors' incomes and that these variances existed even when comparing orders from the same judge.[9] These inconsistencies were attributed partially to the presence of an attorney, the *ability* of the attorney, whether the award was contested or negotiated with the particular judge, and the season of the year. But even after factoring all these considerations, there still seemed to be an unexplained variation in the child support awards.

In reading about cases I have included as examples, please remember that for every case that could be cited *supporting* a particular position, there is most likely another case *opposing* the same position. That is the nature of the law. There are no absolutes.

I have attempted to provide you with all the lessons I learned from my own mistakes as a custodial mother and the knowledge I gained from my own experiences in the system. As you explore the various precautionary measures you can take when structuring your child support requirements prior to divorce and the options and courses of action that are available for enforcement of child support orders, it is my sincere hope that this information will enable you to approach the task with a clear mind and armed with the knowledge that will allow you to succeed. You deserve it . . . and so do your children.

PART ONE
THE PREPARATION

CHAPTER 1

The Starting Point

THE BOOK is organized in a chronological format. It takes you from the process of assembling the necessary data prior to obtaining the services of an attorney to the alternatives for collecting back child support if your spouse fails to fulfill the court-ordered obligations. Before you begin to tackle the job that lies before you, your mind must be clear. This may not be easy to accomplish when you are in the throes of a divorce, but for both your own and your child's sake you must approach the subject of child support rationally, as opposed to emotionally. Child support is a separate issue from spousal support, alimony, or property settlement. The heart of this issue is not your relationship with your spouse but your child's rights and future well-being. In essence you are acting as the guardian of your child and must place the child's needs and requirements first. As your child's guardian it is your responsibility to provide the best life possible through your own means and the means of your spouse.

Experiencing emotions such as guilt, anger, hurt, remorse, and a sense of failure can seriously affect the decision-making process. A wrong decision can be extremely costly. While it would be wonderful if you could wait to approach your legal problems until after your emotions have subsided, in most instances waiting would be unwise and impractical. It is essential that you attain enough self-understanding to avoid making an irreversible error due to your emotional state.

Feeling "responsible" for an impending divorce can bring forth the attitude of not wanting anything from your spouse or just wanting the minimum support and nothing else. You may even resist the advice of your attorney. In this case your emotions may be thinking for you, causing you to make a decision that most likely is not in your child's future best interests. If you are planning to remarry as soon as your divorce is final, you may want to argue that your child's future will be taken care of by you and your new spouse.

This reasoning precludes the possibility, however, that your new marriage may not be successful or that your new spouse may face an economic crisis in the future or may later resent that the noncustodial parent is not contributing sufficiently to the child's welfare. Regardless of the future, the irrefutable fact is that there are two natural parents, and both of you share responsibility for your child.

Wanting to prove that you are independent and totally self-sufficient can also color your judgment. While this desire can psychologically justify the waiving of spousal support, it should not be a factor in any decision regarding child support. As the guardian of your child's future, you must recognize that a minor is not self-reliant and has the legal right to rely on both parents until adulthood; therefore, a decision based on pride fails to meet the criteria of what is in your child's best interests.

The individual who is hoping to save the marriage faces another dilemma: a reluctance to appear too demanding, which might further alienate the spouse's affection. If actions stem from these feelings, then decisions in the area of support may be less than prudent. By not wanting to offend a spouse, you may seriously shortchange a child.

If an individual has been fearful of her spouse throughout the marriage, there is a good chance that this feeling hasn't changed. Unless you can confront it and discuss it with your attorney, you may find yourself unable to "go against" your spouse's demands. Compromising your child's future out of fear can only be detrimental.

You may have spent most of your married life deferring major decisions to your spouse. The fact that you are now divorcing does not necessarily alter the pattern of the relationship. You may find yourself being torn if there is a disagreement over the issues of support. To allow yourself to be influenced on this basis will cloud your judgment.

Feeling hurt and angry can create the desire to obtain a support order for an unrealistic amount. If a spouse winds up obligated to make payments that are beyond reasonable means, chances are that in a short time no child support payments will be made whatsoever. Frequently the noncustodial parent leaves the state and all the parties suffer.

You may not be able to understand yourself thoroughly at this time or even all the elements surrounding your divorce. You may be looking for answers, clues, or reasons to justify your behavior. What you can do as you read this material is attempt to transfer your thoughts about yourself to thoughts about your child's future and recognize that what you will be asking for is for your child who deserves the best life possible.

It may be helpful to bear in mind the following estimates of how much it costs to raise children from birth to their eighteenth birthday: Lawrence Olson, in his 1983 report, *Costs of Children*,[1] estimated in 1982 dollars that a medium-income family will spend $131,277 for one male child over the eighteen-year period, while a high-income family will spend $199,670 over the same time period. In a different study, *Investing in Children*,[2] Thomas J. Espenshade arrived at somewhat lower figures: $106,200 for a medium-income family, estimated in 1981 dollars, and $126,300 for a high-income family. By using the Consumer Price Index Percentage Chart on page 59 you can calculate that an expenditure of $199,670 in 1982 would cost more than $257,634 in 1989.[3] By computing the 6 percent change in the CPI for 1990, the estimate for raising a child from birth to eighteen years of age in a high-income family is $273,092.

You and your spouse will be reestablishing the terms of your relationship after your divorce is final. With the passage of time and your new lives, the intense emotion and stress you may be feeling now will lessen, and eventually a new relationship will evolve. In the future you will have an agreement for the support of your child and a "new relationship" that primarily revolves around your child's well-being. It is essential to remember, therefore, that what you are experiencing emotionally today is temporary. To make a long-lasting, irreversible decision that is based on your present emotional state can ultimately lead to even more emotional and financial turmoil in the years to come.

CHAPTER 2

Taking Inventory

YOU ARE entering a new phase of your life. While the marital relationship you have had with your spouse is ending, your relationship with your child's father will continue for years to come. Once again, the one element of the relationship that must remain constant is what is best for your child. In order to complete successfully the task that lies before you, your mind must be clear. Remind yourself again that this is a time for rational, not emotional, behavior.

The strongest factor determining the amount of child support you will receive is the amount your spouse can afford to pay. This is true if you reach a mutual agreement or if the determination is left to the court in the event you fail to agree. It is extremely important that you record everything you know at this time in the area of finances. It would be nice to proceed on the premise that your husband will be completely aboveboard, opening his entire financial life for review. While this may be true in some situations, unfortunately it is not true in most. It is probably fair to presume that as the stakes increase, there is a greater tendency for a spouse to undervalue assets or omit them entirely from a financial statement. This lack of candor may have nothing whatsoever to do with how much your spouse is psychologically willing to provide for his children. The reality is that any information he divulges regarding his assets and net worth will be taken into consideration in determining the marital settlement, and how much of these assets may be deemed communal in nature will also be determined. Assuming for the time being that he wants to share as little as possible, he will keep his net worth to a minimum.

Every state has adopted a formula or method for calculating minimum child support for families whose income level is below a certain ceiling. When the formula is used, income alone determines the amount of the award. The court takes the child's expense requirement into consideration as the income level increases. In some states, the formula applies even above the income ceiling. If a client can show that the mathematical formula doesn't work in her case, then expenses also play a greater role in determining the amount of the award.

The court is not an investigative agency. It must make its decision based on presented evidence. Your attorney can only provide the court with the information and evidence that he has in his possession. The best source of that information is *you*. It is definitely to your advantage to have as much information as possible in hand during your first consultation with an attorney. This will save both time and money in attorneys' fees. Your first task, therefore, is to take inventory.

If your marriage has been a very open one and you are convinced that nothing could be hidden, then take a notebook and write down everything you know and everything you remember about your finances. How much does your husband earn? Does his job provide for an automatic cost-of-living increase? Is there a bonus or incentive program? Is he on a payroll savings plan? Does he participate in an employee stock participation program? Does his company provide any fringe benefits? Does he drive a company car or does the firm absorb some of his travel expenses? What insurance benefits does the company provide? Prepare a list of the following:

1. jointly held or individual checking accounts
2. jointly held or individual savings accounts
3. life insurance policies
4. IRA account
5. pension plan
6. retirement funds
7. real estate
8. mortgages
9. notes held jointly or individually

10. stocks
11. bonds
12. mutual funds
13. precious metals
14. partnerships
15. personal property
16. outstanding loans
17. monies owed to either or both of you
18. certificates of deposit

In addition you should also obtain copies of all income tax returns filed during the years of your marriage.

Include everything. Do not make any determination as to what may or may not be important at this time. Let your attorney decide if certain information is relevant or irrelevant in determining child support. The following example illustrates the inherent danger that frequently accompanies second-guessing.

Assume your husband obtained a loan five months ago. If you have been thinking in terms of assets and liabilities, you will most likely consider this loan a liability; after all, he now owes the bank the sum that he has borrowed. You may take this line of reasoning one step further and conclude that by considering this loan you will only succeed in hurting your own case because he will be able to argue that he has less money available to pay the amount of child support you require. While this is a logical progression of thought, it fails to take an essential aspect into consideration: In order to obtain this five-month-old loan, there is a strong likelihood your husband had to pledge some collateral (asset) as security for the loan. The bank records of loans taken, which include a list of these assets, are a valuable source of information. The existence of that asset is undoubtedly of importance to you and your attorney.

By preparing all this information prior to seeing your attorney, you are providing yourself with an organized format from which to think and reconstruct the total financial picture. In addition you will be saving time for your attorney, and this could result in saving money for you or your husband, depending on who will ultimately be responsible for your attorney's fees. You will be able to communicate knowledgeably about the finances, which may have a direct effect on your relationship with your attorney. You will spare yourself the ordeal of having to recall periods of your married life and the pain that often accompanies that recollection. Most important, the preparation may result in a larger child support award. While child support is generally based on income, in the case of the individual who purposely keeps his income to a minimum but has extensive holdings, the amount of the child support order should obviously be based on assets and income. You must also bear in mind that there are many sources of potential income outside of a salary.

Yours may have been a marriage in which anything of a financial nature fell into the realm of the "husband's territory." This situation existed in the case of one of my friends who had never even written checks before her husband's death. She had credit cards, charge accounts, and cash but no concept whatsoever of how much they were worth. They had a wonderful marriage, but one day she confided to me that the only thing she felt angry about was that throughout the many years of her marriage she had always felt guilty about buying even a blouse for herself, even though her husband had always encouraged her to go shopping. She never knew what they could afford and was shocked to discover the multimillion-dollar value of the estate left to her and her son when he passed away.

Clearly, if you have never been involved in family financial matters, there is work to do. You are now in a position where you have to become knowledgeable . . . and fast. At first this may appear an impossible task, but it isn't. Write down everything you *do* know. Try to recall anything that was ever mentioned of a business nature. Check through your old diaries for a possible notation of signing documents. Isolated incidents over a period of years may hardly seem noteworthy, but they take on a new significance when put all together. Even if you can't remember when you signed a document, for instance, if it has been recorded, your attorney will be able to obtain the information through a search. If your husband buys securities and you know the name of the brokerage firm he uses and any firms he has used in the past, your attorney will be able to obtain copies of transactions should he determine that will be useful in your case. You should also prepare a list of the names of the attorneys, accountants, and business associates your husband has used during the course of your marriage. Again, copies of your tax returns are extremely important. Do the best you can and don't consider anything you recall unimportant. While assets *can* be hidden from discovery, a sophisticated attorney can flush out a lot of information when motivated. Your determination can make a difference in providing this motivation and affect the ultimate outcome of your case.

There is the possibility that your husband will attempt to persuade you *not* to seek the advice of an attorney, suggesting that the two of you can work out everything together. Depending on your emotional state, you may want to agree with his suggestion—especially if you are hoping that the marriage can be saved or that you can still remain close after the divorce—and he may have the noblest of intentions. This may be the first time you haven't done what he asked of you, but *don't*. If what he is offering is fair, your attorney will recognize it. And if it isn't fair, he will recognize that too. *Always seek the advice of an independent attorney.*

In recording your information, include details on solely owned property (what was owned separately by either of you before your marriage and that has been kept separate throughout your marriage), community property or property that is communal in nature (property in which you both share an interest or may have a vested interest), and any expectancy in property (what he may inherit one day). Do not omit anything, even if you feel that certain information has nothing to do with your divorce; you may be wrong. For example, if you know that your husband's grandmother is going to leave her house to your husband when she dies, you might make the assumption that since you have no interest in this property, there is no reason to make a note of it. But if five years from now your husband owes you a substantial amount of back child support, his grandmother has died, and you can't locate him, that "unimportant information" may be the deciding factor in the success of your collection efforts. Facts that are very vivid in your mind today can become obscured with the passage of time, even to the point of forgetting whether a house is located in Michigan or Minnesota.

All public records of documents are kept at the county recorder's office in the county where the matter occurred. If you want to research recorded documents prior to consulting an attorney, this is the starting place, and you will probably find the personnel who staff these offices very helpful. You will be searching for deeds, conveyances, mortgages, liens, assignments, judgments, notices of default, and any other documents that have been recorded in favor of or against your husband. Be aware that others can have the same name, and what you find may not belong to your husband. In attempting to verify the identity of the party you are searching for, look at the following: signature line, date of the document, and the party's address. Be sure to obtain certified copies of any documents in your husband's name. If you are not certain about the identity, obtain a copy so that your attorney can make the determination.

The tax rolls provide a list of all real property (real estate) within the county and their respective owners. These records are generally kept in the county tax assessor's office and are also open for public inspection. If you believe that your husband owns property out of the county in which you reside, then your attorney can arrange for a search in that area. Even professionals can miss an item during a search, so it is essential to proceed with extreme diligence if you decide to conduct your own search.

Corporate records are maintained by the Secretary of State where the incorporation took place. Information such as names of officers and directors of a corporation are in the public record. A search can be made to see if your spouse is an officer or director of any corporation within the state.

The chances of your being able to generate any information from your husband's close friends or associates are probably slim. You should make their identities known to your attorney, however, and remember that when you are speaking with someone who has a close relationship with your husband, anything you say may very well be repeated. Think before you speak.

Any files you have in the house that might have a bearing on your financial picture become part of your documentation. Always retain the originals yourself and give photocopies to your attorney. Include bank statements if they reflect larger deposits than your husband's reported earnings. Know the license number of his car, his driver's license number, the name of the leasing company if the automobile is leased, or the name of the bank if there is a loan on the vehicle. As you compile this information and documentation, your emphasis must be on thoroughness and detail. Record your husband's Social Security number, credit card numbers, bank account numbers, and the branch locations. If real property is involved, record the parcel number as well as the property location.

If your husband maintains an account with a brokerage firm, record the name of the firm, his account executive (broker), and the account number. If your husband receives a paycheck or steady income from an outside source, record the name and address of the payer, the name of the bank, the account number, and the check's point of origin. Additional sources of income may include gifts, dividend checks, notice of reinvestment of dividends, interest checks, money market statements, and distributions of stock. The information that is accessible to you today might become very difficult for you to obtain in the near future.

Once your records are complete, you are ready to move on to the second phase of preparation before you meet with an attorney.

CHAPTER 3

Your Child's Expenses

YOUR ATTORNEY will attempt to reach an agreement with your husband's attorney over the terms of your divorce and child support. The more comprehensive this agreement and the more factors it takes into consideration, the fewer problems you will contend with in the future.

During the first conference with your attorney, he will most likely hand you a financial declaration form to complete. This form will ultimately be filed with the court and have a strong bearing on your case. Your husband will also be required to file a declaration, and he will have an opportunity to review yours just as you will review his. The form consists of an income and expense statement. Although the format may vary to some degree from one jurisdiction to another, the same basic information is requested throughout the country. It must be prepared carefully and accurately. This financial information should not be hastily prepared while sitting in an attorney's office, although many attorneys expect this of their clients. Completing this paper work prior to your initial meeting with an attorney will save valuable time, and you will avoid placing yourself under unnecessary pressure.

The first part of the form relates to your gross monthly income. You must include income that you receive from any source: salary, wages, pensions, Social Security, retirement, disability and unemployment insurance, public assistance, such as welfare or Aid to Families with Dependent Children (AFDC), child support from a previous marriage, dividends and interests, rents, residuals, royalties, and so on, and contributions to your household expenses

38 CHILD SUPPORT

ATTORNEY OR PARTY WITHOUT ATTORNEY (Name and Address):
John R. MacMillan, Esquire
8500 Wilshire Blvd., Suite 400
Beverly Hills, CA 90212
TELEPHONE NO.: (213) 276-7633

ATTORNEY FOR (Name): Ann Garland, Petitioner

SUPERIOR COURT OF CALIFORNIA, COUNTY OF
STREET ADDRESS: 111 N. Hill Street
MAILING ADDRESS:
CITY AND ZIP CODE: Los Angeles, CA 90012
BRANCH NAME: Central Branch
PETITIONER/PLAINTIFF: Ann Garland
RESPONDENT/DEFENDANT: James Garland

INCOME AND EXPENSE DECLARATION

CASE NUMBER: D 91443

Step 1 Attachments to this summary
a. [X] I have attached completed Income Information and Expense Information forms.
   You must complete and attach the Expense Information form and Income Information form unless b is checked.
b. [ ] My only income is AFDC, so I have attached an Expense Information form only.

Step 2 Answer all questions that apply to you
1. Are you receiving or have you applied for or do you intend to apply for welfare or AFDC?
   [ ] Receiving [ ] Applied for [ ] Intend to apply for [X] No.
2. What is your date of birth (month/day/year)? 3/26/63
3. What is your occupation? Media Consultant
4. Mark the highest year of education completed: Primary 1 2 3 4 5 6 7 8 High School 9 10 11 12 College 13 14 15 ● Postgraduate 17 18 19 20
5. Are you presently employed? [ ] Yes [X] No
   a. If yes: (1) Where do you work? (name and address): _____
      (2) When did you start work there (month/year)? ....
   b. If no: (1) When did you last work (month/year)? 12/86
      (2) What were your gross monthly earnings? 2400
6. What is your social security number? 546-19-2721
7. What is the total number of minor children you are legally obligated to support? 2

Step 3 Monthly income information
8. Net monthly disposable income (from line 13 of Income Information): $17
9. Current net monthly disposable income (if different from line 8, explain below or on Attachment 9): $17

Step 4 Deductions and adjustments
10. [ ] Hardship deductions are requested in the total amount of (item 21 of Expense Information): $ -0-
11. [ ] Child support should be adjusted because of shared custody (item 22 of Expense Information).

Step 5 Expense information
12. Total monthly expenses from line 17 of Expense Information: $2980
13. Amount of these expenses paid by others: .... $ -0-

Step 6 Other party's income
14. My estimate of the other party's gross monthly income is: [ ] unknown $4800

Step 7 Date and sign this form
I declare under penalty of perjury under the laws of the State of California that the foregoing and the attached information forms are true and correct.
Date:

ANN GARLAND
(TYPE OR PRINT NAME OF DECLARANT)

▶ Ann Garland
(SIGNATURE OF DECLARANT)
[X] Petitioner [ ] Respondent

Form Adopted by Rule 1285.50
Judicial Council of California
1285.50 (Rev. January 1, 1986)   **1285.50**

INCOME AND EXPENSE DECLARATION
(Family Law)

761101 — RD041 — 1/86
Civil Code, § 472

Your Child's Expenses 39

PETITIONER/PLAINTIFF: Ann Garland	CASE NUMBER:
RESPONDENT/DEFENDANT: James Garland	D 91443
INCOME INFORMATION OF (name): Ann Garland, Petitioner	

Step 1 Figure your total gross annual income
If your income is irregular, show the total for the past 12 months and indicate that your income is irregular

1. Total gross salary or wages, including commissions, bonuses, and overtime paid during last 12 months: .... 1. $ -0-
2. All other money received during last 12 months **except welfare, AFDC, spousal support from this marriage, or any child support.** *Specify sources below:*
   Include pensions, social security, disability, unemployment, military basic allowance for quarters (BAQ), spousal support from a different marriage, dividends, interest or royalty, trust income, and annuities.
   Include income from a business and rental properties.
   Prepare and attach a schedule showing gross receipts less cash expenses for each business or rental property.

   _____Interest_____ 2a. $ 204
   _____ 2b. $ _____
   _____ 2c. $ _____
   _____ 2d. $ _____
3. Add lines 1 through 2d .... 3. $ 204

Step 2 Gross monthly income

4. Divide the amount on line 3 by 12 months, **total gross monthly income** 4. $ 17

Step 3 Figure the deductions from income each month

5. State income tax withheld: .... 5. $ -0-
6. Federal income tax withheld: .... 6. $ -0-
   a. Number of exemptions claimed on W-4 form: _____
   b. Number of exemptions claimed on last federal income tax return: _____
7. FICA (Social Security) or self employment tax or an amount not greater for persons not subject to FICA, if the amount is used to secure retirement or disability benefits: 7. $ -0-
8. Health insurance: .... 8. $ -0-
8a. State disability insurance: .... 8a. $ -0-
9. Mandatory union dues: .... 9. $ -0-
10. Mandatory retirement and pension fund contributions: ...... 10. $ -0-
    Do not include any deduction claimed in item 7.
11. Court ordered child or spousal support **actually being paid for a relationship** *other* than that involved in this proceeding: .... 11. $ -0-
12. Add lines 5 through 11   **total monthly deductions** 12. $ 17

Step 4 Net income

13. Subtract line 12 from line 4   **net monthly disposable income** 13. $ 17

Step 5 Other income and deduction information

14a. Current gross monthly salary or wages: .... 14a. $ -0-
14b. Current gross monthly *other* income: .... 14b. $ 17
15. AFDC, welfare, spousal support from this marriage, and child support from other relationships received each month: .... 15. $ -0-
16. Monthly costs of child care to permit your work or education: ...... 16. $ -0-

Step 6 Other property ow...

17. Cash and checking accounts: .... 17. $ 650
18. Savings, credit union, certificates of deposit, and money market accounts: .... 18. $ 2960
19. Stocks, bonds, and other liquid assets: .... 19. $ -0-
20. All other property, real or personal *(specify below)*: .... 20. $ 8500
    Automobile - Ford Taurus (1989)

Form Adopted by Rule 1285.50a
Judicial Council of California
Revised January 1, 1986

1285.50A

INCOME INFORMATION   761119 – RD086 – 1-86
(Family Law)

Page two of four
Civil Code, § 4721

from any other source. By adding the entries that you have made in this column, you will arrive at your total gross monthly income. If you have no source of income, then you will enter zero as your total.

The second part of the form consists of deductions from your gross income. Allowable deductions include payments for income tax, Social Security, unemployment insurance, medical or other insurance, union or other dues, retirement or pension plan contributions, and any other bona fide expense directly related to your earned income. By subtracting your monthly itemized deductions from your gross monthly income, you have the net monthly income amount. This figure will show the court how much you have at your disposal to provide for the welfare of yourself and your children.

The third part of the financial declaration is the one that requires the most thought and preparation. This section outlines your monthly expenses, which will indicate to the court the amount of support you require for your children. The monthly expenses are listed on page three of sample form 1285.50. Before you can compute your monthly expenses, you will need your check records and any cash payment receipts that you have available for the last twelve months. You can use the sample form in the appendix as a worksheet, simply filling in the totals as you arrive at them.

Rent This is the amount you are currently paying to your landlord with the following exceptions: If you are planning to move and have signed a lease for your new apartment, then you should enter the amount of your new lease. If your landlord has informed you of a rent increase that will be going into effect shortly, then enter the new amount. Be sure to inform your attorney that you have made this adjustment. The fact that you may be contemplating a move or that your husband has been encouraging you to move to a less expensive apartment has no bearing on this matter.

Mortgage payments This is the amount you pay for the mortgage or mortgages on your residence. This does not include any other mortgages or any other real property that you may own. Enter the amount of the payment or the total payments if you have a first and a second mortgage. If you have an impound account whereby your monthly payment includes taxes and insurance, then you must ascertain how much of the payment applies toward the mort-

Your Child's Expenses 41

PETITIONER/PLAINTIFF:	Ann Garland	CASE NUMBER:
RESPONDENT/DEFENDANT:	James Garland	D 91443
EXPENSE INFORMATION OF (name):	Ann Garland, Petitioner	

1.
   a. List all persons living in your home **whose expenses are included below** and their income:
   ☐ Continued on Attachment 1a.

	name	age	relationship	gross monthly income
1.	Chris Garland	4	Son	-0-
2.	Meg Garland	1½	Daughter	-0-
3.				
4.				

   b. List all other persons living in your home and their income:
   ☐ Continued on Attachment 1b.
   1.
   2.
   3.

MONTHLY EXPENSES

2. Residence payments
   a. Rent or mortgage .... $ __850__
   b. Taxes & insurance .... $ _____
   c. Maintenance .... $ _____
3. Food at home and household supplies .. $ __433__
4. Food eating out .... $ __107__
5. Utilities .... $ __40__
6. Telephone .... $ __79__
7. Laundry & cleaning .... $ __90__
8. Clothing .... $ __241__
9. Medical & dental .... $ __125__

10. Insurance *(life, accident, etc. Do not include auto, home, or health insurance)* $ _____
11. Child care .... $ __100__
12. Education *(specify):*
    Chris - Pre-School
    ½ Day Session .... $ __235__
13. Entertainment .... $ __151__
14. Transportation & auto expenses
    (insurance, gas, oil, repair) .... $ __167__
15. Installment payments (insert total and itemize below at 18) .... $ __297__
16. Incidentals .... $ __65__
    a. Other *(specify):*
    b. Other *(amount):* .... $ _____
17. **TOTAL MONTHLY EXPENSES** .... $ __2980__

18. ITEMIZATION OF INSTALLMENT PAYMENTS OR OTHER DEBTS ☐ Continued on Attachment 18.

CREDITOR'S NAME	PAYMENT FOR	MONTHLY PAYMENT	BALANCE	DATE LAST PAYMENT MADE
Security Pacific Bank	Automobile Loan	219	4,126	7/1/91
Bullocks Dept. Store	Household	40	429	7/15/91
MasterCard	Miscellaneous	38	385	7/15/91

19. ATTORNEY FEES
    a. I have paid my attorney for fees and costs: $1000 The source of this money was: Savings Acct.
    b. I have incurred to date the following fees and costs: $1000
    c. My arrangement for attorney fees and costs is: $150 per hour + Costs
    d. [X] Attorney fees have been requested.
    I confirm this information and fee arrangement. _John R. MacMillan_
                                                      (SIGNATURE OF ATTORNEY)
    Ann Garland   John R. MacMillan, Esquire
    (SIGNATURE OF DECLARANT)   (TYPE OR PRINT NAME OF ATTORNEY)

1285.50B

Form Adopted by Rule 1285.50b
Judicial Council of California
1285.50b (Rev. January 1, 1986)

(Continued on reverse)

EXPENSE INFORMATION
(Family Law)

42 CHILD SUPPORT

PETITIONER/PLAINTIFF: Ann Garland	CASE NUMBER:
RESPONDENT/DEFENDANT: James Garland	
EXPENSE INFORMATION OF (name): Ann Garland, Petitioner	D 91443

This question must be completed if there are minor children

20. Health insurance for my children ☐ is ☒ is not available through my employer. Monthly cost paid by me for the health insurance for the children only is: $ _____
Do not include the amount paid or payable by your employer or others.

Complete section this if you claim expenses that have caused extreme financial hardship. Enter them here, check item 10 on the Income and Expense Declaration, and enter total on line 10 of that form

21. ☐ The court is requested to allow the deductions identified below, which are justifiable expenses that have caused an extreme financial hardship.

	Amount paid per month	How many months will you need to make these payments

a. ☐ Extraordinary health care expenses *(specify and attach any supporting documents)*:
$ _____   _____

b. ☐ Uninsured catastrophic losses *(specify and attach supporting documents)*:
$ _____   _____

c. ☐ Minimum basic living expenses of dependent minor children from other marriages or relationships *(specify names and ages of these children)*:
$ _____   _____

d. ☐ Other *(specify and attach supporting documents)*:
$ _____   _____

e. Total hardship deductions requested *(add lines a-d)*:
$ __-0-__

Complete this section if there are minor children of this relationship

22. Describe the custody arrangement you have or hope to have with the children.

Child's name   Arrangement

If each parent has physical custody of any of the children 110 days or more, check item 11 on the Income and Expense Declaration.

1285.50b (Rev. January 1, 1986)

EXPENSE INFORMATION
(Family Law)

gage. This is the figure that you use for your calculation. The fact that you may be planning to sell your home or that the house may be part of the settlement agreement is unimportant at this time.

Real property taxes This is the amount of real estate taxes you pay on your residence. If these taxes are paid annually, then divide the amount of this yearly payment by twelve to arrive at the monthly expense and enter this figure on the form.

Real property insurance Locate your insurance policy or call your insurance agent to find out the amount of the annual premium and divide that amount by twelve. If your insurance is impounded but you cannot determine how much of your payment is attributable to insurance, call the bank or whoever holds the mortgage; someone at the mortgage company should be able to break it down for you. Also, depending on where you live, you may be required to maintain more than one type of insurance on your residence. A resident in Ohio might carry only homeowner's insurance, but a Florida resident who lives on the water may be required to carry flood insurance as well.

If you have a mortgage on your property, your lender's insurance department will provide the answers to any questions you may have regarding the requirements in your residential area.

Maintenance This includes the cost of employees plus the cost for labor and materials in maintaining your home. It is easier if you compute these amounts on an annual basis and then divide by twelve to determine monthly expense. Since repairs and improvements are made sporadically, it is easy to underestimate the actual cost of maintaining a residence. If you have a gardening, pool, or pest control service, be sure to include the charges for supplies as well as the basic service cost. If you have a salaried employee, such as a housekeeper, you must add the amount of your employer's contribution to her salary. Once you have completed noting these "fixed expenses," you should go through your check records and receipts for the last twelve months and write down each house-related expenditure, with the exception of household supplies. Include amounts paid to plumbers, electricians, and roofers, and expenditures for appliance repairs and replacement, paint, wallpaper—in essence, everything you have spent in order to keep your home in good condition. After you have added up all these costs, you must take one more factor into consideration: A certain degree of maintenance is required on every house, but not necessarily on a yearly basis; for example, your house may require painting once every five years. Assuming that it costs $2,000 to have the house painted, then you should allocate $400 ($2,000 divided by 5) to your annual expenses for painting. Every house has its own idiosyncrasies, so allow yourself some time to reflect before you do your final computations.

Food and household supplies Include the cost of groceries, cleaning products, and eating out, if this is not listed as a separate expense in your jurisdiction. Add up the checks you have written to the supermarket and to any restaurants. If you're accustomed to cashing checks for more than the amount of the purchase at the market, you must deduct the excess amount. Do you always pay by check or credit card, or do you also use cash? If your answer is the latter, you will have to estimate how much you spend. (I have never been able to get McDonalds to take a check, and if I'm only picking up a few things at the market, I use cash.) If you spend only $20 a week in this fashion, your cash expenditures for the year would exceed $1,000. If your children purchase their lunches at school, be sure to compute that cost also.

Assuming that your husband has lived with you for the past twelve months, the grand total of your expenditures will reflect the cost of feeding all of you and must therefore be adjusted. Let's assume that you have two children and your annual expenditure for food and household supplies equals $6,000. That means that the four of you spent $1,500 per person ($6,000 divided by 4). Since your husband will no longer be part of the household, you must deduct his proportionate share of these costs. But this does not mean that you can simply deduct one quarter of your costs: Your household supplies will continue to run approximately the same, but there will be a decrease in the cost of food. If you base your calculations on the same formula used in determining the AFDC minimum child support, decreasing the family size by one person will result in a fifteen percent cost savings; therefore, the amount of your annual expenditure for food and household supplies will be $6,000 minus $900 ($6,000 x .15), or $5,100. By dividing this figure by twelve you will arrive at your monthly expense, which in this example would be $425.

Utilities Since there is generally a wide variance in utility costs during the year, the most accurate way of approaching this expense area is to collect all your bills or canceled checks for the past year and add them together. By dividing the sum by twelve, you will arrive at your monthly expense.

Telephone Your telephone bill includes an automatic service charge that is payable each month whether or not you ever use your phone. Your long-distance calls and message units, if applicable in the area where you live, are listed separately. If you have been separated for some time, you can average the bills you have received since your husband has not been living with you. On the other hand, if you have been together, you will have to analyze the bills to determine how much of the expense you have incurred. If you use an answering service, include that cost as part of your telephone expense. Some telephone companies charge an initial fee plus an additional monthly fee if a subscriber chooses to have his number unlisted. As a single woman, you may decide this is a wise option.

As with every assessment, the issue is your actual telephone expense, not how much or how little you could spend. Since calling long distance is usually an elective choice, this expense may be subject to attack by your husband. I spoke with one woman from Memphis, Tennessee, who told me that her husband spent no less than two hours on the phone with her one night, arguing about the fact that she had listed her monthly telephone expense at $40. Why, he argued, did she have to telephone her mother long distance twice a month? Ironically, this argument came from a man who earned in excess of $80,000 the previous year.

Laundry and cleaning This expense category is likely to decrease. Take into account that a portion of your cleaning expense has been for your husband's garments. However, if you have recently obtained employment and must maintain a wardrobe for the workplace, your cleaning expense will probably go up.

Clothing If you are in the habit of noting on your checks what each expenditure is for, then determining how much you spent on clothing for yourself and your children will be an easy task. If you have not developed that habit, this may be a good time to start. Believe it or not, you may have to repeat this entire process a few years down the line in the event that either you or your husband seeks a modification of the child support order. The better you become at record keeping now, the easier all future accounting will be. Using your checks, department store receipts, and credit card statements, calculate how much you expended, eliminating those purchases made on your husband's behalf. Remember to include purchases made at athletic stores for outfits or shoes. Don't forget gym clothes and items that were purchased on vacation or with cash. Department store and credit card finance charges should also be included. When you arrive at a total, divide the amount by twelve and enter the monthly figure on the form.

Medical and dental This is the total amount spent for you and your children after any reimbursement by an insurance company. Do not include any monthly amount paid for health insurance under this expense category. Include doctor and dentist visits, hospital expenses, prescriptions, eyeglasses, braces, retainers, crutches, and over-the-counter remedies.

Insurance If you are currently paying for life or accident insurance, enter the amount of the monthly premiums. Do not include any expense that you have already listed under your itemized deductions from gross income.

Child care Include any amount that you expend to have another person care for your children, such as a day-care center, nursery school, after-school program, housekeeper, or baby-sitter. If you are in the process of obtaining work, be sure to investigate these costs now. If you have listed the expense of a housekeeper under maintenance, don't duplicate the cost under child care. Don't be too surprised if your husband takes exception to your retaining a housekeeper now that he is no longer a part of the family unit.

Payment of child/spousal support for prior marriages This applies only to child or spousal support you have been ordered to pay an ex-husband from a prior divorce.

Education If your children attend private school, then you must take the amount of the annual tuition and divide it by twelve. If you are currently making monthly payments to the school, they are most likely based on paying the tuition over a nine- or ten-month period, so that monthly payment would not be an accurate figure for this purpose. Let's assume that the annual tuition is $4,800, and you make monthly payments from September through June of $480. It would be an easy mistake to state your monthly tuition expense at $480. But the *accurate* figure is arrived at by dividing the annual tuition by twelve months for a total of $400 per month. Additional expenses to consider are the cost of books, materials, field trips, enrollment fees, school supplies, and lunch boxes. While the cost of some of these items may seem extremely minimal, they do add up.

If your child has been attending private school for a few years, make a note of the previous years' tuition. Most private schools increase their tuition annually. Tuition increased at one Los Angeles private school from $3,300 for 1980–81 to $8,600 for 1990–91. The following chart illustrating tuition and enrollment trends for a California private school provides the Nominal Tuition (the actual cost per year) and the Real Tuition (cost expressed in current dollars).

Entertainment You may feel uncomfortable about claiming too much in this area and therefore underestimate what you actually spend for your entertainment and that of your children. Merely taking two children to the movies each weekend can add up to over $80 per month. Then there is Disneyland, the circus, ice follies, ballet, museum, zoo, theater, Knotts Berry Farm, Adventure Island, Slip 'n' Slide, or whatever weekend excursions have become a part of your children's lives. Be realistic: Entertainment is a necessary part of everyone's life—particularly children's.

Transportation This is how much you incur for transportation other than the use of your automobile. Include your monthly costs for subways, bus fares, taxi fares and gratuities, and airfares. Bus service to transport your children to and from school should also be included.

Auto expense Combine your expenses for automobile insurance, gas, oil, repairs, and maintenance for the past twelve months. If you have had a fairly trouble-free year but the previous year was a real blockbuster, then average the two years' expenses by adding them together and dividing by twenty-four months. What is important here is that you arrive at an accurate accounting of your auto expense.

In Los Angeles the automobile is used almost exclusively. In averaging my auto expense over the past two years, I learned that I spent $4,622 per year, which breaks down to $385.16 per month.

Auto payments Enter the amount of your monthly payment.

Installment payments Make a list of all creditors paid in installments. This includes Mastercard, Visa, American Express, department store accounts, finance companies, and so forth. Even if your husband's name also appears on the account, list the creditor and the amount of the monthly payment. When you have completed the list, compute your total obligations on a monthly basis and fill in the amount. Since the responsibility for these obligations will most likely be a part of your settlement negotiations, you will be discussing these expenses with your attorney, and he will need to see how you arrived at the amount.

Incidentals This includes everything not yet accounted for, from a new toothbrush to your child's bicycle repairs to your son's favorite magazine to your daughter's blush. Go through your checks. If you shop at a drugstore frequently, those figures may be helpful to you. Incidentals are often purchased with cash. A stop at the music store will remind you that popular tapes are currently priced at $9.95, and CDs are introduced around $15.95. Developing a roll of color film with thirty-six exposures currently costs about $9.00. After some consideration you may be very surprised to learn just how much you spend on "incidentals."

Other List any other expenses you may have that do not fall into any of the previously listed categories. Your child may have a special need—medical, educational, or other. This is explored in the next chapter.

It is interesting to note that in 1983 an Arizona report estimated that the monthly average "no frills" cost of raising a child was $302.[1] This is equivalent to $409.54 in 1991.

Once you have compiled all your figures based on actual expenses, add them together and enter the total on the line that asks for Total Expenses. You should feel confident that you have prepared an accurate accounting for your attorney, your husband's attorney, the court, and yourself. Do not worry if you aren't sure about a few expense categories. Make a note to discuss these with your attorney. If the reality of your divorce hasn't quite registered, this exercise can have an incredibly sobering effect. Take a long bath and relax . . . you deserve it. It should feel good to know that the hardest part of your preparation is over.

CHAPTER 4

Evaluating Special Needs

YOUR CHILD'S health is of paramount importance. Have there been any indications or mention by physicians or the school of eye problems, learning disabilities, speech or hearing problems, or lack of coordination? Has your child's dentist advised you that your child will eventually require oral surgery or orthodontic treatment? The potential for illness always exists with or without warning. A child support agreement often contains a provision whereby the noncustodial parent is responsible for medical and dental costs incurred by the children. In the event that an agreement has not been reached, a court will frequently order that the father be responsible for these costs, assuming that a request has been made to the court by an attorney. Despite the obvious importance of this issue, many support agreements and court orders fail to address the subject at all. If your child has a problem that you are aware of, obtain an estimate for professional treatment and make it available to your attorney.

Although your husband may participate in an employee health program right now, you have no assurance that he will be working for the same employer or have similar benefits next month. You also have no control over whom he lists or doesn't list as his dependents. While you may feel that your spouse would never purposely omit the names of your children, out of vindictiveness or another nonapparent reason, it does happen. One custodial mother obtained her divorce while her husband was a member of the Director's Guild of America. The fact that the children were automatically covered by Blue Cross because of guild membership was brought to her attorney's attention. He sought no additional order from the court, deciding that the union membership provided adequate protection for the children. Problems followed: The first claim under this policy was rejected with the explanation: "nonpayment of dues." Since there was no order directing her husband to pay for the medical expenses, the mother had no recourse. This is a prime example of a foolish error made because of false assumptions. While you may currently have coverage through your own employment that provides adequate protection for you and your children, there is no assurance that this will be available to you in the future. You should discuss this area thoroughly with your attorney.

EDUCATIONAL NEEDS

Perhaps your child attends a private school, in which case the tuition expenses will be reflected in your financial declaration. Perhaps your child is too young for school, and you haven't given the matter serious attention. Or you may have always planned to have your child attend private school during his or her last three years of high school. Whatever your feelings are on the subject of private school education, remember that education is of paramount importance to your child's development, and you should explore your viable options. It is crucial that you and your husband reach an agreement on this subject.

Your own educational background will undoubtedly influence your attitude about private school education. The two most important factors for your child, however, are the quality of public school education in your geographical area and your child's potential. I know a couple living in a large metropolitan city who placed their unborn child's name on a private school's waiting list as soon as the pregnancy was confirmed. Both of them had grown up in small towns where they had a public school education, and neither of them felt that private school, per se, was a better alternative, but they believed that the city's overcrowded classrooms couldn't provide the education they wanted for their child. A child who is brilliant or highly gifted in the arts deserves to be in the best possible learning environment, and a child who has a learning problem deserves to be in a supportive learning environment with skilled teachers.

A formal agreement can include anything that the two of you agree on, and it can be written in any way that clearly defines the intentions of the two parties involved. If your husband agrees to provide the tuition fees for your child's schooling and this becomes part of your executed agreement, then he will be responsible for the tuition. If your husband is unable to commit to paying the entire tuition but agrees to provide half of the amount annually, then your agreement can be written to reflect this. But what happens if he cannot afford to pay all or half of the tuition? Let's assume that he agrees your child should attend a private school if possible, but he does not presently earn enough to provide the funds. Your agreement could include a provision whereby he will provide the funds for the tuition or part of it "if he has the ability to pay." There are many advantages in having this type of provision, which I will explain later in this chapter.

This is the time to examine your child's interests seriously and list them in order of their priority. What are the interests, inclinations, and talents that your child has exhibited? Does he take piano lessons or tennis instruction? Has he been attending a computer camp for a month in the summer? Does your daughter enjoy gymnastics or art? Your husband may be willing to pay for his daughter's piano lessons until she no longer wishes to continue. He may agree to do this on the condition that he pay the piano teacher directly. This is fine. Remember that the child comes first: The most important factor is that your daughter will be able to continue to study music. The noncustodial parent often feels that children don't recognize the support he is providing. Although he may be reluctant to offer the amount needed for extracurricular activities in the form of general support, he may be more than willing to do so if he can provide these benefits in a manner that allows the gesture to be recognized. Commit these intentions to paper, leaving nothing to chance.

COLLEGE

The custodial parent should always attempt to incorporate a provision pertaining to college in the child support agreement. Your child ceases to be a dependent once he reaches majority (the age when he is no longer a minor); in most states the age of majority is eighteen. He or she will be entering college at about the same time that the support order terminates.[1] The exception to this is in the event the child has been incapacitated through illness or an accident. The court then determines that he is dependent due to his incapacity to care for himself. In this instance it is within the court's discretion to order the noncustodial parent to continue making support payments beyond the age of majority. Generally the court no longer retains jurisdiction over the support of a child after he reaches the age of majority, and you are not able to go back to court to obtain any financial assistance from your ex-husband for college expenses. For this reason you should attempt to incorporate a provision pertaining to college in your child support agreement. Your attorney will advise you if the court in your jurisdiction will enter an order providing for higher education expenses.

A college education should no longer be considered a luxury. A report to the California Commission for Economic Development stated that "according to the Census Bureau, the median income of college-educated males in 1986 was $34,390. Those without college degrees earned only $24,701. The gap between the two groups has grown in recent years."[2] The report goes on to note that college expenses have risen faster than family incomes, a fact evidenced by the gigantic increase in Guaranteed Student Loans between the 1975–76 and 1985–86 school years. (The largest federal lending program is the Guaranteed Student Loan program.) The Washington office of the College Board in their study titled "Student Loans: Are They Overburdening a Generation?" found that 922,000 students took out GSL-backed loans in 1975–76, and 3,640,000 students took out loans in 1985–86, nearly a 300 percent increase.

There is no guarantee that your husband's agreement to contribute all or part of your child's college expenses will be enforceable. If your ex-husband refuses to pay for these expenses when your child reaches the age of majority, even though he had formally agreed to do so, the court may rule in his favor. (The question lies within the scope of discretion.) Some decisions have concluded, in essence, that the mere fact a person is attending a university or college does not render him or her a dependent person for the purposes of determining entitlement of child support. Seen from a different vantage point, an adult, whether his parents are married or divorced, cannot require his parents to provide a college education for him.

The Colorado Court of Appeals recognized the importance of a college education in their findings in a 1985 case, *In re Marriage of Plummer*. The *Family Law Quarterly*[3] summarized the court's findings in the following manner:

> Attainment of the age of twenty-one merely creates a presumption of emancipation, which may be overcome by evidence that a child expected a college education which was necessary to achieve his desired career goal, and which would be financed, in part, by his or her parents. Failure of a child over the age of twenty-one to actively pursue his or her college education, however, is sufficient for the court to refuse to order child support for the purpose of pursuing such education. In re Marriage of Thompson, 706 P.2d 428 (Colo. App 1985).

In a 1986 case, *Martin v. Martin*, the Indiana Appeals Court reversed an order denying the petition of a student who maintained a 3.37 average on a 4.0 scale at Northwestern University. The court held that the general support order of $22.50 per week "encompassed" educational expenses and that the order could continue after her twenty-first birthday. The Indiana code provides that although child support ceases once a child reaches the age of twenty-one, "an order for educational needs may continue in effect until further order of the court."[4]

Regardless of whether or not your husband challenges the necessity of his providing for college education at some time in the future, it is to everyone's advantage to confront the issue early and spell out the intent of the parties. If a college education is something you envision for your child, then you should broach this subject with your attorney. An attorney who either specializes in or practices family law should be familiar with the cases that have been heard in your jurisdiction and be able to advise you about your chances of prevailing through a breach of contract suit if an agreement is reached and subsequently challenged by your husband.

Once you have completed listing all the needs and requirements of your child, arrange them in order of priority. An organized list will enable you to evaluate realistically which needs are crucial and which are negotiable. For example:

Kaitlin

Medical insurance
Dental insurance
College
Math tutoring
Piano lessons
Marlborough School—10th Grade
Summer camp
Art class

Mentioned earlier in this chapter was the utilization of the phrase "if he has the ability to pay." This can be added to any of the provisions your husband and you agree on that he cannot afford presently. This becomes meaningful when and if your husband's earnings increase or if he experiences a change of circumstances in which he receives benefits that were not available to him at the time of your divorce.

Assuming you reach an agreement regarding child support, that agreement will be incorporated in a court order when you obtain your divorce. Any part of that court order can be modified (changed) later by the court if there is justifiable cause, *but the court cannot modify a provision that does not exist.* In some jurisdictions, courts will consider a modification request for a matter not previously raised. This often requires the addition of a term that was not previously there. There may also be a distinction if there was a previous waiver. If your original court order does not have a provision for medical expenses, you may be barred from returning to the court three years after your divorce to request an order that your husband be responsible for your child's medical bills. The reasons the issue was not raised when child support was being determined are not important. However, if your child support agreement states that your husband will be responsible for the children's medical expenses if he has the ability to pay, you can return to court to have that provision enforced. This would also apply if, for example, you discover three years after your divorce that your husband is working for a company which provides a comprehensive medical plan for him and his dependents. The court will review the original order, and your attorney will provide the proof that your husband now has the ability to pay. The court may then determine that your husband is responsible for the medical bills or for that portion covered by his insurance. The same principle applies if you are seeking to enforce the provision because his earnings have increased since the date of the original court order.

Returning to Court

Let us assume that your support agreement contains no provision for private school tuition, as opposed to a provision with the phrase "if he has the ability to pay." The time comes when you know your ex-husband's earnings could cover the cost of tuition, and you believe your child would benefit from attending a private school. Your course of action would be to return to court to request a modification upward of your child support award.

A hearing of this nature is far more complex than one seeking the enforcement of a provision because the court must take into consideration your ex-husband's earnings, your earnings, the needs of the children, and the change of circumstances of the individuals involved. The following example illustrates this problem.

Paul and Diane were married for seven years. At the time of their divorce, Paul assured Diane that there was nothing within his power he wouldn't do for Jonas, their four-year-old son. Diane felt that she knew Paul better than anyone and was confident that should the day come when Jonas needed something Paul could provide, he would get it. Although her attorney recommended that these intentions be committed to writing, Diane felt this would be demeaning and might destroy what she was hoping would be a friendly, post-divorce relationship.

Paul remarried, had two children with his new wife, and became moderately successful. Diane also remarried, had another child, and she and her husband own and operate a travel agency. When Jonas turned eleven, the school informed Diane that her son was "exceptional" and recommended that he attend a school for gifted children. After investigating she determined which was the best school and learned that the tuition was $3,000 yearly. She called

Paul; he said he would like to help her out, but he had a big tax bite that year, maybe next time.

If Diane goes to court asking for a modification upward, the court will hear testimony about how much Diane is making, that she has remarried (whether material or not, there is another provider in her life), how much Paul is earning, the amount of his expenses (not only is he remarried but he has two more children to support), the amount of Jonas's expenses, and how essential a private school education is for him. The court must then weigh all these factors before a ruling can be made. But had Paul agreed in writing to pay for Jonas's tuition if he had the ability, then the issue at the hearing would be whether Paul's income, considering his expenses, constitutes an ability to pay.

The circumstances surrounding John and Suzanne's divorce were different. Suzanne retained custody of their two minor children, both preschoolers. She had never contemplated private school for either Beth or Tory. John remarried and had two children with his new wife. Suzanne married a man who had two minor children from a previous marriage. When Tory was in second grade, his teacher recognized a learning disability, and the school recommended that he attend a special school for children with dyslexia and other learning disorders. Suzanne went to work to pay for the school and held back from having another child because of Tory's needs. While Suzanne believed that Tory would soon be able to return to public school and keep up with his peers, that hasn't happened. She is currently earning $11,000 annually and believes that John is grossing $36,000, from which he is already paying child support. In seeking a modification upward, the court must consider Suzanne's earnings as well as John's, plus all the other changes that have occurred in their respective lives. The fact that Suzanne would like to have another child and spend more time with her existing children by not working may not carry much weight at the hearing.

As stated earlier, if a child has an incapacity that extends beyond the statutory age of majority, the courts will frequently extend the time provision for child support. A typical example is the 1985 case, *Jackman v. Jackman,* heard in Utah where it was held that "the courts have the authority and should consider awarding child support after a child has obtained majority if the child has some physical incapacity."[5]

Another example of a state recognizing the need for extended support in special situations is evidenced by the revised statutes in New Hampshire. Effective October 1985, the statutory revision provides that handicapped children may be entitled to support for a period beyond the age of majority.[6]

It is crucial to remember that even though your husband may not have the financial ability now to provide your child with extras, it doesn't mean he won't have the ability in the future, which is unforeseeable and generally fraught with surprises, some good and some not so good. The more potential problems you anticipate now, the greater your chances of prevailing in the future. While the courts generally view a parent's primary responsibility to the first children he has fathered, the needs and requirements of additional children cannot be ignored. Remember, you and your husband probably share mutual aspirations for your child's future. The ideal solution is to put these intentions into writing and incorporate them into your support agreement.

CHAPTER 5

Inflation and the Future

WITHOUT A reliable crystal ball, it is impossible to project the cost of food, shelter, utilities, and clothing for the duration of a child support order. Inflation is a reality. The table[1] below shows the annual rate of inflation for all urban consumers from 1979 to 1989. The 12.5 percent inflation rate for 1980 means that there was a 12.5 percent increase in prices that year. Please note that the categories listed are the most essential tangible needs of your child.

Table 1. **Percent change in Consumer Price Index for All Urban Consumers, by major group, 1979–89**

[12 months ended December]

Category	1980	1981	1982	1983	1984	1985	1986	1987	1988	1989	Average annual change
All items	12.5	8.9	3.8	3.8	3.9	3.8	1.1	4.4	4.4	4.6	5.1
Food and beverages	10.1	4.3	3.2	2.7	3.8	2.8	3.7	3.5	5.1	5.5	4.4
Housing	13.7	10.2	3.6	3.5	4.3	4.3	1.7	3.7	4.0	3.9	5.2
Apparel and upkeep	6.8	3.5	1.6	2.9	2.0	2.8	.9	4.8	4.7	1.0	3.1
Transportation	14.6	10.9	1.8	3.9	3.1	2.6	-5.9	6.1	3.0	4.0	4.3
Medical care	9.9	12.5	11.0	6.4	6.1	6.8	7.7	5.8	6.9	8.5	8.1
Entertainment	9.7	7.2	5.6	4.0	4.2	3.1	3.4	4.0	4.6	5.1	5.1
Other goods and services . .	10.1	9.9	12.1	7.9	6.0	6.3	5.5	6.1	7.0	8.2	7.9

The *Wall Street Journal 'Guide to Understanding Money & Markets'* provided the following chart to illustrate the buying power of the dollar.[2] The projected cost of living for the year 2000 is based on a 16 percent annual rate of inflation, but the costs reflected for 1967 and 1985 are actual.

59

The buying power of a dollar declined dramatically during the inflation-ravaged years of the early 1980s. Inflation seemed to many a way of life that would never end. This chart shows the rise in the cost of living from 1967 (the base year used in calculating the CPI) to 1985. It also shows the projected cost of living in the year 2000, based on a 16% annual inflation rate which, at the time, many considered a realistic estimate.

item	1967	1985	2000
monthly housing expense	$114.00	$678.00	$6,288.0
monthly auto expense	82.00	369.00	3,428.0
loaf of bread	.22	2.02	18.7
coffee (2 lbs)	.49	2.59	24.0
steak (lb)	.98	2.49	23.0
gasoline (gallon)	.23	1.21	11.2
resident college tuition	294.00	1,581.00	14,655.8

It is practically inevitable that the amount you require for support this year will not suffice in years to come.

One solution to this problem is to have your child support payments aligned with the cost-of-living index. In this way the amount you receive for child support will increase along with the cost of living. If this provision is included initially, it will save you the time and expense of returning to court to modify your child support award upward. If your husband's earnings are more than adequate to meet the support requirements or if he has an employment contract that contains an automatic cost-of-living increase allowance, your chances of obtaining his agreement on this issue or having the court grant your request in relation to this issue are obviously greater than if he is presently barely making ends meet.

An alternate approach to aligning the payments with the cost-of-living index is to decide that the support amount will increase in specific increments as your child reaches certain ages. For example, if your son is five years old and you have agreed to $400 per month, this figure could increase to $475 per month after your son's tenth birthday and to $525 per month when he is fifteen.

California now provides an "Appendix A Information Sheet" to help a petitioner calculate a potential increase in spousal or child support when attempting to modify an existing court order. You can begin to understand the true effects of inflation by reviewing the California All Consumer Price Index.

There is another factor that will increase your future expenses:

As a child grows older, his financial needs and requirements become greater. If you have any doubts about this, talk to someone who has a teenager or price a shirt for a three-year-old compared to one in a size sixteen. Your little ones may not yet have heard of Jordache, Calvin Klein, or Polo, but don't count on this for long. One judge in St. Petersburg, Florida, frequently points out the high cost of raising children by relating how he cringes every time one of his teenage sons opens the refrigerator. That children become more expensive as they grow older is a reality you should face at the inception of framing a support agreement.

The following table shows estimates of the cost of raising children from birth to age seventeen. Although these independent studies produced different actual dollar amounts, the pattern of increased expenses is similar. The figures were arrived at by two separate reports written to assist in developing state guidelines for the issuance of child support orders. Turchi's figures are much closer to the 1981 Bureau of Labor Statistics' figures which are based on a budget for specific expenses as opposed to actual family

ESTIMATES OF CHILDREN'S EXPENSES BY AGE[3]

Age of Child	Turchi (1983)	Olson (1983)
	(1981 $)	(1982 $)
0	3,754	7,118
1	3,225	6,216
2	2,812	5,325
3	2,510	4,747
4	2,311	4,437
5	2,210	4,357
6	2,201	4,441
7	2,276	4,645
8	2,431	4,994
9	2,658	5,473
10	2,951	7,870
11	3,305	8,530
12	3,712	9,227
13	4,167	10,519
14	4,663	11,073
15	5,195	11,541
16	5,755	11,882
17	6,338	12,062

ESTIMATED COSTS OF A CHILD BY AGE GROUP[5]
ESTIMATED COSTS AND PERCENT OF TOTAL

Age of Child	Turchi (1983) 1981 $		Espenshade (1984)* 1981 $		Olson (1983) 1982 $		USDA† 1980 $		BLS Urban Family‡ 1981 $	
	Dollars	Percent	Dollars	Percent	Dollars	Percent	Dollars	Percent	Dollars	Percent
0–5	16,882	26.9	21,094	25.6	32,200	24.3	20,285	29.3	9,852	16.1
6–11	15,822	25.3	29,829	36.2	35,953	27.2	22,564	32.6	24,078	39.3
12–17	29,830	47.7	31,477	38.2	64,125	48.5	26,383	38.1	27,360	44.6
0–17	62,474	99.9	82,400	100.00	132,278	100.0	69,232	100.0	61,290	100.0

*One-child household, mother employed part-time, full year.

†Moderate-cost level, north central region.

‡Intermediate budget level.

expenditures. There have been many studies done on the cost of raising children, resulting in considerably varying estimates. It is relatively easy to determine the minimum cost of raising a child on a basic diet that meets minimum nutrition needs. But as the overall household income increases, more is expended on a child. Therefore, the cost will vary according to the socio-economic level of the family.

In "Development of Guidelines for Establishing and Updating Child Support Orders," Robert G. Williams, Ph.D., states that "expenditures on children vary systematically with the age of the children. Below the age of twelve there is disagreement about the pattern of the variation. But for ages twelve and above all studies agree that there is substantial increase in expenditures relative to the level of spending for younger children."[4] The author also included another table estimating the amount spent on different age groups. Note that the dollar amounts are from 1980–1982.

Aligning your support payments with the cost-of-living index will not take your child's specific growth needs and expenses into consideration, but it will provide a buffer. There are two distinct issues: inflation and the fact that children's needs and desires increase as they grow. The cost-of-living index addresses only the easier of these two issues. Your child's growing needs require both thought and conjecture on your part, but they are just as real.

There is also a danger in structuring an automatic increase *based on some future event*. An example of this occurred in a 1985 case heard in South Dakota. In *Fossum v. Fossum*,[6] the court struck down an automatic increase in child support payments that was to go into effect on a particular date when some of the husband's debts would be paid; it found that support should be based on the child's present needs and the obligor's ability to pay.

An agreement which incorporates automatic support increases does not preclude the possibility that the increased amounts will be insufficient for your child's needs. The inclusion of a provision that takes the future into consideration will not bar you from returning to court to seek an additional modification if necessary. Farsightedness may avoid the unpleasantness of a future court appearance without giving up any of your rights or the rights of your child.

CHAPTER 6

Insurance

YOUR CHILDREN'S needs will have to be covered either by you, the noncustodial parent, or jointly. Your husband may agree to assume the responsibility for medical payments for the children by maintaining insurance, in which case you should request a copy of the policy for your records. Complications may arise if he agrees to assume the responsibility but has no insurance. In this case you will either have to pay for your child's medical or dental services when they are rendered and then proceed to obtain reimbursement from your husband or request that the office submit the bill to your husband directly. While some practitioners may be willing to go along with the latter billing procedure, many hospitals, physicians, and dentists require the bill to be paid at the time of the visit or the responsible party to sign a medical form or questionnaire establishing financial responsibility. It is generally unimportant to the practitioner who bears the responsibility according to your support agreement and court order. If the doctor agrees to bill your husband directly, your hope will be that he pays promptly lest you find yourself in an uncomfortable situation during your next visit. This may also create the necessity of communicating with your husband more than you had desired. Insurance coverage minimizes potential problems of this nature. If your husband does not have coverage, you may wish to discuss with your attorney the idea of his obtaining coverage or even providing a portion of the premiums as part of the settlement.

Some states require that a child support order contain a provision covering insurance obligations. In Arizona, for example, a revised statute requires that an order for child support assign the responsibility for providing medical insurance for minor children. The statute goes further in requiring the assigning of the responsibility for any costs not covered by the insurance.[1]

The term "reasonableness" is frequently used in court orders. Even if your husband has been ordered to be responsible for medical expenses for your children, he has the right to challenge the "unreasonableness" of medical or dental expenses. This was the subject of the 1985 Mississippi case, *Clements v. Young*, where the noncustodial parent charged that the medical bills incurred on behalf of his children were excessive. The court, finding for the mother, held that "the custodial parent has discretion to make day-to-day decisions regarding the welfare of the child, including medical and dental care. While such decisions are subject to the challenge of unreasonableness of costs to the noncustodial parent, proof that such medical bills were incurred is *prima facie* (on the face of it) evidence that such bills were necessary and reasonable."[2]

The fact that less than 50 percent of all women awarded child support seek and/or obtain health insurance provisions in their child support awards can be seen by reviewing the following table prepared by the U. S. Department of Commerce, Bureau of the Census.[3]

Life insurance is another matter. Life insurance assures you that your child will be supported in the event that your husband dies prior to the termination date of the support order. You cannot purchase a policy covering your husband's life without his consent. If your child is now three years old, he will require support for a minimum of fifteen years. A support order of $400 per month for a period of fifteen years amounts to $72,000, even without any support increases. The potential loss of this support poses a viable threat to the well-being of your child. If your husband dies, then his estate may be responsible, assuming there were sufficient assets. With no estate and no insurance, you would find yourself padding upstream for a long, long time.

If your husband agrees to maintain a life insurance policy naming your child as beneficiary, you will be assured of receiving the amount your husband is obligated to pay over the life of the support order. Since your minor child would be the beneficiary, the proceeds would be held in trust until a guardian is appointed.

Table G. Child Support Award Status and Health Insurance Inclusion, by Selected Characteristics for All Women and Women With Incomes Below the Poverty Level in 1987

(Numbers in thousands. Women with own children under 21 years of age present from absent fathers as of spring 1988)

Characteristic	Total	Awarded child support payments		
		Total	Health insurance currently included in award	
			Number	Percent of total awarded
ALL WOMEN				
Total	9,415	5,554	2,160	38.9
Current marital status:[1]				
Married[2]	2,386	1,957	759	38.8
Divorced	2,958	2,284	974	42.6
Separated	1,381	757	323	42.7
Never married	2,625	517	95	18.4
Race and Hispanic origin:				
White	6,467	4,448	1,912	43.0
Black	2,686	956	197	20.6
Hispanic[3]	937	397	185	46.6
Age:				
18 to 29 years	3,169	1,346	475	35.3
30 to 39 years	3,924	2,631	1,087	41.3
40 years and over	2,321	1,577	598	37.9
Years of school completed:				
Less than 12 years	2,349	1,007	320	31.8
High school: 4 years	4,486	2,665	1,002	37.6
College: 1 to 3 years	1,739	1,235	581	47.0
4 years or more	842	648	258	39.8
Number of own children present from an absent father:				
One child	5,111	2,896	1,119	38.6
Two children	3,026	1,979	793	40.1
Three children	862	487	186	38.2
Four children or more	416	193	62	32.1
WOMEN WITH INCOMES BELOW THE POVERTY LEVEL IN 1987				
Total	3,191	1413	450	31.8
Current marital status:[1]				
Married[2]	167	131	26	19.8
Divorced	791	587	233	39.7
Separated	710	361	145	40.2
Never married	1,498	319	42	13.2
Race and Hispanic origin				
White	1,659	879	347	39.5
Black	1,431	490	96	19.6
Hispanic[3]	473	180	74	41.1
Age				
18 to 29 years	1,562	553	168	30.4
30 to 39 years	1,201	622	199	32.0
40 years and over	427	238	83	34.9
Years of school completed:				
Less than 12 years	1,403	519	124	23.9
High school: 4 years	1,373	651	207	31.8
College: 1 to 3 years	353	201	110	54.7
4 years or more	62	42	9	21.4
Number of own children present from an absent father:				
One child	1,423	604	215	35.6
Two children	1,034	480	140	29.2
Three children	449	207	51	24.6
Four children or more	285	121	43	35.5

[1] Excludes a small number of currently widowed women whose previous marriage ended in divorce.
[2] Remarried women whose previous marriage ended in divorce.
[3] Persons of Hispanic origin may be of any race.

Generally, you will be named as guardian. It is wise to discuss with your attorney what provisions can be made to assure you of the shortest possible time delay in receiving your monthly support payments.

There are two distinctly different types of life insurance policies. Type A covers the insured only in the event of accidental death and is less expensive. Type B provides coverage for death by either accidental or natural causes. It is extremely important to specify which type of insurance you require for the benefit of your child. You could easily end up with a policy that provides zero coverage in the event your husband should die from natural causes.

Assuming your husband is young, in good health, and does not skydive or participate in other death-defying feats, the premiums for a full-coverage, term life policy are not exorbitant. For example, a twenty-four-year-old healthy male can purchase a type B policy having a $50,000 face value for $13.46 per month, or $161.50 annually. Although the rates increase as the insured gets older, the face amount of the policy can decrease, assuming he is making his child support payments, and these two factors should balance each other out, keeping the premiums at approximately the same amount.

The rates for insurance premiums are based on existing statistics. While you may have a difficult time imagining that your husband could die from any cause other than an accident, if the insurance companies were in agreement with you, the cost of a term life policy that covers death from any cause would be but a fraction higher than the cost of a policy that pays only in the event of accidental death. This is not the case. No one is immune to illness; therefore, no matter how healthy your husband appears to be, there is always a chance that he could die young from a natural cause.

If your husband's earnings are not sufficient to pay for child support and a life insurance policy, then you should think about obtaining his consent in writing to take out a policy on his life in the future. Even if you can't afford the premiums now, you may be able to later, and you will want to retain the option. Your husband may feel somewhat squeamish about this suggestion, but if the purpose of having such a policy is properly explained to him, preferably by his own counsel, any negative feelings should be dispelled.

I wish I could say that if you have an experienced domestic relations attorney, all the pertinent specifications regarding insurance will automatically become part of the settlement negotiations for your case, but that is not necessarily true. A friend of mine, an attorney, made an equitable settlement with his wife when they divorced several years ago. His wife was represented by a highly regarded and experienced family law attorney. My friend is a dedicated father who has never been late with a support payment and has never been late calling for his child on a visiting day. Yet during one of our discussions during the writing of this book, he confided that his wife has no idea to this day that he carries only an accidental death policy because the premiums are so much less. Her attorney never drew the distinction in the settlement agreement. While she believes her child's future is protected, the truth is that this "oversight" could result in a very uncertain future for that child.

CHAPTER 7

The Education Trust

THE COST of enrolling as a nonstate resident at Tulane University in the fall of 1977 was $4,930. In 1987 the cost was $15,950. During the same time frame, the yearly cost of attending the University of Colorado rose from $3,802 to $10,200, while the annual cost at Harvard University increased from $7,000 to $17,100. In 1990–91, the yearly cost at the University of Colorado was $12,755 and at Harvard University $19,575. Bear in mind that these amounts reflect *only* tuition and room and board for one school year.

From 1977–78 to 1987–88 the average increase for a four-year undergraduate program in a public institution was 130 percent, while private institutions increased 160 percent. Using these figures as a tool for projecting approximate expenses in the years to come, a four-year undergraduate program costing $67,364 at the University of Pennsylvania in 1987 would cost $87,573 in 1997 and $113,845 in 2007; Johns Hopkins University would jump from $63,720 (1987) to $101,952 (1997) and $163,123 (2007).

On February 14, 1991, the University of California administration proposed a 40 percent increase in student fees, the largest hike in the institution's history.[1] The increase was approved, and student costs rose $650, to $2,274 for the year, not including room, board, parking, or activities charges.

The following chart[2] prepared by Life Insurance Marketing and Research Association illustrates the increase in college tuition and room and board over a ten-year period:

A 1989 *New York Times* article, "College Tuition to Be 5% to 9% Higher This Fall," reported that the College Board's annual survey

The Spiraling Cost of Education

Name of Institution	Annual Cost¹ 1977-1978	Annual Cost¹ 1987-1988	% Increase
Alabama, University of	$2,663	$6,350	138%
Arizona, University of	2,925	7,396	153%
Baylor University	2,835	7,458	163%
Bucknell University	5,465	14,740	170%
Colorado, University of	3,802	10,200	168%
Cornell University	6,420	16,320	154%
Denison University	5,400	13,580	151%
Denver, University of	5,265	12,813	143%
Duke University	5,115	14,124	176%
Grambling State University	2,132	4,614	116%
Harvard University	7,000	17,100	144%
Howard University	3,204	7,418	132%
Indiana University	2,869	7,740	170%
Johns Hopkins University	5,675	15,930	181%
Massachusetts Institute of Tech.	7,028	16,970	141%
Michigan State University	3,393	8,042	137%
Michigan, University of	4,785	11,588	142%
Nebraska, University of	3,011	6,037	100%
Northwestern University	6,420	15,636	144%
Notre Dame, University of	4,630	12,500	170%
Oberlin College	5,741	15,884	177%
Oklahoma, University of	2,781	4,971	79%
Oregon, University of	3,637	6,455	77%
Pennsylvania, University of	6,800	16,841	148%
Purdue University	3,180	8,018	152%
Seattle University	3,820	10,520	175%
Smith College	5,935	15,650	164%
Stanford University	6,665	16,835	153%
Syracuse University	6,019	13,240	120%
Tennessee, University of	2,595	4,982	92%
Tulane University	4,930	15,950	224%
Vanderbilt University	5,235	14,685	181%
Vermont, University of	4,870	11,634	139%
Virginia, University of	3,307	8,646	161%
Yale University	6,950	17,020	145%
Average Cost 4 years Undergraduate			
Public	$3,282	$7,620	130%
Private	5,550	14,344	160%

of college prices for the 1989–90 school year showed the rise in tuition outpaced inflation for the ninth consecutive year. The article provided the following average tuitions and fees for the 1989–90 academic year: $1,694 for a four-year public college, up 7 percent from 1988; $842 for a two-year public college, up 5 percent; $8,737 for a four-year private college, up 9 percent; $4,713 for a two-year private college, up 7 percent; and $20,000 at "the nation's most elite colleges."[3]

Kathleen Brouder, director of information services and association affairs for the College Scholarship Services (CSS), the financial aid division of the College Board, stated that "the pace of college price increases has slowed somewhat since the early 1980s when annual rates of change were expressed in double digits. But covering their share of the costs still requires *effort and sacrifice* of most families."[4]

When both parents want to provide for their child's attendance at college—assuming the child has the ability and potential motivation—they may want to consider establishing an education trust. A fund of this nature can be structured in various ways, depending on the financial capabilities of the parties.

Before we explore various investment options, you should ask yourself some basic questions:

1. Do I want to be involved in a long-term, ongoing financial arrangement with my husband that will probably require frequent communication?
2. Despite his intentions, what are the chances of his failing to fulfill his commitments?
3. Should we avoid those investments where we would be at risk if ongoing contributions couldn't be made?
4. Could he carry the full load in an emergency? Could I?
5. Would it be better if we each established a separate account with a joint understanding?
6. Are we both emotionally ready to tackle this problem together?

While it is a wonderful gift for a child to have a college fund created by two parents that he loves (even if they are divorced), it may not always be possible. Any of the following savings programs can be established and maintained by one or more people, with the necessary financial capability.

Endowment policies were a very popular means of providing for a child's college education not too long ago. Parents would take out a policy when their child was young, and by contributing on a regular basis, his college needs were met at the appropriate time. This type of policy fell out of favor when interest rates from other investment vehicles yielded a much better return, but an endowment policy may be a viable option in today's money market and worth some consideration.

Another option is a savings vehicle structured around life insurance. This type of investment is generally thought of as a tax-deferred savings plan with a preset goal. The following example illustrates the accumulated value after ten, fifteen, and eighteen years of contributing $2,400 annually into the fund at the projected rate of 12 percent. In this example, the death benefit is $100,000

College Education Funding[5]
USING JOHN HANCOCK FLEXIBLE LIFE INSURANCE AS THE FUNDING VEHICLE

		Policy Cash Value		
Age	Annual Deposit	10 Years	15 years	18 years
25	$2,400	$35,835	$74,436	$107,764
30	$2,400	$35,707	$74,554	$107,728
35	$2,400	$35,290	$73,997	$106,634

The initial death benefits for the above illustrations are $100,000. This value is subject to increase based upon investment performances.

These values assume a 12 percent return on the investments.

All figures assume the insured is a male "preferred nonsmoker."

The required premiums for ages 25, 30 and 35 are $708, $820 and $1,006, respectively. However, any deviation from the above planned premiums will have a direct effect on the cash values.

John Hancock Flexible Variable Life Insurance is an insurance policy in which the cash value portion is invested in a family of mutual funds. The growth of the cash value is dependent on the performance of these funds. The death benefit growth is directly related to the changes in cash value. The initial death benefit is guaranteed as long as the minimum premiums are paid.

until the eighth year, at which time it increases. Savings can be accessed in either a lump sum or on a periodic basis through withdrawals or loans to meet tuition requirements. The amount of the annual contribution can vary, without forfeiting the amount invested to date, but the required premium amount must be paid. This type of investment can solve the problem of your receiving support payments if your ex-husband dies and the problem of offsetting a substantial amount of tuition costs. An investment of this nature is not insured by the U.S. government. The recent upheaval in the insurance industry is a timely reminder to always seek a company that has a good history and a good industry rating.

Zero-coupon bonds are also frequently used as an investment tool for educational purposes. A zero-coupon bond does not pay any interest while the loan is outstanding. All the interest accrues and is paid at maturity along with the original investment, which will equal the par value or face amount of the bond. These bonds are sold at "deep discounts." The amount of the discount depends on the amount of time it will take for the bond to mature and the current interest rate. For example, zero-coupon treasury bonds selling in January 1991 and maturing in January 2004 at 8.2 percent return cost $342.40 per $1,000. By paying $6,848 now you would receive $20,000 when redeeming the bond thirteen years from now. If you purchased the same bonds in 1995, the cost per thousand would be much higher since there would be less time before the bonds mature.

Zero-coupon bonds are popular because they allow investors to purchase more bonds for their money. There are several different types of zero-coupon bonds—treasury, municipal, corporate, and CD—and there are different tax ramifications governing these investments. There is no state tax on treasury bonds, and there is no federal or state tax on municipal bonds if you are a resident of the state that issues the bonds. You are obligated to pay both state and federal tax on nongovernment bonds.

There is a tax, known as a phantom tax, with zero-coupon bonds whereby tax must be paid on the interest you would have received had it been paid out to you. Frequently these bonds are purchased in a child's name in order to report interest income under a lower tax bracket. This type of planning should be made with a professional tax advisor.

Other types that might be considered for a college fund are the following:

Municipal bonds are issued in multiples of $5,000 by a political entity smaller than the federal government. Their maturity varies from one month to thirty years, and a specific amount of interest and principal is paid each year. These bonds are exempt from federal tax and from state tax if purchased from the state where you reside.

Well known are *agency bonds* from mortgage associations, nicknamed Ginnie Mae, Fannie Mae, and Freddie Mac. They are issued from $1,000 with a varied maturity from thirty days to twenty years. These bonds have fully taxable interest.

T-bonds are issued in amounts from $1,000 and mature in periods over ten years from the date issued; *T-notes*, also issued in amounts from $1,000, mature from two to ten years after issuance. They have a relatively low rate of return and are exempt from state and local taxes. These investment "instruments" are actively traded and therefore can be sold at any time.

Establishing a *trust* with a bank and naming the bank as trustee is a possibility, although it may not be a very viable solution because the amount of money involved may not justify the administrative costs charged by the bank for their services.

You may want to consider a *savings account* for your child, with you and your husband as trustees. While a regular passbook account has a lower rate of return than a money market account, treasury bills, or certificates of deposit, there is no risk factor in maintaining a savings account *as long as the institution is insured by the Federal Deposit Insurance Corporation (FDIC) or the Federal Savings and Loan Insurance Corporation (FSLIC)* and the account balance does not exceed $100,000. Despite the current savings and loan crisis, individuals who maintained savings accounts within insured institutions are protected. The horror stories that resulted from the collapse of Lincoln Savings and Loan, for example, resulted from investors who purchased bonds from the institution that were not insured. Institutional bonds are not insurable instruments.

Depositing a nominal amount of money into a savings account each month can assure that your child's tuition needs will either be met or, at least, greatly offset. For example, if your son is five years old and your husband deposits $40 per month between now and your child's eighteenth birthday into a savings account paying a nominal annual rate of 5.25 percent, the compounded amount would be $8,961.19. If you were able to match that monthly amount, your son would have $17,922.38 available upon entering college. While this amount would not enable him to attend Harvard or Yale, it would cover the expenses of attending a public four-year college. This amount could also allow him to obtain his education at various institutions if used in conjunction with scholarships or loans.

Once the fund has accumulated a certain amount of equity, other alternatives become available. If you and your husband are on good terms, it is conceivable that the funds could be invested in certificates of deposit (CDs) or treasury bills that would provide a higher rate of return. Many institutions also offer Liquid Asset and Money Market accounts which have certain minimum balance requirements and withdrawal limitations, but offer a better interest rate. While joint cooperation can result in a larger balance, only you and your husband can determine if you can work together in this way.

The following chart is a comparison of yields for various financial instruments as of January 22, 1991:[6]

Regular savings passbook	5.01%
3-month certificate of deposit	7.30%
6-month certificate of deposit	7.25%
3-month T-bill	6.20%
6-month T-bill	6.47%
Money market account	6.88%

Other investment alternatives are available if your husband earns a large income. A good accountant will be able to offer considerable beneficial advice.

There are many professionals who will be pleased to explain the various ways to structure an education trust. The establishment of this trust—whether an endowment policy, an annuity, bonds, an irrevocable trust, or a savings account—will solve one of your largest problems in the future. The solution can be as creative as you, your husband, your accountants, and your respective attorneys want it to be.

CHAPTER 8

Evaluating Your Spouse

DURING YOUR marriage you have had the unique experience of observing your husband's attitude toward responsibilities. You must now sit down and draw an honest analysis and profile of what you have observed. The more accurate you are in pinpointing his behavioral patterns, the better prepared you and your attorney will be for anticipating future problems before they arise. Review the following:

1. Is your husband conscientious about paying bills on time?
2. Is he budget-oriented?
3. Is maintaining good credit one of his priorities?
4. Does he plan his purchases in advance, or does he buy items impulsively, only to worry about paying for them after the fact?
5. Will he take his child support obligations into account before he selects an apartment, or will he rent the apartment of his choice first and see how much he has left?
6. If he had debts in the past, what methods did he use to resolve the problems?
7. Did he work out payment schedules with creditors? If so, did he honor them?
8. Did he use attorneys and the courts as delaying tactics?
9. Did he run away and hide his head in the sand, hoping the problems would go away?
10. Did he wait until judgments were entered against both of you?

11. Did he look to you to solve the problems?
12. If you had problems, was it the most important creditor or the one who yelled the loudest who got paid first?
13. Is he mature enough to handle his own finances?

This is a good time to assess yourself as well. Try to be objective and ask yourself:

1. How financially responsible am I?
2. Did I demand unnecessary money from my husband?
3. Would my husband be justified in believing that no matter how much support I receive, I will insist it isn't enough?

In your notebook that includes your financial obligations, your husband's income and assets, and your children's special needs, devote an additional page to your husband's patterns of meeting financial obligations. Make a note if he indulges in any excesses such as gambling, alcohol, clothes, and so forth. At the same time, confront yourself with these same questions.

Once your marriage is dissolved, your ongoing creditors will look to you for payment. The telephone company, the utility company, and the landlord need to get paid at specified times, not when it is convenient for you. The support that you are supposed to receive can make the difference between your survival and nonsurvival.

For all intents and purposes you will become another creditor to your ex-spouse. Whatever situations the two of you may have faced together in the past, the noncustodial parent will now confront that alone. While both of you historically faced obligations and creditors together, you have now crossed over into the other side's camp. Child support is entered on your asset side of the ledger and becomes a liability on his.

If you have grown accustomed to justifying your husband's actions during the course of the marriage, you may find yourself still making excuses for him and not honestly addressing the reality of the situation. You cannot assume that someone will change. (In marriage counseling one of the most frequently heard complaints is "If only she would change!" Counselors are quick to point out that people do not change.) Nor can you muddy up the analysis through the rationalization that the amount he will be obligated to pay to you is for your child and "that changes everything." Once your divorce is complete, your husband, like you, will become involved in self-survival. He will have a certain amount of income and his own living expenses, and he will have been ordered to pay a certain sum to you. He must ultimately decide the order of his priorities.

I spoke with one young woman who has been struggling over child support payments since the early eighties. The support order she requested and received was for $300 per month for her daughter. She told me that at the time of her divorce, her attorney assured her she could receive more but she felt $300 was an amount her husband could comfortably afford, and she was anxious not to alienate him. Child support, she believed, would be his highest priority. Now, after sporadic payments and years of imploring him to make his payments, he has moved out of the state. She is seeking enforcement through the district attorney's office. When I asked her how her former husband dealt with his obligations while they were married, she thought for a moment and then said that he always had bills and "paid whoever screamed the loudest." Understandably, she never related this behavior pattern to his failure to make his support payments.

When you meet with your attorney, review your observations about your husband's behavior patterns. If he is conscientious about his obligations, then you may very well have no problem in this area. If you do anticipate a problem, familiarize your attorney with this possibility. Your attorney may be able to avert it or take certain steps to minimize the risk. For example, if your husband acknowledges that budgeting is not one of his strong points, he may agree to a voluntary wage assignment whereby child support payments are automatically deducted from his paycheck. This is an ideal solution because everyone benefits. You will be able to attend to your child's needs as they arise, and he will be spared your expressions of tension caused by financial pressure. Your child will be spared overhearing confrontational telephone conversations or witnessing arguments between you and your husband over delinquent child support payments. Since many fathers who have failed to make their payments tend to stop visiting their children, your child will stand a better chance of spending time with his father if there is a voluntary wage assignment. Your husband will be able to experience the self-respect that comes with meeting his obligations to his child; he will avoid the danger of exhausting his income before he has met this responsibility and will avoid the harassment, the court appearances and legal fees, and the threat of incarceration that hangs over the heads of nonpaying spouses. You won't have to fall behind in your obligations, see your child do without, or spend time, energy, and emotions attempting to collect sums that should have been paid. In addition to these benefits, the payment of child support in a timely fashion leads to a healthier relationship between mother, father, and child.

I witnessed a hearing at the Los Angeles Superior Court where the judge was reprimanding a father who was seriously delinquent in his child support payments. "What kind of a father," the judge asked, "doesn't see, telephone, or even send his children a birthday card for over six years?" The father explained how he had fallen behind in making his payments and how the amount he owed compounded month after month. He felt that because he owed the money, he couldn't maintain his relationship with his two children. "Finally," the father said, "I felt it would be better if I just cut myself off from them."

Despite the many advantages of a voluntary wage assignment, your husband may not agree to one. (See Chapter 20 for a complete discussion of wage assignments.) One major concern is that it brings his personal life into the workplace. While the courts enjoy a broad latitude in issuing orders to assure a custodial parent's receiving child support payments, you would probably be expecting too much to assume that a court would issue an anticipatory order, that is an order based on what you expect is going to happen.

If your intuition is accurate and your husband does fail to make the payments after he has been ordered to do so, then the court's creative ability can come into play, but by anticipating the problem, you and your attorney can preplan a course of action. Even though you have filed for a divorce and have been awarded child support through a court order, there is no guarantee that you will receive those payments. A 1986 study found that fewer than half of the women entitled to child support received the full amount, and those who received any support at all were likely to receive it on a sporadic, unpredictable basis.[4] If the worst case scenario occurs, you will appreciate the importance of having made contingency plans.

If your husband will not agree to a voluntary wage assignment, requesting that he make his child support payments directly to the court is an alternative worth discussing with your attorney. This is common practice in some jurisdictions. The authoritative nature of the court can instill a sense of urgency and compliance in a noncustodial parent, resulting in a better manner of payment than when payments are sent directly to the custodial parent.

An outstanding judge in the South implored me to make women aware that obtaining their divorce is just the beginning. He described how he sits on the bench day after day and watches the same scenario repeat itself: Women come in with their attorneys and believe that this figure, robed in black, presiding in the austerity of the courtroom, wields the power to order her husband to make support payments, and by virtue of his power, these payments will be made automatically. They are unprepared and frequently financially unable to act effectively when their ex-husbands defy the court order. For the most part the custodial parents never thought they would need their attorneys again.

This is precisely the situation you want to avoid. If you believe there is a good probability you may have a problem, then you should discuss fees for enforcement procedures with your attorney. The evaluation and preplanning strategies discussed in this chapter should help you focus now on surprises that may occur in the future.

PART TWO

THE PROCEEDING AND THE AFTERMATH

CHAPTER 9

Selecting an Attorney

DECIDING WHO is going to represent you as counsel may be the most important decision you make when you obtain your divorce. If you have followed all the steps outlined thus far and have completed all your "homework," you are now ready to retain an attorney. But how do you decide which attorney is the right one for you?

In the event that you have already retained an attorney but are dissatisfied, you will be going through the same selective process. In this case, however, you must be sure to obtain your complete case file from your original attorney. This file should include *all memos* that relate to your case. Your attorney will undoubtedly require that his fees be paid to date. While it is costly to change attorneys midstream, it can be more costly to remain with an attorney who is not providing adequate representation.

Because divorce is a domestic issue, you should find an attorney who has expertise in domestic matters. Many attorneys limit their practice to family law. Specialists in this area are aware of recent court decisions, whereas a general practitioner may have to spend time (which is money) reviewing cases and recent decisions. A specialist should be familiar with the inclinations of the courts and individual judges in your jurisdiction; he should be aware of the emotionalism that often accompanies the divorce process, understand the ramifications of the poorly drawn settlement agreement, and be better equipped to handle your divorce. Just as you would choose to see a dermatologist instead of a general practitioner if you were experiencing a skin problem, you should choose a family law specialist as well. In essence, when you retain an attorney, you are paying for expertise—and that is precisely what you should receive.

An attorney I have known for many years told me that he has never had a client ask him if he is skilled in the legal area of his case. It never ceases to amaze him that in over twenty years of practice clients have never asked him the most fundamental question: "Is this an area in which you have expertise?"

If you are acquainted with an attorney you admire or have used the services of an attorney in an area outside of family law, you may want to ask him to provide you with references for attorneys who specialize in divorce. An attorney can often be the best source for a recommendation since he may be aware not only of the qualifications and reputation of the individual but also his fee structure. Always seek a referral from an attorney whom you know and trust to minimize the risk of being given the name of an attorney who is not highly qualified.

If one of your friends recommends an attorney that she has used, ask questions to find out what that attorney accomplished. *Be specific.* The mere fact that a person has already obtained her divorce doesn't necessarily qualify her to determine whether or not her attorney excelled in representing her. You now know what child support issues should be raised, and it is important to ascertain to what extent her attorney pursued those issues. You may be surprised to learn that some of the previously mentioned support issues were not raised at all. While listening to a subjective appraisal of an attorney, you must attempt to discern if your friend's criticisms are based on reasonable complaints or stem from having entered the divorce process with unrealistic goals. In addition to the issues and the results of your friend's case, there are three questions you should ask: Did the attorney return her phone calls within a reasonable time? Was he responsive to her suggestions and questions? Was he supportive of her position?

Community support groups may provide you with the means of finding the appropriate attorney for your case. Members of support groups have already gone through the divorce process and have firsthand experience they will be pleased to share with you. Appendix B is a listing of child support advocacy groups by state. The child support enforcement agency in your jurisdiction may also be able to provide you with the names of support groups in your area.

The key to selecting an attorney is to be objective. A relative or close friend who happens to be a lawyer may not necessarily be qualified to handle your case. If that person is experienced in the practice of family law, however, and you believe he has represented clients fairly in the past, he may be a fine choice.

Once you have the name of an attorney, it is important to learn which side he generally represents. Some attorneys are known for representing wives in divorce proceedings, while others always represent husbands. An attorney who is usually extremely successful representing one party may not do as well representing the other.

If you have no one to ask for a referral, one of your options is to call the state bar association, which will give you the telephone number of the lawyer's referral service. You should be aware, however, that the bar association will give you the name of a law firm based on the rotation system; that is, the names of attorneys who want clients referred to them are included on a list, and the bar association rotates these names as requests are received. Unless the referral service states otherwise, there are no special tests administered to ascertain the qualifications of individual firms.

Around 1985 several new firms emerged doing business under the heading of legal referral services. The basis of these services is as follows: Lawyers become "panel members" of the service. The service refers clients to the lawyers on a rotation basis, and the service receives a percentage of the fees collected for the referral. On October 26, 1989, the California Supreme Court Order[1] went into effect establishing standards to discourage abuses in these enterprises. The state bar of California established minimum standards a referral service must meet to be certified by the bar. If you decide to use such a service, select one that is required to maintain the highest standards.

If you find yourself staring at the yellow pages, having no idea which firm to choose, you will find the following disclaimer or words to this effect in the "Attorney Guide":

> This guide does not necessarily represent a complete list of all attorneys practicing in the fields shown. Also, appearance in this guide does not mean that an attorney has had special training or has been certified as a specialist.[2]

An attorney who chooses to list his firm under the heading of Family Law Practice hasn't necessarily met any state bar specialist requirements in this area, nor is he necessarily any more qualified than any other attorney in the field of family law. He has simply made the choice of placing his firm's name under this category heading. In checking the phone book you will notice that many firms place their name under several headings. You should also bear in mind that many experienced and successful attorneys decide not to advertise in the yellow pages of the directory, preferring to obtain clients through their reputations.

In some states attorneys must meet certain requirements in order to become members of a group of attorneys who specialize in family law. In California, for example, while all licensed attorneys can practice family law, an attorney can become a certified family law specialist by meeting standards of education and experience in family law set by the California Board of Legal Specialization of the State Bar of California. By calling your state bar association you can find out if this applies in your area as well.

Another resource is The American Academy of Matrimonial Lawyers, or AAML. The AAML is a professional organization of highly qualified matrimonial lawyers and has chapters in two-thirds of the states. Membership in the AAML requires ten years of family law practice and a referral or sponsorship from a sitting judge.[3]

Another option is the Legal Aid Society, which in some regions will assist low-income individuals in the divorce process. Legal Aid generally refers callers to a foundation that will provide advice on self-representation. I recommend seeking advice from Legal Aid over approaching storefront lawyers, who are about as reliable as a name randomly selected from the Yellow Pages.

Another option is available to those in search of an attorney: You can see an attorney in action by going to family court and observing cases as they are heard. You might find an attorney who would be right to handle your case. Many attorneys who primarily practice family law practically live at the courthouse. The county clerk of the court can tell you when and where domestic matters are heard. Going to court also provides the opportunity of seeing the "mechanics" of the court, which may help to remove some of your apprehensions if judicial proceedings are foreign to you.

There is no reason to feel intimidated about going to court as an observer because the courts are accustomed to nonparticipating observers. On a typical day in Santa Monica Superior Court you can spot the faces of a few "professional courtwatchers" who are always hoping to catch an exciting hearing or trial, perhaps with a celebrity.

The Santa Monica courthouse may not be your "typical" courthouse. Attorneys there may be every bit as theatrical as their clientele and use all their powers of voice projection when mentioning a personality's pending suit or settlement. There is a standing joke that on certain days you would have to stand in the hallway outside Department J with a vacuum cleaner in order to pick up all the names that are dropped. While this is a bit of an exaggeration, several years ago I was outside Department J, the courtroom for domestic matters, waiting for my ex-husband's contempt hearing for failure to pay child support, when I heard one attorney mention "Liz and Richard" at least a dozen times.

COURT PROCEDURES

The usual courtroom procedure is for the attorneys to identify themselves when their cases are called and to inform the court whom they are representing. The standard dialogue is as follows: "Greg Hamilton for the petitioner." This may be the only time that the attorney's name is mentioned within the proceeding. If you have observed an attorney whom you would like to contact but are unsure of his name, you can ask the clerk of the court for the attorney's name during a recess or at the close of the court session. In the event that several matters were heard during one session, provide the clerk with the case heading, as in Smith versus Smith, so that you get the right attorney's name. (See Chapter 11 for a full discussion of courtroom procedures.)

FEES

Some attorneys have a set fee for a divorce. Others base their fees on the complexity of the issues involved in obtaining a settlement and the projected cost of litigation. There are attorneys who handle only the bigger cases that have larger settlements and higher fees. The fact that a particular attorney may be the most well known or the most publicized in your area does not necessarily mean he is the best attorney for you. If your case involves substantially less in assets than the cases he generally handles, he may agree to represent you but not be able to maintain the level of enthusiasm you would like to have from an attorney. In essence, if in financial terms your case simply doesn't warrant the amount of time you would like him to invest, you may find yourself feeling shortchanged with a high-profile attorney.

Many attorneys have a set fee for what they term a simple divorce, which often means a divorce where there are no children involved and no property matters to settle. Some attorneys have a set fee for a divorce with children as long as no custody issue is involved. In any case, fees will be incurred, and for the time being anyway, you may as well assume you will be the one paying those fees. At this point one of your primary considerations must be whether or not you can afford the fees of this particular attorney. This is also the time to raise the subject of what kind of costs you will be looking at if you have to go back to court in order to enforce your child support order. It is important to be aware of these cost factors *before* you enter into an agreement with an attorney rather than after. It is almost always less expensive to be represented by the same attorney if you have to return to court. Your original attorney will be familiar with your file, whereas you must pay for the time it takes a new attorney to acquaint himself with the history of your case. In addition to the expense factor, finding new counsel means repeating the same process you are going through now. Keep in mind that inexperienced does not necessarily mean inadequate. Flat fees are often established by inexperienced lawyers in the field. Many talented young attorneys gain experience by taking on divorce cases with children.

COSTS

Costs are generated in a number of ways: through filing fees imposed by the court, serving your husband with documents, long-distance telephone calls, postage, faxing documents, and court reporter fees for depositions. The filing fees vary depending on the jurisdiction, but in California, for example, it costs $145 to file a petition for divorce where there is property and children involved and $29 to file for a modification of child support. Depositions are expensive because you have not only the court reporter's time during the deposition but also the cost of transcribing the proceeding to produce hard copies. You are therefore looking at several hundred dollars before you even factor in your attorney's time.

Most attorneys work on an hourly fee basis rather than a set fee. The fee structure is generally based on the success of the attorney's practice and the "going rate" in that part of the country. The following is a sampling of attorneys' average hourly rates in various cities throughout the country in 1986:[4]

Atlanta	$50–125
Boston	60–125
Chicago	50–85
Denver	75–95
New York	40–125
Philadelphia	50–100
San Francisco	75–125
Washington, D. C.	45–125

Currently, fees range from approximately $100 to $200 per hour. This fee range does not take into account the expertise and reputation of the experienced family law specialist. If there are substantial assets, an attorney may suggest a contingency agreement whereby he would receive a percentage of your settlement.

If you select an attorney who will charge you on an hourly basis, he should set forth the fee agreement in writing and give a rough estimate of how many hours the case will require. This should provide a clear understanding for both parties. Keep in mind that the estimate is generally based on "best case scenario." In other words, his estimate assumes that both sides will cooperate and appear for scheduled depositions and hearings. Because hourly billings are made in time increments, the billings are not a precise amount. For example, if John Smith, Esq., charges $100 an hour and bills in fifteen-minute increments, each activity he performs on your case that requires less than fifteen minutes will be billed at $25. A phone call lasting three minutes will be billed at $25, and the preparation of a document that takes seventeen minutes will be billed at $50. Therefore, the smaller the billing increments are, the lower the fees should be.

It is possible that the court will order your husband to pay your attorney's fees for the divorce. It is also possible that in a contempt hearing for failure to pay child support, the court will order the offender, or citee, to pay the legal fees incurred in bringing the matter to court. You must bear in mind, however, that your attorney will look to you for payment of his fees and costs unless you have an agreement to the contrary. Assuming your husband complies with the court order for payment of fees, you will be reimbursed, but in the event he doesn't pay, you will have to bear the costs.

Be bold and frank during your first meeting with an attorney. Ask him how frequently he handles your type of case. An attorney who is secure should be happy to respond to your questions. If he becomes defensive or attempts to intimidate you, then you probably have the wrong person for the job. Ask him if he usually represents wives or husbands in divorce matters. Ask him how long he has been practicing law, and family law in particular.

A good divorce attorney should be self-confident and a strong negotiator because everyone comes out ahead if a negotiated settlement can be attained; he must also be a good trial lawyer in the event that there are contested issues. Spending an hour with an attorney in his office will not afford you the opportunity to witness firsthand whether or not he has these qualifications, but the combination of his demeanor and his experience will provide sufficient data on which to base your decision.

Once you have decided to meet with the attorney, call his law firm and set up a conference. The first conference will be an exploratory meeting: The attorney will decide if he wants to handle your case, and you will decide if you want him to represent you. You should ask the attorney or his secretary about his fee arrangements *before* you make the appointment. Find out if there is a consultation fee. Some attorneys will not enter into a discussion regarding fees over the telephone, while others will, especially if they have a set fee for each service rendered to the client who is seeking a divorce. You may want to limit your question regarding fees to the amount he charges for the initial conference. If after you have had your initial conference, you are not satisfied that he is the proper person to represent you, you may or may not be obligated to pay for the consultation depending on that attorney's policy. If he elects not to handle your case, you generally shouldn't owe him anything.

It is most important that you do not lose sight of the main purpose of your initial meeting, which is to determine if this is the attorney you want to represent you. Does this attorney seem knowledgeable about the divorce process? Is he experienced? Does he generally rep-

Selecting an Attorney 91

resent the custodial parent? Are you able to communicate with each other easily? Is he treating you as a credible individual?

If you have been able to prepare all the facts beforehand, you will be able to cut through the superfluous information and give him the "bottom line," which is your husband's earnings, your expenses, and your joint and separate assets. This information should enable him to give you some indication of what he believes is feasible and what areas may be "iffy." Of course he has no way of knowing what your husband may or may not agree to, but he should certainly know how the courts in your jurisdiction customarily treat the issues of your divorce.

When you are sitting across from an attorney's desk, it is difficult to gauge how he will handle himself in the courtroom or at the negotiation table. If he has an authoritative manner in his office, it is likely that this carries over into the courtroom. Ask him about his methods of negotiation: is he prone to use trade-offs, guilt factors, "Getting to Yes" techniques, face-to-face meetings? How much will you participate in the negotiating? The more familiar you are with his negotiating strategies, the more confident and relaxed you will feel during the actual process.

If you allow yourself to become too emotionally distressed when relating the events that led up to your divorce—which is easy to do under these circumstances—you may find yourself leaving his office and returning home without knowing any more about him than you did before your meeting.

As in any profession, there are good attorneys and there are bad ones. A good attorney deserves to be respected for his expertise, but sometimes respect is replaced by intimidation. If you permit yourself to feel intimidated, you are bound to find yourself at a disadvantage. You may find yourself continually compromising on issues and blaming your attorney in the years to come.

Attorneys occasionally turn a case over to another attorney in their firm without advising the client. You should make certain that whoever you meet with will be the one representing you in court; otherwise, you might find yourself in court with someone you don't even know. This could happen for various reasons: The attorney whom you have chosen may feel that your case is small and doesn't justify his time. He may be "trailing" (waiting for a trial judge) on another case when your case is scheduled to be heard and therefore be unavailable. He may be in the middle of a trial that has taken longer than anticipated. In these instances you can request that your case be continued until such time as your attorney can be present. You have selected an attorney, and you should be represented by him, not a substitute, unless you choose otherwise.

I had firsthand experience with this problem several years ago. While waiting at the courthouse for the attorney I had retained, one of his associates approached me, introduced himself, and informed me that he would be handling this matter since my attorney had a conflict in his schedule. I was disappointed but didn't object. Very early in the hearing it became painfully obvious that this attorney was not only unfamiliar with my case but seemed to be inexperienced in family law as well. He suggested that we request a dismissal without prejudice; I agreed, but it was a fiasco. It left me worse off than I had been prior to the hearing.

By the time your initial meeting is over, you should sense the attorney's interest or lack of interest in your case and act accordingly. Fine, expert attorneys make every effort to obtain a fair and equitable agreement on behalf of you and your children; therefore, you shouldn't have to settle for something less in an attorney. Years after your divorce you may find yourself fighting to get what is supposed to be yours. By immediately choosing an attorney who is understanding and empathetic to your needs, you can eliminate one unnecessary fight.

You are going to be required to put a great deal of faith and trust in your attorney. He may represent your interests when you are not present, an all-important factor that you should take into consideration as you sit in his office and discuss your case.

Finally, there is that certain intangible thing called chemistry, vibrations, or just plain intuition. This has nothing whatsoever to do with an attorney's reputation, knowledge, success, or previous list of clients. It is simply a matter of your own personal feelings. If it doesn't feel right, then pass and look elsewhere.

How should you feel? Ideally, you should feel confident, trustful, relaxed, open, and secure. No written law states that you must make your decision at the close of this initial conference. While an attorney generally will recommend that you file for your divorce as soon as possible, with justifiable reasoning, a few days one way or another is not going to make a great deal of difference. If you are uncertain, then allow yourself the time to come to an intelligent, well-thought-out decision.

CHAPTER 10

The Attorney-Client Relationship

Now that you have chosen your attorney, the presumption is that this new relationship has all the necessary qualities and characteristics of a good attorney-client relationship: You feel confident that your attorney cares about your case and will make every effort to achieve what is best for you and your child. You are comfortable expressing your views and concerns with him, and he listens to what you have to say with an open mind. You are equally receptive to his expert opinions. You will begin to feel more confident if you organize your thoughts and list your questions in order of priority.

Interacting with Your Attorney

The relationship that now exists with your attorney is professional. Every effort should be made to preserve it, by both you and your attorney. You may be extremely vulnerable during this time and find yourself gravitating toward anyone who exhibits a degree of empathy and caring or offers a shoulder to lean on. Your attorney should not be one of these people. His time is not only valuable, it also constitutes his livelihood. It is unfair to expect him to chat with you to lift your spirits when you are feeling low. An attorney logs his phone calls and maintains time sheets in order to charge his clients accordingly. If you are paying by the hour, you would be much better off talking about your feelings with a friend or even a therapist. If your attorney has quoted you a flat price to handle your divorce, then he has based that quote on his projection of how much time he will devote to your case. If you start misusing this time—wasting it, to be more precise—then something is bound to change. Most likely it will be the relationship, but there is also the danger that the outcome of your case will be adversely affected.

If you enter into an hourly fee arrangement with an attorney or a flat figure that is later to be adjusted upward or downward, based on the number of hours he ultimately spends on your case, you should be particularly conscientious of his billing time. By becoming too casual in this area, you may incur an unnecessary legal expense, as shown in the following scenario.

You have a five o'clock meeting with your attorney. Since it is the end of the day, there are a few phone calls he must accept, some documents he must sign, and so on. The meeting ends at 6:30, at which time you have completed your business. You are probably both hungry, and one of you suggests grabbing a bite, so you proceed to a nearby restaurant. As you are eating you discuss various aspects of your case, and you hear about some of his brighter moments in court. After dinner he picks up the check, and you both say good-bye and go off in your separate directions. You may have just purchased one of the most expensive dinners in your life. From your attorney's point of view he has spent more than an hour discussing your case with you. It is useless to say later that you would have passed on dinner if you had known you would be paying for his time. The only way to know for sure if the "meter is running" is to ask beforehand.

On the other side of the coin, if you have a viable concern, one that may affect your divorce proceedings, you should inform your attorney immediately. An active attorney's time is often divided between his office and the court; he will therefore quite often be unable to speak with you. Some attorneys return their clients' calls from the courthouse while they are waiting for a case to be heard, some return them at the end of the day. If your attorney is in the middle of a lengthy trial, he may not return your call for a day or so. There is no excuse, however, for an attorney to fail repeatedly to return calls for days on end—but, unfortunately, some fall into this category. If your attorney does not return your call within a reasonable length of time, then you must address this problem right away. If you are unable to reach him by phone, inform his secretary of your dissatisfaction; if that doesn't bring quick results, *put it in writing* and mail the letter. The latter alternative will almost always bring an immediate response. The relationship you enjoy with your attorney is no different from other relationships: Once there is a lack of communication, a loss of faith, or an abuse felt by either party, the relationship begins to deteriorate. If deterioration begins and is allowed to continue, there is little chance for restoration.

A client who becomes emotionally and/or sexually involved with her attorney virtually eliminates the possibility of maintaining a professional attorney-client relationship. This also holds true for the male client of a female attorney. Some men believe that every woman represents a sexual challenge, regardless of professional dynamics. The client who feels her self-worth is tied to her ability to attract men can also be the catalyst in this situation. Some women clients, experiencing a loss of self-esteem, seek their attorney's reassurance that they are desirable. Others believe that an attorney will work harder on their case if he is emotionally involved. While I haven't seen any statistics on how many attorneys become involved with their clients, it does happen—and, yes, stories are circulated over cocktails about conquests made over the conference table.

Just how detrimental sleeping with one's attorney can be is best illustrated by the following examples from actual cases. In California a woman who had filed for divorce and was being challenged by her husband for custody of their children was having an affair with her attorney. Since she didn't want to leave her children alone at night, this woman and her attorney spent time together in her home. When the trial was in progress, her husband's attorney alleged that she was having an affair with her attorney and offered into evidence photographs of her attorney's car parked in her driveway overnight on several occasions. The relationship and their lack of discretion proved to be not only a source of immense embarrassment for her and her attorney but also severely damaged her case. Another young woman told me the story of how she and her attorney arrived at a "nonverbal" agreement, whereby he would handle her case without a retainer because he liked her, and he felt she liked him too. As weeks passed they shared more than time with each other, and he "worked" on her case. After several months her case had yet to be filed, let alone heard in court. It was only after the relationship cooled and he didn't return her calls that she realized he hadn't done any work on her divorce.

The state bar of California started examining potential problems stemming from attorney-client sexual relationships in 1988 and issued a formal opinion on the subject. The *Los Angeles Daily Journal* article, "Clients and Sex Don't Mix, State Bar Panel Warns Attorneys," reported that "the opinion listed a variety of potential clashes between attorney-client sexual entanglements and the bar's Rules of Professional Conduct, extending well beyond the personal dilemmas regularly encountered by [Arnie] Becker, the philandering divorce lawyer on the NBC TV series."[1] The bar's Standing Committee on Professional Responsibility and Conduct cited examples: A lawyer who has a sexual involvement with a client might have a conflict of interest in zealously pursuing a reconciliation; a lawyer who has tired of a sexual relationship with a client might try more strenuously to get them to reconcile than is appropriate. The committee provided the following examples of how a lawyer could fail to represent his client competently: the client in a custody battle is questioned about extramarital relationships; the lawyer has to plan strategy regarding the custody while he is living with the client; the spouse, aware of the live-in relationship, retaliates by blocking a settlement.

In 1989 the *California Lawyer* article, "No Sex Please, We're Lawyers," reported that the California state legislature was considering directing the state bar to ban lawyers from having sex with clients. Robert Unetic, a member of the bar's Family Law Section, led a group of Orange County attorneys in seeking a resolution barring attorney-client sexual relations. He stated that his interest was piqued by an acquaintance's experience: "She was constantly being hit on by her attorney. He [the attorney] told her eventually she was going to go to bed with him. When I told her [the lawyer's] conduct was inappropriate, she became defensive. People say, 'Well, get another lawyer,' but her finances were restricted. The combination of vulnerability and the likelihood that this may be the client's first contact with the legal profession [places the lawyer] in a position of unique power and influence."[2]

The state bar of California is currently considering a rule barring—or, alternatively, restricting—attorneys from having sex with their clients. The *Los Angles Times* article, "Lawyer-Client Sex May Be Banned by State Bar,"[3] reported that any rule adopted by the bar would be sent for final approval to the state supreme court. The article states that Assemblywoman Lucille Roybal-Allard, author of the 1989 law that required the bar to adopt a rule governing lawyer-client sex, says that "a specific ban on lawyer-client sex is needed to protect clients against manipulation and intimidation—particularly those clients involved in emotionally draining divorce, child custody, or probate cases."[4]

The results of an affair between a client and an attorney may not always be disastrous, but there is no way that the relationship will be unaffected. Since your case must stand on its own merits, becoming emotionally involved can't really do much good and *can* result in harm.

Experienced divorce attorneys are familiar with the fact that there is a great deal of "hand holding" in their practice. Many attorneys won't practice family law because of this reality. The attorney specializing in divorce usually acquires an understanding and concerned demeanor, but this shouldn't be mistaken for a welcome mat to listen to all your problems. Through a complete appreciation of your attorney's goals and your particular case requirements, a good working relationship can be established and can help lead you to a good resolution of your case.

ORGANIZING YOUR QUESTIONS

If you have done the preparation outlined in the earlier chapters, you will have your notebook, your documents and, it is hoped, a sense of mental order when you meet with your attorney. The subjects you will want to discuss thoroughly with your attorney are as follows:

1. assets and earnings—yours and your husband's
2. living expenses
3. medical and death benefits
4. education requirements
5. children's special needs
6. tax ramifications
7. responsibility for legal fees
8. potential problem of nonpayment of support
9. jurisdiction's guidelines for child support

It is important to "stay on point." Deal with one issue at a time and avoid the trap of rerunning your entire married life. Jumping from one subject to another when you are relating an incident because it reminds you of something else that occurred can confuse your attorney and the issues. By staying on point you should have a productive meeting that will be mutually beneficial.

Assets and earnings go to the top of the list since any support order is going to be predicated on these figures. Provide your attorney with the photocopies you have prepared for him of pertinent documents. Once he has reviewed this material he should be able to give you a good idea of the amount of child support you can reasonably expect.

If you have prepared your financial declaration by using the sample previously provided, your attorney will have an immediate overview of your living expenses. If you have any questions regarding any of the expenses, you must bring them to his attention. He may ask how you arrived at certain amounts, and this should be taken in a positive manner—it does not mean he doubts your honesty or your figures. It is extremely important to understand that when an attorney represents that a specific claim of yours is true, he must be able to substantiate the claim with proof. If a particular expense is proven to be exaggerated, you have lost some credibility, and all the other expenses become suspect, so if he spots something that he feels your husband's attorney may question, he must know the answers beforehand.

THE CHILD SUPPORT SETTLEMENT AGREEMENT

Everything you and your husband ultimately agree upon is written into your settlement agreement; it will be reviewed by the court and incorporated into the court order at the time of your divorce. The court may withhold its approval if an issue seems to oppose your children's best interests. For example, a judge may take exception with an agreement that provides the non-custodial parent with visitation rights only during the holidays and for one month each summer. Any issues you have not resolved must be presented to the court for determination at the time of your hearing. If you have failed to come to terms on several issues, then you and your attorney must decide priorities and what should be presented to the court. Your living expense requirements, your child's special needs, and insurance and education requirements are fundamental issues that your attorney and your husband's attorney will attempt to resolve and incorporate into your support settlement agreement. There is no prescribed format for this settlement. It can be as creative as you and your attorney wish to make it. Even though your child will benefit from all the requests your attorney makes, you have to remember that everything is negotiable, which is why it is essential to define your priorities. This is also the area in which you have the right to expect both expertise and innovation from your attorney. Every issue that is resolved and becomes part of your settlement is one less issue on which the court must make a determination. One word that clients often use but that doesn't really fit into the legal vernacular is "fair." Many things that may not seem fair to you or to your husband are part of reality. For example, your daughter may want to be a ballerina more than anything in her whole life, and she may live for Saturday mornings when she takes her ballet lesson. Through negotiation your attorney may ask that your husband, knowing how much this means to his daughter, to agree to have the provision made part of a support agreement. But if the court determines how much of your husband's salary should be paid to you for child support, it is highly unlikely that it will then order him to also pay for her dancing lessons. In the matter of college tuition, you may feel it's unfair that your support order terminates at age eighteen, a crucial point in your child's educational life; however, this will not seem like a prime issue to everyone compared to food, clothing, and shelter. The education need cannot be met through the court but through a tailored support agreement. There are various ways to structure an agreement as long as both parties are intent on solving the problem.

Since an agreement is also a contract, the more specifically it is constructed, the less chance there is for interpretive problems to arise in the future. If a clause states that your husband agrees to pay any "reasonable" expenses your child incurs while attending a university, the word *reasonable*, in itself a vague term, opens up all kinds of potential problems when the provision goes into effect. Is your child living on campus at reasonable expense? Are transportation costs going to and from school reasonable? The bottom line is that ambiguous wording or wording that keeps the door slightly ajar for interpretation can be a potential source of conflict in the future. If an agreement specifically states that your husband will pay for tuition, board, and books while your child is attending college, the meaning is quite clear.

If your agreement incorporates reimbursements for specific expenses, you must detail how and when payment will be delivered. To include merely a provision providing for reimbursement is too vague and will be difficult to enforce. It is more effective to define the terms specifically: for example, by stating that you will send him receipts for reimbursable expenses within two weeks of when the money was spent, and that he will reimburse you within two weeks of the date the receipts were mailed.

STRUCTURING YOUR AGREEMENT

While a multitude of options are available in structuring a support agreement, it will be your attorney's job to come up with a formula that works for you. If your husband is uncooperative, however, your attorney may find himself able to do little and may have no choice but to present the issues to the court. You can never generalize about how the courts will rule since so much is left to the discretion of the particular judge who hears the matter in addition to what is customary in your jurisdiction, but there are two very important factors to remember: First, *you cannot modify a provision that was not mentioned in your original court order without the addition of a new term.* To modify is to change, and in order to change something, it must exist. If medical expenses are not mentioned in your court order, then for all practical purposes the matter is lost. That is why any order you can obtain in this area is far better than nothing. Without it, you may have allowed the door to slam forever. The second factor is that *if you don't ask for a provision regarding an issue, you won't find anyone offering it to you.* For example, should your attorney fail to request that your husband be responsible for your child's speech therapy bills if he has the ability to pay, then no one will bring up the subject of speech therapy later on.

TAXES AND LEGAL FEES

You should know one important fact about taxes as they apply to child support versus alimony or spousal support: The amount of child support you receive is not taxable income. You do not declare the amount on your income tax return, and your husband cannot deduct the support on his return. Conversely, spousal support or alimony is both a deduction for him and taxable income to you. You will fare much better by obtaining a more generous child support order and less spousal support than vice versa. Tax ramifications often play an important part in the negotiation process and can also be used as a bargaining tool. Under special circumstances, your ex-husband's attorney may make certain concessions in return for increasing the spousal support and lowering the child support payments. Occasionally, a father in a higher tax bracket can pay more to a mother through alimony than through child support. The government will subsidize the payments because of the tax bracket differential. Aside from child support you should know about other tax consequences that can result from your property settlement. I suggest that you not only discuss this area thoroughly with your attorney but also seek the advice of a good certified public accountant if there is a question of any tax liability on your part. A family law attorney may not be a tax specialist, so it is wise to seek an expert opinion.

Declaring a child as dependent has considerable tax consequences, as children of divorced parents fall under a specific category for the IRS's dependency test. The right for a noncustodial parent to declare a child as dependent is frequently used as a negotiating tool. For a 1990 return, a custodial parent divorced after January 1, 1985, and who has physical custody for more than six months a year can claim the child as dependent, assuming all other dependency qualifications are met. The IRS Publication 17 provides an in-depth guide to dependency requirements.

Unless your husband volunteers to pay your legal fees, your attorney must request that the court order your husband to pay for the amount of fees deemed reasonable. It will be up to your attorney to bring the issue to the court's attention. In all likelihood your attorney will ask you for a retainer that will enable him to proceed with the case. This amount can vary from his projection of out-of-pocket costs, such as filing fees, photocopies, telephone costs, witness fees, and so forth, to his fee for handling the divorce. If your attorney intends to ask the court to order your husband to pay your legal fees, then this fact should be incorporated in your agreement with your attorney. The premise is as follows: You give a retainer to your attorney, your husband is ordered to pay for your legal fees, your husband pays the court-ordered fees to your attorney, and your attorney then returns to you the amount of your retainer. If the court determines that your husband should not be obliged to pay the fees, then there would be no reimbursement to you, and you must bear the burden of your own legal costs. This sounds so logical that it seems almost inconceivable for it to present any problems or require the need for it to be put in writing. This actual case history illustrates how a verbal understanding of a "given" can become a problem.

Sally M. retained an attorney to obtain a divorce in 1976. The attorney is a well-known Beverly Hills divorce specialist who at the time was associated with an extremely celebrated law firm. He asked for a retainer of $1,500 and stated that he was confident the court would order her spouse to pay her fees for the divorce. The court did exactly what he had anticipated, ordering her husband to pay her attorney the sum of $1,500 for legal fees paid to date. Since Sally had advanced this amount initially, she felt secure that she would be reimbursed and saw no reason to put the understanding in writing. When her husband failed to make his support payments, the attorney filed a motion requesting the court to find him in contempt. This was the first of several contempt hearings that were calendared during the next three years. At each hearing the court ordered Sally's husband to pay her attorney's legal fees for lodging the contempt action, in accordance with her attorney's request. During that period her attorney requested additional fees, which, of course, she gave him. At the hearings her husband was found to be in contempt not only for failing to pay the child support but also for failing to pay the legal fees for dissolution and the subsequent contempt hearings. When Sally and her attorney concluded their association, she asked him to assign to her his rights to any fees that might be collected from her husband since she had paid him directly for his time. After hedging a bit, he stated that he had actually put in much more time than he had billed her for, and he felt entitled to keep any funds he either received or was able to collect. Had their initial agreement been in writing, this "misinterpretation" of their agreement would never have occurred.

While your attorney will represent you in court, you must also represent yourself with your attorney. It is always better to document a mutual understanding: Remember that an agreement worth having is worth having on paper.

Your Husband's Ability to Pay

Your child's needs must be balanced with your husband's ability to provide. Your husband may be in a situation that precludes the possibility of your obtaining certain important benefits for your child. As an example, your husband may work for a company that offers no benefits. If his salary is low, he will be ordered to pay the minimum amount of child support. While he is currently unable to provide medical insurance for your child, this situation could change in the future if he goes to work for a company that provides insurance to their employees and their dependents or one that offers optional dependent coverage. In the latter case, he may agree to pay all premiums for your child or one-half of them. He may agree to pay for medical and dental expenses *if he has the ability to pay*. The support agreement can outline precisely the intent and obligations of both parties should circumstances change, while always protecting your child's interests. If you agree on the necessity of establishing an education fund, then the particulars should be outlined in the support agreement. Will both parties be contributing to the fund? Will contributions be made monthly, quarterly, annually? What form of investment vehicle will be used? How will the funds be disbursed? The support agreement offers the only opportunity you will have to obtain a written commitment that can be used in court regarding tuition.

Manner of payment One area for consideration is the manner of payment. In some jurisdictions it is not uncommon for the court to order the husband to make the child support payments directly to a court officer (the court trustee, clerk of the court, or another title the court assigns). A small fee is generally included for the court's service. This practice offers a tremendous advantage: First, the court automatically maintains a very accurate accounting of payments received and payments owed, which is beneficial if you return to court at some later date because of nonpayment of child support. The court accounting will be deemed correct without your having to present records of payment and your husband offering evidence of canceled checks, and so forth. It saves time for you, your husband, and the court. Second, a notice to your husband from the court regarding the status of his payments may carry far more weight than a telephone call from you asking for last week's payment. There is no guarantee that this method will make your husband pay in a timely fashion, but it may make a considerable difference. Some jurisdictions will not grant a request for payments to be made to the court unless the mother is receiving Aid to Families for Dependent Children because it creates additional paperwork and costs for the court. If payment directly to the court is available in your jurisdiction, it is worth discussing. While some states provide for wage deduction automatically, others provide for it when payments have been missed.

Many states have statutes requiring the obligor to make support payments directly to the court. Arizona requires that all child support payments or spousal maintenance payments be made through the clerk of the court unless the parties agree otherwise. In Kansas, every child support order must be paid through the clerk of the district court or the court trustee, except in exceptional circumstances. Arkansas' act 989 of 1985 provides that payments for spousal and child support be made through the registry of the court.

Your husband may also agree to a voluntary wage assignment, although this is relatively rare. It is more common to establish a trust out of which support payments are made. However, if he recognizes that he has a problem budgeting he may see the wisdom in having child support payments automatically deducted from his wages and sent directly to you. This suggestion may be acceptable to him if he recognizes that (a) it will mean less contact between the two of you, and therefore less potential conflict, (b) the timely payment will eliminate the possibility of returning to court for enforcement, which could result in additional legal expense and/or incarceration, and (c) the fulfillment of his responsibility can help strengthen the parent-child relationship. For a more complete discussion of wage deduction, see page 165.

These options may not be viable in your case or in your jurisdiction, or your husband may refuse to agree. In fact, there may be no protective measures that your attorney can initiate at this time. But you can plan a course of action that you will follow if your husband fails to comply with the court order once it is entered. It is very important to make this plan. When it comes to child support, adopting the attitude of "let's cross that bridge when we come to it" can be destructive. The fact that in 1987 only about half of all women awarded child support payments received the full amount[5] should speak for itself. It is infinitely better to discuss your options with your attorney early and never have to implement them than be totally unprepared when the worst happens.

One of the many attorneys I met with while preparing this book made a statement that haunted me long after the interview was over. She had been stating her views and relating some of her success stories for about an hour when I posed a question regarding the enforcement of her clients' child support orders. She said she didn't like to practice in that area and added, "Just because I handle a divorce for someone doesn't mean I'm married to him for life." While this is not an isolated attitude—I have heard these sentiments expressed in less vivid terms by many other attorneys—it does underline the importance of determining if your attorney will proceed with gusto to represent you for the purpose of the enforcement of a court order if your husband fails to comply.

As you continue reading your will learn about various options that are available for enforcement. I strongly recommend that you familiarize yourself with these methods prior to discussing this matter with your attorney. If you have already met with an attorney, learning now can only strengthen your case. Your attorney should know the best action to take as well as the enforcement agencies that exist in your jurisdiction. If he suggests that the best method for enforcement is for him to continue representing you and filing a contempt action against your husband, then you should discuss the fees required and whether these fees are recoverable; that is, find out if your husband will be ordered by the court to pay your legal expenses for bringing the contempt action.

If you were selling a piece of real estate and retained an attorney to handle the agreement, he would undoubtedly explain all your options and the legal courses of action available to you if the buyer failed to perform. When it comes to obtaining a divorce, however, many attorneys don't even mention the possibility of their client's not receiving the support and the remedies available should nonpayment occur. This is the time to find out where your attorney stands on this issue. After your divorce is final, for all intents and purposes your attorney has completed the services for which he was hired.

The concessions that your attorney obtains at the bargaining table and the court order that is entered on your child's behalf are only half of the solution. The total solution requires that your husband live up to his agreement and comply with the court order. By preparing the assessment of your husband's patterns, you have given yourself some time to think about how your husband functions in terms of his obligations. The one element that is missing in your assessment is how he will feel in the future, after the divorce, toward you, your child, and his child support obligations. If you feel there is going to be a problem, then by discussing it with your attorney, the two of you may be able to come up with ideas to minimize it.

Educating yourself about every aspect of your case will not only make you feel secure but also make the difference between your losing months or even years of support while you are floundering for solutions. As in any situation, knowledge alleviates the feelings of confusion and helplessness that occur when you don't know what to do.

Finally, since communication and understanding are prerequisites for any relationship, they are essential elements of the attorney-client relationship. When you are discussing aspects of your case with your attorney, he may use terms that are foreign to you. Since you are not necessarily an attorney yourself, you may not understand everything, so ask him to explain in terms that you can comprehend. If you allow statements to go by without grasping their meaning, you may hurt yourself and the relationship because your attorney might assume you have a level of understanding that you don't. There will be times when you will be called upon to make a decision, but making an informed decision on a matter you don't fully understand is impossible. Help yourself and your attorney to sustain a good relationship through openness and honesty.

CHAPTER 11

Your Day in Court

THE DAY you have been anticipating has arrived: the forum for presenting the results of your many hours of preparation. In this public arena you and your husband will be sitting on opposing sides, perhaps for the first time in your lives. Today you will find out the effects of all your preparation.

Seeing your husband across the courtroom may or may not be a highly emotional experience for you, depending on the circumstances of your divorce. If your emotions are running high and you find the court experience unsettling, nothing beats having an attorney that you have faith in and who is supportive. You may find some comfort in knowing that you are not alone in feeling anxious. Anyone who has sat in on family court with any frequency will confirm that the party who is calm and remains detached emotionally from the proceedings is the exception.

Any new environment becomes less formidable once you become educated about it, and the court is no exception. Visiting a domestic court prior to your own court hearing will help relieve some fears and/or anxieties. You may gain a degree of confidence by simply grasping the format of the court procedure. In the time I spent waiting in superior court I witnessed various situations that not only increased my knowledge but also allowed me to feel comfortable and develop some objectivity.

One morning I sat through one and a half hours of a husband and wife divorcing, neither of whom was represented by counsel. Theirs was a relatively simple divorce with no children or substantive assets involved. They were arguing over the division of a headboard, mattress, boxspring, bed frame, and dresser. It became obvious that the basis of their arguments went deeper than these possessions, but nevertheless the commissioner sat there patiently as each side presented his or her response to what the other had said. Eventually it was obvious that these two people would never agree. The division was made by the court.

On a different occasion I watched as a clerk from one of Century City's most prominent law firms specializing in divorce requested a continuance on a case that had been dragging on forever due to continuances previously granted, on the basis that the attorney was ill. In this instance the judge surprised some in attendance by stating that he didn't care if they had to bring the attorney in on a stretcher, the request for a continuance was denied and he expected the attorney in his courtroom when court reconvened after lunch.

Another time I saw a new attorney's disbelief when the clerk of the court rejected the papers he was attempting to file because he had used blue ink instead of the required black ink in filling out the forms. In this particular case it was my former husband's newly retained attorney who was representing him regarding his failure to make child support payments.

Your attorney will file a petition for the dissolution of your marriage, and a court date will be set for the hearing. Your name will appear as Petitioner or Plaintiff, and your husband's name will appear as Respondent or Defendant. If your husband has already filed for the divorce, the reverse will be true. A case number will be assigned, and in the future any information you seek from the court or any other papers filed in relation to your divorce must include this case number. To prepare you for this hearing your attorney should "walk you through the process" so that you will know what to expect. Generally you will be asked a few questions to establish for the court that you wish to obtain a divorce. These questions may be posed by the judge or by your own counsel. If the divorce has been mutually agreed upon by you and your husband, this procedure will take but a few minutes of the court's time.

If you and your husband have reached an agreement on your marital settlement and no issues are left to be resolved that would require a trial, the court at this time may enter an order for child support. If, on the other hand, you have not reached an agreement, your attorney will have to request a temporary support order, often referred to as a TSO. A Temporary Support Order is entered by the court and remains in effect until the hearing to determine support is held. He may choose to make this request concurrently (at the same time) with the petition for dissolution or subsequent to (after) this hearing. Prior to obtaining a temporary support order you have no legally enforceable way to collect support from your husband. It is in your best interests, therefore, not to delay this hearing any longer than is necessary. Your attorney should have all the pertinent information and proof regarding your husband's assets and income at the time of the hearing. Frequently, the custodial parent is not required to appear and the attorney can obtain a TSO with an affidavit.

You should not dress down for the occasion. Some women mistakenly believe that they have to prove to the court by their attire that they need the money. Your financial declaration speaks for itself and states precisely your needs and requirements. Your appearance reflects your respect for both the court and yourself, and you should dress as nicely as you can. Until a stop was put to it, some individuals were appearing in the Santa Monica courthouse in shorts and with bare feet. It is hard to imagine how a judge's attitude could not be affected by someone appearing before the bench who didn't seem to care enough to put on a pair of shoes. Such an affront to the court can antagonize a judge long before the individual's case is heard.

In some jurisdictions your case will be set to be heard at a specific time. In other jurisdictions a number of domestic matters will be set for a morning session or an afternoon session, often with a list of the cases scheduled to be heard posted on the courtroom door.

An attorney usually plans to meet his client at least fifteen minutes before court convenes or before the time the matter is set to be heard. If you are in the courthouse and for some reason your attorney does not arrive on time, you may find yourself being approached by your husband or his counsel. You should resist entering into any discussion with them. You may feel strongly about wanting to make some point, you may wish to make your husband's attorney understand your position, or you may even feel that he is operating from misinformation provided by your husband, but you must remember that *he represents your husband*. Anything you say may expose a vulnerability on your part or even damage your own case. Your husband's attorney is aware that if he has a question to ask, the appropriate and ethical behavior is to ask it of your attorney. The safest rule to follow is that you do not converse with opposing counsel. If you are alone in the courthouse, keep to yourself. Too many times a woman may find herself nervous and apprehensive about facing the court and strike up a conversation with anyone who will listen. Once she is inside the courtroom she may discover that she has supplied the opposing side with a variety of information because the "friendly ear" is a friendly witness for the other side.

Generally the first occurrence in the courtroom is the calendar call whereby the clerk calls out the cases that are scheduled or "calendared" to be heard. When your case is called, your attorney informs the court that both of you are present, and your husband's attorney responds similarly (assuming they are both present). There is a second calendar call for those who are running late. Some of the cases that are called will probably not be heard that day for any number of reasons; therefore, your wait may not be very lengthy. Conversely, a case scheduled to be heard before yours may take an inordinate amount of time even though no major issues are being contested. When a microwave oven or a set of dishes becomes the object of an emotional battle in the courtroom, the opposing arguments can go on endlessly, and you simply have to wait.

If your attorney has not arrived by the first calendar call, you should inform the court that you are present and that your attorney has not yet arrived. If he is running late, he may have called the court, which the clerk will state. In any case, it is not the end of the world. You should find the nearest telephone, however, and speak to your attorney's office to be sure he is on his way. Even in the event that your attorney fails to appear, which is highly unlikely, you will not be required to represent yourself. The court will either push the date forward or take the matter off the calendar, in which case your attorney will have to obtain a new date for the hearing. I would like to emphasize that the chance of this happening is very, very slim.

You are not permitted to communicate aloud with your attorney once your matter is before the court; however, you can write a message to him on a pad if an issue is raised that you failed to discuss earlier and on which you have something to say. Since this will interrupt his train of thought and pull his attention away from what is momentarily occurring, you should employ this device only if what you have to tell him is extremely important.

When your case is called, both attorneys will offer their respective clients' financial declarations to the court and present their case. What happens next depends on you and your husband. If your husband's attorney takes issue with your expenses, you will be in a defensive position. If your attorney challenges your husband's income or expense declaration, you will be taking the position that he is lying. If both of you are in agreement with each other's declarations, there will be harmony, the hearing will be short, and the decision will rest solely with the judge.

While your husband should have filed an accurate income and expense declaration prior to the hearing, giving you and your attorney sufficient time for review, this is not always the case. Frequently an attorney requests permission from the court to submit a modified declaration, and you will need time to review the financial declaration before the case is heard. Your attorney and you should go over the declaration carefully to be sure it reflects what you know to be true and accurate. If your husband has omitted or understated his income or assets, then your attorney should have the necessary documentation to challenge these inaccuracies.

If you have to defend your declaration, remember that the figures you prepared were not pulled out of a hat but were arrived at through precise accounting. People frequently don't realize how much everything costs until they are forced to prepare or review an accounting, so while your expenses may be characterized as excessive by the other side, you can be assured that your accounting is true and accurate.

If your husband's declaration shows a change in circumstances from what you have known to be true, such as a decrease in income, you may not be able to contest it during this hearing due to lack of proof. The change may even be something you know is an outright lie. This is not the time to lose control. As difficult as it may be, you must refrain from saying anything directly to your husband or to the judge in court. Remember, if testimony can be disproved at a later date, a child support order can be modified by the court.

A great deal of potential trauma can be eliminated if you and your husband have entered into a Stipulation to Establish Child

112   CHILD SUPPORT

ATTORNEY OR PARTY WITHOUT ATTORNEY *(Name and Address)*:	TELEPHONE NO.:	FOR COURT USE ONLY
ATTORNEY FOR *(Name)*:		

SUPERIOR COURT OF CALIFORNIA, COUNTY OF
STREET ADDRESS:
MAILING ADDRESS:
CITY AND ZIP CODE:
BRANCH NAME:

PETITIONER/PLAINTIFF:

RESPONDENT/DEFENDANT:

STIPULATION TO ESTABLISH OR MODIFY CHILD OR FAMILY SUPPORT AND ORDER	CASE NUMBER:

1. We agree that we are fully informed of our rights under the Minimum Child Support Standards Act.
2. We make this agreement freely without threat or duress **and** the needs of our children will be adequately met under this agreement.
3. *Complete a, b, or c.*
   a. ☐ The right to support has not been assigned to any county and no application for public assistance is pending.
   b. ☐ The right to support has been assigned to *(county name)*:
   c. ☐ An application for public assistance is pending in *(county name)*:
   If you checked b or c, a district attorney of the county named must sign below before the court will accept your stipulation.
   Date:

   ....   ▶   ....
   (TYPE OR PRINT NAME)   (SIGNATURE OF DISTRICT ATTORNEY)

4. Petitioner's net monthly income: $ _____ Respondent's net monthly income: $ _____
5. *Check one.*
   a. ☐ We agree that child or family support will be ordered in a sum which is **equal to or greater than the current AFDC payment** for the number of children we have. The AFDC payment is: $ _____
   b. ☐ We agree that child or family support will be ordered in a sum **less than the current AFDC payment** for the number of children we have. The AFDC payment is: $ _____
   c. ☐ We agree that child or family support will be ordered in a sum less than that provided by the Minimum Child Support Standards Act and no change of circumstances need be demonstrated for a modification.
6. We agree that ☐ child ☐ family support will be payable as follows beginning on *(date)*: _____

Name of child	Monthly amount	Payable by	Payable to	Payable on (dates)
a.	$			
b.	$			
c.	$			
d.	$			
e. Family support	$			

▶ ....   ▶ ....
(SIGNATURE OF PETITIONER/PLAINTIFF)   (SIGNATURE OF RESPONDENT/DEFENDANT)

ORDER

7. a. ☐ Child support is ordered payable as set forth in item 6. All provisions of previous orders relating to the child or children remain in effect unless specifically modified by this order. Child support payments shall continue until further order of the court or until the child marries, dies, is emancipated, reaches 19, or reaches 18 and is not a full-time high school student residing with a parent, whichever occurs first.
   b. ☐ Family support is ordered payable as set forth in item 6e. The payments shall continue until the death of the recipient or until further order of the court.

Date:

....
JUDGE OF THE SUPERIOR COURT

Form Approved by Rule 1285.27
Judicial Council of California
1285.27 (Rev. January 1, 1986)
1285.27

STIPULATION TO ESTABLISH OR MODIFY CHILD OR FAMILY SUPPORT AND ORDER
(Family Law)

76S693 — RD084 — 1/86
Civil Code, § 4728

Support prior to the hearing. A sample of a stipulation form is provided at the end of this chapter. In the absence of an agreement, the judge or commissioner will make a determination as to the amount of the payments, when they should be paid, and for whom they are being paid. Depending on the nature of the proceedings, you will leave the court with either a temporary support order or a final support order. Once the order has been prepared and signed by the judge, your attorney should send you a copy for your records.

It is possible that after the hearing is over you will find yourself feeling confused about what actually happened. For a person who has had little exposure to the judicial system, court proceedings can be extremely difficult to follow, and, combined with the emotions experienced during the hearing, it is easy to understand how you can leave the courtroom feeling bewildered. If you have questions or there are areas you don't understand, ask your attorney for explanations. It is very important in the long run that you not only understand what happened but also *why* it happened.

CHAPTER 12

Maintaining a Diary

ONCE YOU have received your court order, you must keep accurate records of everything that occurs from that time forward. The solution to many of the problems that may arise will often be dependent on your records and their accuracy. Relying on your memory alone won't work.

You should establish a file for the divorce documents generated from your case. Your attorney will provide you with a copy of any document filed with the Court. He should also give you a copy of any court memorandums and correspondence that are generated between him and opposing counsel. Whenever you write a letter to your attorney, be sure to make a copy for your file. By developing this organizational habit you will save yourself an incredible amount of time and avoid potential frustration in the future. Certain documents are required if you decide to change attorneys or seek assistance from a child support agency. You can always obtain a copy from the court of any document in the court file, but this is time consuming and costs money. If an attorney has to go to the courthouse to review your file, this also generates more fees. If you ever have a question about something that has transpired, you can review your file in the clerk of the court's office at the courthouse.

Unless you and your ex-husband arrive at an agreement determining when he will make the child support payments, the judge will choose the dates. Frequently, a support order provides that monthly support be made in two equal payments. Unless your state requires obligors to make payments to the court directly, your ex-husband will mail the checks to you. It is crucial to outline every aspect of how you will receive payment. If the guidelines for arranging are nebulous, your ex-husband may use manipulative strategies for payment—like asking the child to deliver checks, paying late or less than the amount called for, or not signing the checks. In your payment agreement, be sure to specify whether "payments shall be made on June 1," "payments shall be received by June 1," etc.

If you do not receive your child support payments and must seek enforcement of the order, you will do so in one of three ways: by retaining an attorney, by using the services of a child support enforcement agency, or by bringing an action on your own behalf. (A thorough discussion of enforcement proceedings appears in Part III.) In order to commence seeking enforcement proceedings of a child support court order, you must have both the actual court order for child support and your *precise* record of the amount of support you have received to date, including the dates of receipt. Since this history dates from when the very first payment was due, can you imagine the difficulty you would encounter trying to reconstruct a payment schedule five years after the order was entered if you had failed to keep a good record of payments received?

The records you maintain will become the most valuable source of data you have should you ever seek enforcement or modification of your court order. Regardless of who would ultimately bring an action on your behalf, you are the one who will be required to swear to the veracity of the arrearage. (*Arrearage* is the total amount of child support payments an obligor fails to make.) For example, if you were to go to court, after having sworn in your documents that you have received a certain amount of support, and your husband presents canceled checks that prove he has paid you $250 more than you credited him with, your credibility would suffer a severe blow. The fact that your mistake was unintentional can't be proven to the court. The reality is that you declared you had received an amount that was *proven* to be erroneous. Even if your husband is obviously guilty and this error results in his owing you $3,000 instead of the $3,250 you had claimed, you have still harmed yourself in the courtroom.

I strongly suggest that you purchase a book to serve as your diary. You will be using this diary during the years your child grows to adulthood, and its purpose is to record all events that relate to child support: court orders, legal fees, record of payments, actual ongoing expenses, and so forth. The diary should have ample pages to accommodate this information.

COURT ORDERS

Your first entry in the diary will be the court order. Copy it down word for word. If the order includes an agreement between you and your husband, write down the part that pertains to child support and visitation. Include all information about the order: your case number, the name of the judge who presided, the name and address of the court, the date the order was entered, your attorney's name and address, and the name and address of your husband's attorney. Leave several pages blank for future orders that may be issued by the court.

THE CHILD SUPPORT PAYMENT SCHEDULE

You are now ready to prepare your child support payment schedule, which will consist of five columns: Date Ordered, Amount Ordered, Date Paid, Amount Paid, and Balance. The court order designates whether the payments are to be made weekly, bimonthly, monthly, or on specific days of the month. The order should also include the commencement date of the payments. You will want to refer to a calendar to fill in the Date Ordered column. The Amount Ordered is a constant factor. Accuracy is crucial.

Sample Child Support Schedule

Date Ordered	Amount Ordered	Date Paid	Amount Paid	Balance
3/15/87	600	3/15/87	600	0
3/31/87	600	3/31/87	600	0
4/15/87	600	4/20/87	600	0
4/30/87	600	4/30/87	300	300
" "		5/15/87	300	0
5/15/87	600	5/15/87	600	0
5/30/87	600	6/07/87	500	100
" "		6/15/87	100	0
6/15/87	600	6/15/87	600	0

Promise yourself to conscientiously record each payment as it is received. Above is a sample schedule.

The Recording of Events

This section of your diary can be structured in one of two ways. You can maintain it either chronologically, recording each event as it occurs, or you can create separate sections for specifics such as visitation, husband's financial information, hearings, and so forth. I prefer the first method. You can always transfer information into separate areas at a later date, but the recording of events as they happen provides a comprehensive picture that may be extremely useful to you and your attorney. Here is an example of diary entries:

June 7, 1990   Received a check for child support that was ordered for June 1. The check was drawn on a different bank. This account is with Bank of America, Westside branch, and the account number is #241-365771-08. Check number 39.
June 15, 1990 The children were picked up on time, went to the movies, and had a great time.
July 3, 1990   I called my attorney to tell him that I haven't received a payment since June 7. He was out, and I left word for him to call.
July 4, 1990   Spoke with my attorney, and he suggested that if I haven't received a payment by the 15th of this month we file an OSC—a motion to find Sam in contempt. He said it will take about three weeks from the filing date to be heard. Spoke for ten minutes.

The more comprehensive your diary, the more valuable it becomes. Any new information you may garner regarding your husband's earnings or assets should be noted. If he changes his residence or purchases goods of value, record as many details as you can. You never know what information may be useful in the future. Your husband may attempt to modify his support payments downward or may fight you on a modification upward on the basis of his living expenses. If his expenses have escalated, not out of necessity but due to his chosen life-style, it is unlikely the court will grant him relief in the form of lower support obligations. The more factual your records, the stronger your case. This is not to imply that you should spend every wakeful hour tracking your husband's activities; that would be extremely destructive. It means that you should be aware of and record any information which could have a direct impact on you.

Your Children's Expenses

The final section of your diary is devoted entirely to your children's expenses. As the chart on page 62 indicates, a child's expenses increase dramatically after twelve years of age. This record of actual costs incurred can be used as supporting evidence should you later request a modification upward. You should indicate what expenses will be reimbursed by your ex-husband, the date of the expense, and the date you receive reimbursement. Maintain each child's expense records separately and leave ample pages.

Your diary will constitute evidence should your husband's attorney request that you produce any records, journals, or diaries maintained for the purpose of determining child support arrearage. If your husband has no justifiable defense for his failure to pay child support, his attorney may well mount an offensive in an attempt to discredit your claim. He may challenge the amount you claim is owed by attempting to demonstrate to the court that you are a poor record keeper and are disorganized. How strong a bearing this has on the court is highly speculative, but you should understand the enormous value of having your records in order and in a book that has been established specifically for that purpose.

CHAPTER 13

Post-Hearing Evaluation

AFTER YOUR first appearance in court, a period of time generally elapses before your divorce is final. The length is determined by the nature of your divorce proceedings and the jurisdiction where you have filed. This "waiting period" can often provide a window to what you can expect in the future. If the amount of your child support order is based on an agreement between you and your husband, there should be no element of surprise regarding the amount. If, on the other hand, the child support order exceeds the amount your husband wished to pay, he may believe that he is being treated unfairly.

From your diary you know the amount you are due to receive and the dates on which you are supposed to receive it. As you record the payments you want to be watchful for any patterns that start to emerge. Are you receiving the payments consistently on time, or are they usually four or five days late? Are the payments getting further and further apart? As soon as you notice a problem, bring it to the attention of your attorney. If you are lucky, your attorney will be able to resolve the problem by communicating with your husband's attorney. An attorney recognizes how important it is that a client adhere to a court order, and learning that a client is behaving in a manner that could be deemed contemptuous of the court should prompt an attorney to improve his client's behavior. It should not take very long for you to see the outcome of such an attempt, but if your husband continues to fall into arrears on the support payments or fails to pay anything at all, then a stronger course of action must be initiated.

I cannot express strongly enough how important it is to take action the moment a problem arises. Your failure to act may lull your husband into believing that nothing will happen if he fails to make the support payments, and then taking him back to court may be your only strategy for changing his mind. All tears, shouts, begging, and threats will fall on deaf ears. It is crucial that you establish a precedent early. If he believes he is in a "power" position because you are dependent on his money and he has gained some degree of control over you, then you may face many years of manipulation. By taking a positive step, which may mean returning to court to seek enforcement of the support order, you will be able to bring everything back into perspective. He knows that if he fails to make his automobile payments, they will take his car away; he will learn that if he fails to make his child support payments, he will be forced to answer to the court.

You may discover during this time that your evaluation of your husband was wrong. Having informed your attorney that there was no chance of his failing to comply with a court order, you may now be reluctant to admit that his actions are falling short of your expectations. In that case you must bury your pride and realistically face the truth. If you were making excuses for him all your married life, you may be unwilling to recognize the truth now and rationalize his failure to pay. He may be very aware of your tendency to justify his behavior, but if you permit yourself to fall into this trap, you could pay dearly for years to come.

Your ex-husband may not make his support payments for any number of reasons, and they are examined in the next chapter. People change, and so do their priorities. If he is exhibiting a reluctance to pay, then it is your obligation to your child and to yourself to face the reality and take affirmative action.

CHAPTER 14

Intimidation and Rationalization

It is not uncommon for individuals to behave unethically and replace feelings of guilt with rationalization in order to feel better. The belief can set in quickly that the rationalization is true. How does a father rationalize not providing for the support of his child? Every nonpaying individual will have his own method, but let's examine a few.

If you are the one who wanted the divorce, that alone can provide the reasons. You should have known what was in store for you. You wanted to be on your own, so be on your own. You've taken his child away from him, so why should he have to pay you for that hurt?

What if the court has ordered more than your ex-husband believes he can afford? He can prove to the court that he was right by not paying. After all, didn't he say he couldn't afford the payments?

Support payments are supposed to be for food, shelter, clothing —the child's necessities. Well, his child has a place to live, clothes to wear, and food to eat even when he doesn't make his payments. The custodial mother will always make sure of that.

Perhaps you have remarried, and your new husband has a nice income. Why shouldn't your new husband take care of the child's expenses? After all, he knew what he was getting into when he married you.

Look at the way you spend money. Every time he sees you in a new dress, he figures he bought it for you. Why should he be struggling to add to your wardrobe?

He can't afford it. He never realized how much living on his own would cost.

You have a good salary and don't really need any money from him.

He has a new life now. He is remarried, and his new family must come first.

He doesn't like the way you're raising his child. If you will change, he'll be happy to start paying support.

You don't have enough money to take him back to court. Anyway, what good would it do to throw him in jail?

Look at how much he spends on the children for Christmas, weekends, birthdays, and vacations. This should offset anything he owes you for support.

The list can go on forever, but the chances are that if he isn't making support payments, he has found a rationalization for his behavior. Regardless of which rationalization your ex-husband uses, remember that it is just that—a rationalization. It has nothing to do with you and your legal situation and should not influence your course of action. The danger lies only in your believing his self-deception and excuses.

Intimidation is another issue completely. Problems that may arise in this area should be brought to the attention of your attorney. If your ex-husband threatens to try to obtain custody of your child, discuss this with your attorney immediately. There has to be very strong evidence to prove you are an unfit mother or that it would be in the best interests of your child to remove him from your custody. Having threats concerning your "relative fitness" as a parent looming over your head can be frightening, but your attorney may be able to dispel your fears in one conversation.

Your ex-husband may threaten to tell your child that you are trying to put Daddy in jail if you file a contempt action against him. He may say that you are bankrupting him, that you have more money than he does, and that you are unfair. By permitting yourself to be manipulated in this fashion, you are eliminating the most common remedy at law that is at your disposal.

He may threaten to leave town or even the country. While this would create problems for you and would also buy him some time, it would not relieve him of his child support obligations. Child support orders are enforceable throughout the country under the Uniform Reciprocal Code which enables a custodial parent to file a petition for failure to pay child support in their state of residence for a hearing to be held in a different state. This topic is addressed later in Chapter 19.

If your husband threatens you with physical abuse, you must inform your attorney. He can obtain a restraining order against your husband for your safety. This type of order places a restraint on a party's behavior. A T. R. O. is a temporary restraining order, used when there is a pending case between parties. The order might state, for example, that your husband is to stay at least one thousand feet away from you, your residence, and your workplace.

Intimidation is only useful if it is effective. When you refuse to be a party to this intimidation and proceed along the proper, legal channels, then you, your child, and your husband will benefit in the long run.

Even though your marriage is over, your ex-husband may want to remain feeling in control. If you have sole custody, he may sense that he has lost control over his child's life, and his making or not making child support payments may offer him the only opportunity to restore his feeling of control.

Just as you may feel that you know your husband, he feels the same way about you. He undoubtedly knows your vulnerabilities, your weaknesses, what causes you to procrastinate, and what makes you feel guilty. A psychologist might say he knows which of your buttons to push, just as you know his. The ongoing issue of child support payments may be the only battlefront left between the two of you to keep the conflict going.

If you allow yourself to become involved in an overt confrontation over child support, chances are you will come away with nothing but anger and frustration. To allow your child to overhear a confrontation of this nature is incredibly unfair. Remember, there is no reason for you to justify your need for support. The court order exists and speaks for itself: Your ex-husband was ordered by the court and must comply with the order.

If you are the one who seeks the confrontation, then you are acting against your own welfare. You should examine your motives. Whether or not your husband is complying with the support order, the court has a level of authority over him. It is a powerful authority. Use it.

Arguing outside of the court, one on one, will inevitably work in his favor. If he begins to believe that future battles are going to take place in this arena where he may very well exert more psychological control, then you may unwittingly be encouraging him not to comply simply by continuing to debate him without your attorney present. As the result of many unresolved problems and conflicts that led to the deterioration of your marriage, you may need to vent emotions such as hurt, frustration, and anger, causing you to welcome any opportunity to confront your ex-spouse. If this is true, then you must accept that only you can resolve the past, either by yourself, with friends, through therapy, or just with the passage of time.

During this period when your relationship with your ex-husband is being redefined, it is possible that (a) he is using the child support issue as a means of staying attached to you in the event that he is unable to "let go," or (b) he still needs to feel that he is in control of you, and this is the only area in which he can assert control. If you react to these types of misdirected motivations, the dynamics of control and attachment can remain intact for years. The fact that you have a court order means that you don't have to be a willful participant in a destructive scenario. You can seek enforcement, if necessary, and therein lies your strength.

CHAPTER 15

Visitation

YOUR AGREEMENT will contain a provision that outlines when your ex-husband will have visitation[1] with your child if you are in accord on this issue. If you have not agreed on a visitation schedule, then the court will set forth the visitation terms within the court order. Your attorney will be familiar with what the court in your jurisdiction deems "reasonable visitation rights" and will be able to give you a good indication of what the court will order. There is less variance among the different jurisdictions on the issue of visitation than on child support. Visitation provisions differ considerably depending on the ages of the children and other factors.

Many visitation provisions provide for the noncustodial parent to have the child every other weekend from 6 P.M. Friday to 6 P.M. Sunday, every other major holiday, meaning Christmas and Easter (or half of Christmas vacation and half of Easter vacation), and a period of time in the summer, generally one month or six weeks. Of course, visitation can be structured in any manner that is agreeable to both you and your husband. One unmarried father I spoke with believes that it would be terribly unfair to have his daughter sitting at home while he works on the weekdays during the summer. In lieu of this, he calls for his daughter after work on Thursdays throughout the year, at which time they go out to dinner. She spends the night at his home, they enjoy breakfast together, and then he drives her to school. This has become a ritual, one that his daughter looks forward to every week. He has found a viable alternative to summer visitation, and in this case it works.

It is essential that visitation be structured. Even if you feel that you want your ex-husband to spend as much time as possible with your child, there must be guidelines. If your ex-husband exercises his visitation rights regularly, your child will adapt to the pattern, increasing his sense of security. He will grow to understand that he sees his father at certain times on certain days and that this is what happens when your parents are divorced. If there is no prescribed timetable, a child feels that his father can see him whenever he wants to. It is emotionally difficult for the child to deal with all the time his father does not visit him.

Just as the court has taken various factors into consideration in determining child support, it will also concern itself with any particular circumstances that are relative to visitation in your case. Once the court has reached a decision, an order will be entered spelling out the visitation rights. Whereas the support order is directed at your ex-husband, requiring him to pay you a specific amount for the purpose of child support, the court order pertaining to visitation is directed at you. You are ordered to have your child prepared to be called for at specific times for visitation. To deny your ex-husband his visitation rights, therefore, or to frustrate his attempts to exercise those rights is not only morally wrong but is also an action for which you can be found guilty of contempt of court.

Your child has the right to be supported, and he also has the right to be with his natural father. These are two separate and individual rights; one issue has nothing to do with the other. Your ex-husband has certain visitation rights that have been ordered by the court whereby the court acknowledges that (a) your child will benefit from spending time with his father, and (b) a parent's right to spend time with his child should never be abrogated. Even if your ex-husband fails to make child support payments for a week, a month, or a year, visitation privileges should not be withheld or used as a weapon. Your child has also been granted the right to spend time with his father.

If you refuse to let your ex-husband have your child on visitation days, he can bring an action against you. If he does, at no time during the hearing will the fact that he failed to make his support payments be an issue. The only issue will be that you were under court order to permit visitation for specified periods, and you failed to comply with that court order. In addition to being guilty of contempt of court, you would also be guilty of depriving both your ex-husband and your child of their rights.

In several recent cases mothers were held in civil contempt for refusing to comply with scheduled visitation schedules. In Diane J. Vogt's article, "Civil Versus Criminal Contempt,"[2] she relates how in 1981 a California court found Faye Henderson in contempt for refusing to allow her ex-husband visitation rights with their two-year-old daughter based on her allegations that he had sexually abused the child. The visits in this case were stopped when the child was found to have injuries after having visited her father.

Another example in the same vein is the widely publicized case of Dr. Elizabeth Morgan who placed her daughter in hiding rather than comply with a visitation order. The court determined that there was insufficient evidence to support Dr. Morgan's allegations that her husband, Dr. Eric Foretich, had sexually abused their child. Dr. Morgan, a surgeon trained at Harvard, Yale, and Oxford, was jailed on August 28, 1987. By the fall of 1988 she had served over a year in jail, and her fine had reached over $1 million. Both of these cases involve sexual abuse allegations, but they do reflect the reluctance of courts to treat lightly the failure to comply with visitation orders.

Frequently, a noncustodial parent will use the fact that he has been deprived of visitation privileges to justify his failure to pay child support. This argument generally constitutes no better defense for his case than his failure to pay support justifies your withholding of visitation. Courts hear these arguments over and over again, but they are two separate issues.

An example of how the courts maintain the separateness of child support and visitation is illustrated by the ruling in the 1986 North Carolina Appeals Court case of *Appert v. Appert*. The court held that "conditioning payment of child support upon the custodial parent's compliance with the order granting the noncustodial parent visitation privileges is 'inherently detrimental' to the child's best interest and contrary to state law."[3] In *Biamby v. Biamby*, however, a 1985 New York case where a mother had denied her ex-husband visitation and was seeking a judgment for arrearage, the court held that denial of visitation precluded a judgment for arrears in support.[4] The court stated that a noncustodial parent's right to visitation is a right more precious than any property right, and the custodial parent should not ordinarily be allowed to enjoy the benefits of a support order when visitation is being denied.

The court will more often supervise a noncustodial parent's visitation than deny it altogether. If substantial evidence was presented to the court that your child would be exposed to danger or an extremely undesirable environment during visitation, the court would then weigh the potential damage against the benefit of the visits. For example, a noncustodial father who was convicted of selling a controlled substance was permitted to continue visitation privileges with the added provision that his child's parental grandmother be present during the visitations. If this sort of situation applied in your child's case, your attorney would seek a lawful resolution to the problem, asking for either an injunction or a modification of the visitation court order to ensure the child's safety and well-being.

A custodial parent may subjectively consider a noncustodial parent's environment "extremely undesirable" based on personal beliefs that would not be embraced by the court. Philip and Gloria's divorce resulted from their differences in beliefs that developed after they were married. After the birth of their daughter, Gloria joined a particular religious group. Philip was unwilling to convert, and the marriage disintegrated. Gloria was awarded sole custody of their two children, and Philip received reasonable visitation rights. The religious group did not believe individuals should accumulate material possessions, forbade female members from wearing makeup, required members to adhere to strict dietary rules, discouraged the bestowing of gifts, and held that those who violated the doctrines of the group were sinful. Philip, embracing none of these beliefs, lived in a spacious home with a swimming pool, drove a foreign sports car, enjoyed giving gifts to his children, and married a woman who was never seen without makeup. Gloria believed that Philip's environment was not only "undesirable" but also sinful. For a long time she and her new husband, who was also a member of the same religious group, did everything possible to frustrate Philip's visitation rights. The children were torn—enjoying the swimming but fearful for their father's eternal life. With time the situation diffused, and the children grew up exposed to both parents' worlds, but not without a great deal of emotional turmoil.

Unfortunately, there is frequently a tendency for divorced parents to communicate with each other through their child, thus making him "the messenger." The perfect opportunity for delivering messages exists when your child is about to spend some time with his father, but this creates a heavy burden for the child and is truly unfair. If you find yourself gravitating toward this kind of behavior, you must fight the temptation. Instead, allow him to luxuriate in being a son while spending time with the other parent that he loves.

It is unforgivable to frustrate your ex-husband's attempts to visit and develop a bond with his child. No matter how sensitive you may be to the feelings of your child, there is no way to shelter him from all the hurts that result from a divorce. The best you can hope for is that your child continues to enjoy healthy and loving relationships with both you and his father, relationships that reinforce the fact that he is deeply loved by both of you. Your constructive behavior and maturity can help your child receive the love he needs for his emotional well-being.

PART THREE

YOUR REMEDIES

CHAPTER 16

Contempt Proceedings

Between 25 and 33 percent of women entitled to receive child support never receive even their first payment.[1]

IN THE courtroom you heard the judge tell your husband when and how much he must pay for your child's support. The judge may have warned him that the failure to make these payments would bring serious ramifications. Generally, during the hearing to determine child support your attention was focused on how much the court would order. At that auspicious moment you believed you would receive those payments. You may have even left the courtroom elated if the support award exceeded your expectations. But if you are not receiving your payments, you have learned that *the fact you obtained an order for child support does not necessarily mean you will receive it.* A court order is useless unless it can be enforced. The court does not automatically enforce its own orders. If your husband is not complying with the child support order, enforcement can only come after you take affirmative action.

The filing of a contempt action is the most commonly used remedy for the enforcement of a child support order. This is true whether enforcement is sought through a child support enforcement agency or private counsel. While there are some minor differences between jurisdictions regarding the amount of time required to give notice to the other party, the time it takes to obtain a hearing date, and the form of service that is appropriate, contempt actions basically follow the same format throughout the

133

country. Every state has its own rules of civil procedure, and the courts have their own rules. The following example outlines the steps and procedure for bringing a contempt action in the superior court of Santa Monica, California.

In order to obtain a hearing date for any case, "moving papers" must be filed with the court. These papers set forth the nature of the hearing and include all supporting documents. A specific preprinted court form must be used in filing a contempt action. In California, the form is called an OSC RE: CONTEMPT, which is an abbreviated version of Order to Show Cause why this party should not be held in contempt of court. It is also referred to by the rule number that appears at the bottom of the form, 1285. This number indicates that the form was adopted by Rule 1285 of the Judicial Council of California.

The following information is required to complete this form: case number, your case number (which is the same case number assigned to your divorce proceedings), the style of the case (that is, Smith v. Smith), the order that was entered by the court that has not been complied with, the total amount of child support that was ordered, the amount that was paid, and the amount owing as of the date of filing. One of the supporting documents to be attached to this form is your declaration. In some jurisdictions it is referred to as an affidavit. This declaration will set forth that a court order exists, that your husband had knowledge of it, that he has failed to comply with it, and that his failure to comply was willful. These four elements must exist in order to prove contempt. The declaration must be dated and signed by you.

If you are using an attorney to bring the contempt action, he will prepare the declaration for you once you have provided him with the record of child support payments maintained in your diary. Below is a sample declaration:

DECLARATION

I, Susan L. Brown, do hereby declare that:

WHEREAS, on September 24, 1990, the court ordered Respondent to make child support payments to the Petitioner in the amount of $1200, said payments to be made on the 1st and the 15th of each month, commencing on October 1st;

WHEREAS, Respondent was present in the court when the child support order was entered;

WHEREAS, Respondent has failed to comply with said order as set forth in the schedule of child support payments, "Schedule A," which is attached hereto;

WHEREAS, Respondent's failure to comply was willful in that he had the ability to pay.

That the foregoing is true and correct to the best of my ability.

DATE: _____   _____
                                                            SUSAN L. BROWN

As the declaration indicates, a schedule of child support payments must also be attached. Generally, the precise wording of the court order is entered at the top of the page. This schedule lists in columns the amount the court has ordered, the date it was due, the amount that was paid, the date it was paid, and the amount still owed for each payment ordered during the period for which you are filing the contempt action. In California the courts will only consider finding a person in contempt for failure to pay child support for the previous twelve months: If your filing date for a contempt proceeding was September 24, 1990, your husband could be found guilty of contempt from September 25, 1989, through the date of filing. The format for this schedule follows the same form to record your receipt of support payments shown in Chapter 12, which is designed to facilitate the preparation of this supporting document. A copy of the court order is frequently included.

Once these papers are completed, they must be taken to the courthouse and filed with the clerk; he enters the date for the hearing, which is generally three weeks from the date of filing. A filing fee must be paid, and a conformed copy—that is, a copy that has been stamped by the clerk with the date of the hearing and the date of filing—must be served on your ex-husband no less than ten days prior to the hearing date. Because a contempt action is quasi-criminal in nature, in this jurisdiction, there is a requirement to effectuate service in person, as opposed to mailing a copy of the papers. Your attorney will arrange service through either an attorney's service or the marshal's office; this is one of the "costs" of bringing suit. In addition, a copy of the moving papers may be sent by your attorney to your ex-husband's attorney as a courtesy. Unless you are planning to subpoena witnesses or use other documents to substantiate the fact that your ex-husband has the ability to make his child support payments, there is nothing more to do until the time of the hearing.

If you have counsel, you are generally not required to be present in the courtroom at the time of the hearing. If you do not attend the hearing, however, you will be unable to hear any testimony from your ex-husband that might be contrary to what you have sworn to be true in your declaration. Were your ex-husband to claim, for example, that he had given you cash payments for which you have not credited him, you would be unable to refute his testimony if you were not in the courtroom. The court will not automatically believe your ex-husband's testimony, of course, but your attorney will probably prefer to have you present in court.

There are exceptions, of course. In a 1985 Utah case, *Utah State Department of Social Services v. Toledo*,[2] the state brought an enforcement action. The court held that the mother may be a necessary witness, that she was not an indispensable party, and she was required to attend the hearing.

THE CONTEMPT HEARING

At the beginning of the hearing your attorney will establish for the court the four prerequisites to prove contempt: your ex-husband's failure to comply, the existence of the court order, your ex-husband's knowledge of the court order, and his willfulness in not complying though he had the ability to pay. The counsel for your ex-husband will present his defense. Your ex-husband may or may not testify[3] since he will have the right, if he so chooses, to take the Fifth Amendment on the basis that he may incriminate himself.

After the judge or commissioner has listened to all the testimony, he will make his decision, which will be entered into what is sometimes referred to as a minute order that the clerk of the court will prepare. He will also establish for the record the amount of the arrearage owed. Your attorney will obtain a copy of this minute order and should provide one to you for your records, which you should enter into your diary. If you have to return to court again for enforcement, you will need to attach a copy of the minute order to your new moving papers.

INABILITY TO PAY

Assuming that the first three prerequisites for the hearing are valid—that there is a court order, which there must be to bring this action; that your husband had knowledge of the order (either he was in court when the order was made or he received notice of the order); and that he has not made the payments as ordered—there is only one justifiable defense available to him: He didn't have the ability to pay. Inability does not mean that there wasn't enough money left after his living expenses or that he wasn't working and therefore didn't have any money. An individual may be considered to have a valid inability to pay if he has had an accident that has disabled him or an illness that prevents him from working. Most courts are fairly consistent in expressing the opinion that if a man is healthy and capable of working, it is his obligation to find work in order to comply with a court order. This also holds true when it is the woman who has been ordered to make the child support payments. The burden of proof will theoretically be on the nonpaying spouse—that is, he must prove to the court that he was unable to make the payments.

In the 1982 New Mexico case *Niemyjski v. Niemyjski*, the court held that an obligor can be found guilty of contempt if he had the ability to pay during the period for which he failed to make his child support payments, although he may not have the ability at the time of sentencing. To the father's repeated claim that he needed all the money for his own personal and business uses, the supreme court of New Mexico remarked: "If he did so, it was bad judgment on his part and clearly a willful violation of the obligation. It is unfortunate that he ignored *his most important single obligation*, namely *the support of his minor child*."[4]

The burden of proving that a noncustodial parent has the ability to pay does not exist only when a nonpaying spouse lacks funds. In the *Creighton Law Review* article, "Civil Versus Criminal Contempt,"[5] Diane J. Vogt writes that "contrary to popular belief, most men not making child support payments can afford to pay something. One study found that fathers earning $30,000 to $50,000 a year were just as likely not to pay child support as fathers making less than $10,000 a year."

The term "counts," as it applies to a contempt matter, is the number of times the father has failed to comply with the court order. If your ex-husband was ordered to make twenty-four support payments during the year and made only thirteen, you would be asking the court to find him guilty on eleven counts of contempt. It is within the discretion of the judge to decide how many counts your ex-husband will be cited for, should he be found guilty. In California, contempt can be punishable by up to five days' imprisonment for each count. In the above example, the judge could find him guilty and cite him for one to eleven counts. If the court finds him guilty, sentencing is usually put off to a future specified date. This affords your ex-husband the opportunity to bring his payments up to date and to illustrate to the court that he now understands the ramifications of not paying his child support. The court also has the right to sentence your ex-husband and suspend the sentence, place him on probation, or simply give him a warning. The last option is often referred to as a "slap on the wrist" and is frequently received by the first-time offender. Although jurisdictions differ and judges deal with this problem differently, in many cases the nonpaying spouse will be reprimanded by the court and sternly informed that if there is a next time, he will be sentenced and have to serve time.

The other issue that the court must take into consideration is the arrearage, the amount of money owed to you to date. The ultimate goal of the court is to see to it that your husband becomes current and remains current. If he owes you $1,800 in arrearage, it may be impossible for him to become current because whatever he pays you is generally applied to the arrearage. If he has been ordered to pay $300 per month and after his appearance in court proceeds to make his payments at the rate of $300 per month, that amount will be applied to what he owes you from the past. For all intents and legal purposes, he has failed to comply with the court for the current period. He will continue to amass more counts of contempt for which he may be found guilty at some future date.

To head off this problem, the court will frequently order him to pay a specific amount per month toward the arrearage and to stay current on his future support payments. He will also be instructed that he will not be held in contempt if he complies with this new court order.

Some attorneys will argue against this type of order. While the court has a valid reason to enter a long-term repayment order, there is also a valid reason not to. When viewed from a different perspective, the court is actually rewarding the nonpaying spouse for failing to pay child support. After all, if someone owes you $1,800 and is given the opportunity to pay you at the rate of $25 per month, he is really coming out ahead. This type of order provides no incentive for faster repayment. Meanwhile, the custodial parent may have had to borrow the funds to compensate for the amount not received. Naturally, a great deal depends on the individual circumstances surrounding a case.

What I have described so far is primarily the procedure followed in bringing a contempt action. Now you must examine the other factors that may come into play if you elect to utilize a contempt proceeding to collect back child support.

To date, you have hired an attorney to handle your divorce. You have paid him—whether reimbursed by your ex-husband or not—to file your divorce papers, work out a settlement, appear on your behalf for the dissolution of your marriage, and attend to the follow-up paper work. By the time your ex-husband has fallen behind on his child support payments, for all practical purposes you are without representation. This does not apply, of course, if your ex-husband fails to make his payments prior to the time that you have received your final divorce decree. If this is the case and you want your attorney to represent you in a contempt hearing, you will have to retain him to do so. This means that in addition to not having received the support you need, you must advance money in an attempt to collect what is owed and, it is hoped, get your husband to start paying you on a timely basis. This is not an unusual situation; any creditor who brings a debtor into court faces the same reality. What is unique in the custodial parent's case is that you are not a business and therefore this expense cannot be written off as a cost of doing business; also, if you are dependent on the support that you have not been receiving, you are already in a financially depressed situation—which you must compound in order to hire an attorney.

LEGAL FEES

Once again the issue of recovering the amount you must expend on legal fees arises, and what happens will depend mainly on the jurisdiction in which you file and the judge before whom you appear. Your attorney may be able to answer this for you. In many ways it is difficult to understand why a court would *not* order a nonpaying spouse who is found guilty to bear the cost of bringing an action for contempt.

Let's examine the scenario: A parent has been ordered to provide support. Because of his failure to abide by the court order, the custodial parent is forced to return to court to seek enforcement of that order. Though the ex-husband has behaved in a contemptuous manner toward the court, in many jurisdictions the custodial parent must absorb the cost of bringing the action. The reason I have been given for this is that the court wants the money to go to the children, not the attorneys. This attitude does not exist in all jurisdictions; in some places the party having the strongest financial capability bears the cost of bringing the action.

In Los Angeles County, fees are generally awarded to the petitioner's attorney if the court finds the respondent guilty of contempt. But even where fees are awarded almost automatically, there are exceptions. One hearing I observed in Los Angeles County resulted in the father's being found guilty on several counts of contempt. At the hearing's conclusion the attorney for the wife routinely requested that the court order the citee to pay the custodial parent's legal fees for bringing the action, but the presiding judge, who was from a different district and was substituting for the commissioner, denied the attorney's request. He then addressed the wife, saying that she should think of herself as a collection agency and the fees as a cost of doing business. If she had chosen to spend more money in the appeal process, the possibility exists that his decision could have been reversed.

It is the nature of the system that there are no guarantees. The important lesson is that in a jurisdiction where the awarding of fees is practically a given, they were denied. This may help explain why attorneys guard against speaking in terms of absolutes. Too many factors come into play in law, including human nature, to allow anyone to be absolutely positive about the outcome of any particular event.

Let's assume you have gone to court for a contempt hearing, and the court has ordered your ex-husband to pay a specific amount for your legal fees. This will become part of the court's minute order. Because your ex-husband has failed to make his child support payments in the past, he may fail to abide by the court order to pay the legal fees as well. If this occurs, your remedy will be to file another contempt in the future. Bringing a contempt action may make him understand the gravity of the situation and force him to comply with all the court orders that have been issued. This is your objective and the reason you have initiated the action in the first place.

In some cases the mere service of the motion of the contempt hearing on your spouse will bring forth the desired results—many checks have passed through hands on the courthouse steps. If your ex-husband realizes that you are not going to remain passive over the issue of child support and that you are prepared to do whatever is necessary to make him comply, he may somehow find the money he owes. If your ex-husband is able to pay you the arrearage prior to the hearing, your attorney may suggest that you dispense with the hearing altogether, possibly saving you additional attorney's fees and accomplishing most of what you set out to do. The problem that can arise, is that your ex-husband may start to think he can allow the payments to slide until the last moment and still avoid a confrontation with the court. If this pattern emerges, your attorney may be less willing to withdraw a contempt motion in the future, preferring to have the court take notice that your ex-husband does not remain current and hoping that the court appearance will encourage him to start paying on time.

When there is a hearing on contempt, the court wants to know if the nonpaying spouse has been cited for contempt before. While you may have been experiencing problems for three years, there is no history of noncompliance if the matter hasn't reached the court. Your court file may contain the motions for contempt filed by your attorney, but it is doubtful that these motions will be brought to the court's attention. Your case file is brought to the bench at the hearing. The judge generally reviews the orders that have been entered and disregards motions that have been filed but not heard by the court. Many considerations must be weighed when determining whether or not to proceed with a hearing.

There is always the chance that your ex-spouse will not appear for a hearing. If this happens, your attorney must provide proof that he received notice of the hearing—a summons. If he fails to appear, some state courts may issue a bench warrant for his arrest. If his counsel appears, the court may be inclined to set a new date and perhaps issue a bench warrant, but order that it be held until the date of the new hearing. This affords your ex-husband a second chance to appear. The effectiveness of a bench warrant frequently depends on where it is issued; it may produce immediate results in a small town but be totally ineffective in a large city. The sheriff's department in Los Angeles County has many responsibilities and few employees; to seek a father who has failed to appear in court when he hasn't made his child support payments is not one of its top priorities. The bench warrant can be effective, however, if an ex-spouse is stopped for a traffic violation and the computer picks up the outstanding warrant on a routine check. Fortunately, most nonpaying ex-spouses do appear for their hearings.

Your ex-husband may appear in court at the appropriate time and ask the court to grant him more time so that he can obtain an attorney. He has the right to be represented by counsel, and if he hasn't yet retained an attorney, the court will afford him this opportunity and set a new date for the hearing. Although he had at least ten days prior to the hearing to find an attorney, the courts must be lenient with this request and take the human element into consideration. In legal terms he has asked the court for a continuance, which means exactly what the term implies: By granting this request, the court agrees to continue the hearing on this matter at a future date.

Your ex-husband may appear in court with his attorney who may request a continuance. The reason generally given is that he has just been retained and has not had sufficient time to prepare for the hearing. Under most circumstances his request is considered reasonable and is granted. Only if the court sees this request as one more stalling device after a long series of delaying tactics will it be denied.

You are the one who is hurt the most by continuances. Your attorney's fees may increase because of the additional appearances in court and the generation of paperwork, but the most damaging factor is that you are losing time. If no effort has been made to pay you during this period, you will have nothing to show for your efforts to date and must wait—while the amount of arrearage grows.

If your attorney informs you that the opposing side is asking for a continuance without any viable reason, then you do not have to agree, or "stipulate," to such a continuance. Your attorney must have your approval before he can enter into a stipulation to continue a hearing. You may wonder why your attorney would want to agree to the request. As with all professionals, there is a level of cooperation between most attorneys that is deemed professional courtesy. If both attorneys work primarily in the field of domestic relations, there is a good possibility that they have been on opposing sides in the past. They may see each other at Bar Association meetings and share a friendly competitive relationship. Your husband's attorney may be preparing for an important trial, taking his wife on a long overdue vacation, or simply waiting for a retainer from his client. Perhaps your attorney wants to reciprocate due to the opposing counsel's cooperative attitude in the past. Before you automatically agree to a continuance, discuss your options thoroughly with your attorney.

Your attorney may inform you that your ex-husband has offered to pay a certain amount if you will stipulate to a continuance. Now you have something substantial to consider. The bottom line is that you want your unpaid child support and you want to set a precedent whereby you will receive your support on a current basis. Any sum received under this agreement would be applied to the arrearage and would not alter the fact that your ex-husband was in contempt when he failed to pay you within the time frame ordered. Ideally, part of this agreement should include the amount you have had to pay or are obligated to pay your attorney to date for bringing the contempt action. Consider the following example: You are owed $1,500 in back child support and have been offered $750 if you will stipulate to a continuance. You have given your attorney a retainer of $250. You might agree to the continuance on the basis that you will accept the $750, applying $250 toward your attorney's fees and crediting your ex-husband with $500 toward the child support arrearage. This way you have been reimbursed for your legal fee outlay, have reduced the amount due by $500, and will have a scheduled hearing at a later date. If your ex-husband's intention is to become current prior to the new hearing date, your agreement can assist him to get on the right track, whereby everyone benefits.

The more prepared your attorney is when you go to court, the better the outcome. Just how much time he will be required to spend on preparation may depend on you and your record keeping. You benefit greatly from having developed the habit of recording information.

The three common methods for obtaining additional information for your case are through the use of subpoenas, interrogatories, and depositions.

Subpoenas To subpoena information your attorney will have an individual served with the notice to appear in court. A *subpoena duces tecum* is the form he will use if he wants that individual to produce specific documents. Your attorney may inform the subpoenaed witness that he need not appear as a witness if he produces the requested documents. If you have kept a record of the banks your ex-husband has used, your attorney will be able to subpoena the bank records. The subpoena must be served at the branch of the bank where your ex-husband maintains his account and is served on the person the bank personnel indicates will accept service, as the "keeper of the records." Generally that individual will not be required to appear as a witness as long as the bank has complied by producing the requested records. Some banks charge a fee for their document preparation costs, and the witness must receive a witness fee, which is attached to the subpoena. The witness fee and any fees assessed by the bank are passed on to you as costs.

Interrogatories Interrogatories are written questions directed to a party of a lawsuit. Your attorney may send interrogatories to your ex-husband, which is an effective way of obtaining information while keeping costs down. The charge for preparing interrogatories is based on your attorney's time in establishing the questions and the preparation of the document.

Deposition A deposition is an appearance, either at the courthouse or in the office of a reporting service or an attorney. If your ex-husband is "deposed," he will be sworn in and requested to answer questions posed to him by your attorney. If your ex-husband has counsel, his attorney will also be present. Your attorney may or may not ask you to be present during the deposition. It is very likely that your attorney will request your ex-husband to produce documents for this deposition.

A deposition is by far the costliest method of pretrial discovery. It requires preparation by your attorney, your attorney's time during the deposition, the cost of the reporter, and the cost of transcribing the testimony and providing the other side with a copy. In Los Angeles a court reporter typically charges $5 per page for an original and one copy of the deposition. In San Francisco the average page rate is $3.95 for an original and one copy of the deposition in addition to a flat rate for the reporter's time of $75 for a half day and $150 for a full day. The rates quoted within this paragraph were applicable as of January 31, 1991.

If your attorney believes there is vital information he must obtain prior to your hearing, he may elect to depose your ex-husband. Since this is expensive, your attorney will undoubtedly discuss the advantages, disadvantages, and costs with you before making this decision. The potential risks in scheduling a deposition are as follows: your ex-husband may not appear, he may appear but refuse to answer questions, or he may appear but fail to produce requested documents. If he fails to appear or fails to produce, your attorney can return to the court and obtain an Order to Compel Discovery. Again, there will be a larger outlay of time and effort. Even though the law provides certain remedies, the meter is always running. Sometimes one side will postpone or not show up simply to wear down the other side—emotionally or financially.

By being able to provide information to your attorney you can lessen your costs. Thorough fact-finding may preclude the necessity of using any form of pretrial discovery. If your ex-husband is renting an apartment, for example, then you should find out the name of the rental agent. If he leases a car and you know the name of the leasing company, you can easily determine the amount of his monthly payments. Information you may consider relatively meaningless can become very meaningful in the hands of your attorney.

Technically, the burden of proof is on your ex-husband to show that he did not have the ability to pay. In reality your attorney must show the court that he did have the ability. Consider the following scenario: During a contempt hearing, Will Jones claims that he was unable to make child support payments to his ex-wife Louise. He informs the court that he is a free-lance writer and hasn't had any writing assignments for over five months. He explains that his agent has high hopes for the future but hasn't found him any work lately, and he expounds upon all the effort he has made to secure work. Unless there is evidence presented to the court contrary to this testimony, it would be very difficult to find that Will Jones *willfully* failed to pay. Louise Jones's attorney then shows the court that Will has been paying $900 a month for rent and $300 a month for his automobile; he has been able to eat and has paid to retain an attorney for this hearing. The question now is where did the money come from?

In California the law states that the noncustodial parent's obligation to pay child support supersedes any other creditor obligations. This means that before he pays his Visa or MasterCard bill or whatever other bills he has, the noncustodial parent is obliged to make his child support payment.

While states recognize that child support obligations are a priority, many obligors don't. A study reported by Joseph I. Lieberman in *Child Support in America* concluded that two-thirds of the men involved in the study paid more in monthly car payments than they paid for child support.[6] The courts and public agency attorneys are quite familiar with the overused excuse that a nonpaying spouse would be happy to make his child support payments if he had any money left over at the end of the month. It is because the absent parent fails to pay child support that single-parent families, most often headed by women, are forced onto the welfare roles.

Preparation is the key to prevailing in the courtroom. Your attorney must be prepared, and you should do everything in your power to help him in this preparation to ensure success.

Trailing

In some congested courts there are many more cases to be heard than there are available courtrooms. To "trail" is to wait in the courthouse for a courtroom assignment. It can be very expensive, as can be seen by the following case.

The respondent, Tom Brent, appeared in front of the same commissioner on several occasions. He was warned, reprimanded, and cited for contempt at various times. In the superior court of Santa

Monica an individual has the right to stipulate that the case be heard by the commissioner or else choose to be heard by a judge. Deciding that he had used up all the goodwill that was coming to him from the commissioner, Tom would not stipulate to having the case heard by him. The matter was therefore sent to another courtroom which had its own calendared cases, but the Brents were fortunate to be heard at the end of the afternoon session. It could have been carried over to the following day. By 4 P.M. Sarah Brent's attorney had spent eight hours in court, of which fifteen minutes was spent in front of a judge, and Sarah was responsible for her attorney's fees for the entire day.

This type of maneuver brings another factor into play. Tom Brent, failing to make his child support payments in the past, was brought up on contempt charges various times in front of the same commissioner. He had been found guilty at prior hearings, but this time he appeared in front of a new judge. While it is true that his file provided a history of the case, noting several motions for contempt and orders resulting from the hearings, the judge hearing the matter for the first time chose to proceed in his own way. Since this was the first time Tom was appearing before him, he granted a "reprieve" followed by a severe reprimand and warning.

There are usually several judges in each courthouse. While no one could employ this method of avoidance for too long, it does offer another delaying tactic to the nonpaying parent "who would rather die than pay." This could not occur in those jurisdictions where procedure requires that any matter pertaining to a specific divorce be heard by the same judge.

Most attorney's don't have any problems requesting fees from the court. The request that your ex-husband be ordered to pay the cost of bringing the contempt action must be made either in the moving papers or at the conclusion of the hearing. In either case your attorney must make the request since the judge will not raise the issue. If fee awards are viable in your jurisdiction, then be sure to discuss with your attorney prior to the hearing how this request will be made. I witnessed one situation where an attorney simply forgot to raise the issue of fees. One attorney who represented me was too intimidated by the judge to enter a fee request. This attorney had relocated from Washington, D.C., approximately one year earlier, was now with a well-established law firm in Los Angeles, and was experienced in family law. We discussed the subject of fees, and there was no question that even though I was responsible for my attorney's fee, he would ask the court to order the respondent to pay the fee and costs for bringing the contempt action. As the hearing was drawing to a close, he hadn't mentioned attorney's fees even though we prevailed in proving contempt. I wrote on his legal pad and whispered the word "fees" to him to no avail. The hearing concluded. It was only in the parking lot when he asked me for a check that the subject of fees was raised again. While he could be assertive outside the courtroom, he had been too intimidated to make the request of the court.

If you want to collect your child support but cannot deal with the thought of your ex-husband going to jail, you would be better off having your attorney appear without you. If you decide that you will not do anything that might result in your child's father being sentenced, then you eliminate one of the strongest remedies of law available to you and the easiest route that a divorce attorney can pursue. While there are other alternatives for enforcement, the contempt proceeding is the one most commonly employed. If you have retained a specialist, his services may not be available for alternate remedies.

The thought of your ex-husband, your child's father, going to jail is not pleasant. It is important to remember, however, that in order for him to be found in contempt and therefore face the possibility of being sentenced to jail, it must be proven that he *could* have made child support payments if he had wanted to but *chose* not to make them. The court is saying, in essence, "What do we have to do to get you to understand that you have brought a child into this world who needs to be taken care of?"

In his comprehensive article, "The Child Support Problem: Credible Threat and Use of Incarceration Works," Judge Robert L. Gottsfield weighs the philosophical problem of using incarceration to enforce child support orders against the results, stating that

> the empirical evidence from Chambers' study and earlier studies examined by Robert H. Mnookin[7] may be summarized as follows:
>
> 1. The use of jail leads to considerably higher support payments where the county also has a well-organized, self-starting enforcement system (that is, where it has a policy of initiating enforcement action in cases without waiting for complaints from the mother about nonpayment).

2. It is the frequency with which jail is used and not the length of the jail term that is significant.
3. The credible threat of jail in a well-organized county raised the payment rates for every group of fathers (whether classified by age, type of employment, race, income, or events following the divorce).
4. Not only did the credible threat and use of jail produce more income than would be produced without it, but many fathers who went to jail thereafter paid proportionately more than before the jail sentence.
5. There is little relationship between income and the father's failure to comply with court-ordered child support.[8]

In summary, the question remains: If the father is not compelled to pay, then *who* is going to pay?

Some jurisdictions have established a special forum where women who are not receiving their child support payments can bring the matter to court without counsel. The court generally sets aside a particular session on a specific day of the week or month for this type of proceeding. You can find out if this is offered in your jurisdiction by contacting the clerk of the court. South Dakota legislation has initiated an administrative procedure that currently allows a contempt action to be filed through the Department of Social Services without counsel for a $5 fee. The matter can be reviewed by a referee, and the respondent is given ten days to file a response. If there is no response, an order will be entered by the court; if a response is filed, a hearing will be held. A representative of the Department of Social Services stated that they are pleased with the results they are achieving—primarily through the use of wage assignments.

If you proceed with a contempt action effectively, your ex-husband will understand that you won't allow him to fail to make his child support payments. He will also realize that you will continue to do everything in your power to make him comply with what the court has ordered him to do. He will see that there is nothing enjoyable about going to court, standing in front of a judge, being reprimanded, and facing the possibility of incarceration. If your contempt action is less effective, your ex-husband may continue to act irresponsibly, figuring that it has taken you some time to get him into the courtroom, it has cost you money in attorney's fees, he has been scolded and gotten off without being sentenced, and you'll give up before he ever has to pay.

In speaking with attorneys, individuals who work in district and state attorney offices, and judges, I have learned that many people believe the courts are too lenient when it comes to child support. If a nonpaying parent does not equate his failure to pay with any serious ramifications, what is going to make him comply with the court order? If you don't pay your rent, you will be evicted; if you fail to make your car payments, your car will be repossessed; if you don't make your child support payments . . . it depends. One judge in the Sunbelt is known for his consistency. The first time he finds a spouse guilty, he reprimands him and puts him on probation. The second time, he sentences him to serve time. A different judge in the same courthouse can't bring himself to sentence anyone to serve time for nonpayment of support. He leaves the bench before sentencing, and someone else renders the sentence. Some judges who pay child support themselves resent any man who doesn't face up to his responsibility. Other judges bend and bend and bend. Many judges feel that the ex-husband is in a no-win situation because there frequently just isn't enough money to go around.

The Honorable Robert L. Gottsfield wrote that "the basic conclusion . . . from a review of the recent literature on the subject and the author's own experience as a domestic relations judge is that the credible threat and use of incarceration in a systematic and unbiased way can and does produce additional payments for needy children that would not be recovered any other way."[9]

In California a custodial parent can ask the court to find her ex-husband in contempt of court only for failure to pay child support for the previous twelve months. If you wait for two years before setting a hearing for contempt, you will still be asking the court to find your ex-husband guilty for failure to pay only for the last twelve months. This does not mean you are not owed the amount that accumulated prior to that one-year period, but it does mean that by waiting you have created more problems for yourself. Each time a contempt hearing is held, the amount of arrearage owed to you is confirmed by the judge. If your husband is six months behind, it is very simple for the court to determine the arrearage. If six months later you must bring him back to court again, the amount previously determined is on record, and the new amount is simply added to the old figure. By going beyond a twelve-month period, the court may require more testimony to determine the arrearage, and the hearing may become more complex than necessary. You may even have to go through a special hearing just to determine the arrearage. Attorneys always encourage their clients to bring contempt charges as soon as possible when nonpayment occurs.

By now you can see the psychological effect on your ex-husband of allowing a great deal of time to pass before choosing a course of action. That time, compounded by the time it takes to go through the court system, the time that can be bought through legalistic maneuvering, and the time afforded by judges in the hope that individuals can mend their ways, can sometimes lull a nonpaying ex-husband into a false sense of security and result in frustration for you.

A good family law attorney should be able to project to some degree the results of the first contempt hearing he files on your behalf. He will know his jurisdiction and know the judge's leanings. Your contempt hearing may result in perpetual compliance, or it may not solve the problem at all at first. But it is a course of action you must take if you are to succeed. A hearing on contempt can only be put into action by you, and even if it fails to bring all the desired results immediately, to do nothing is to ensure failure. In many cases the action will have to be repeated, but through your understanding of reasonable expectations and the mechanics of working within the system, you will gain the knowledge and patience required to prevail.

CHAPTER 17

Child Support Enforcement Agency

> "As of spring 1988, 9.4 million mothers were living with their own children under twenty-one years of age whose fathers were not living in the household; 5.6 million . . . were awarded child support payments . . . 2.6 million had, at some time, contacted a government agency for assistance in obtaining child support."[1]

IF YOU are not receiving your child support payments, you have the right to utilize the services of your local child support enforcement agency. You have this right whether or not you have the means to retain private counsel. Bringing an action for enforcement of child support orders is the same whether it is brought on your behalf by independent counsel or by the district or state attorney, with one exception: In the majority of states the district or state attorney has the option of bringing an action under the civil code (contempt) or the criminal code and may elect to go forward under the statute that is criminal in nature. This requires a jury trial and the case is heard in criminal court instead of superior court. In Orange County, California, the district attorney's office experienced a much higher success rate when it switched over to enforcement through criminal proceedings, but the idea of a criminal action may be met with shock in other jurisdictions. In Los Angeles County Bureau of Family Support Operation seeks enforcement of child support orders by bringing charges under section 270 of the penal code, which is "Failure to Provide," a misdemeanor. If the noncustodial parent fails to appear in court, a warrant is issued for his arrest.

Legislation

On January 4, 1975, President Gerald Ford approved Public Law 93-647 (H.R. 17045), which established the Child Support Enforcement Program as an addition to Title IV-D of the Social Security Act, for the purpose of "enforcing the support obligations owed by absent parents to their children, locating absent parents, establishing paternity, and obtaining child support." After reviewing the results of the act, it was determined that while there had been substantial improvements in the collection of child support, the overall noncompliance was still at epidemic proportions.

In 1982 the U. S. Department of Health and Human Services, Office of Child Support Enforcement, issued a report stating that "the problem of increasing welfare costs in the United States is, to a considerable extent, a problem of nonsupport of children by their absent parents."[2] The agency reported a dramatic increase in divorce and desertion and the following statistics:

- approximately one-half of the children born [today] will spend considerable time in a single-parent household, which means primarily female-headed households
- the years spent in a single-parent household will be spent either in poverty or in a significantly lower standard of living than in a two-parent family
- in 1980 the poverty rate for female-headed families was over three times that for married couple families
- nine out of ten children receiving Aid to Families with Dependent Children have an absent parent.

In 1983 the Maricopa County Family Support System 80 of the Human Resources Department in Maricopa County, Arizona, reported that out of the very small percentage of single-family households receiving regular child support payments, the main source of income came from the custodial parent's earnings, the second source from welfare, and the third source from child support. This report estimated that of those custodial parents receiving support, 50 percent received less than 10 percent of the custodial parent's total income. In reviewing these reports, the Honorable Robert L. Gottsfield wrote that "Increased public awareness of the correlation between the failure to pay child support and the increased tax burden of welfare has created an emerging view that we must get tougher in the establishment and enforcement of child support obligations."[3]

Congress reevaluated the Child Support Enforcement Program and passed the Child Support Enforcement Amendments of 1984, Public Law 93-378, which, among other items, required every state to develop guidelines for child support orders by October 1987. This has resulted in the use of various methods to calculate child support obligations throughout the country, referred to as formulas, models, and/or guidelines. All states have complied and have established minimal child support guidelines for the courts. (The Delaware Child Support Formula and the Wisconsin Percentage of Income Standard are reprinted in Appendix F.)

The Family Support Act of 1988, Public Law 100-485, is an act "to revise the AFDC [Aid to Families with Dependent Children] program to emphasize work, child support, and family benefits, to amend Title IV of the Social Security Act to encourage and assist needy children and parents under the new program to obtain the education, training, and employment needed to avoid long-term welfare dependence, and to make other necessary improvements to assure that the new program will be more effective in achieving its objectives."[4]

The services offered to the custodial parent through this program are available to recipients and nonrecipients of Aid to Families with Dependent Children. AFDC is available to qualified applicants through the Welfare Department. In most states the child support enforcement agency is located in the "umbrella" social services or the U. S. Department of Health and Human Services, but in a few states it is located in a department such as the Department of Revenue. Most states have cooperative agreements between the child support enforcement agency and other state agencies, such as the state or district attorney's offices, probation department, court, domestic relations offices, and county clerk offices. Some cities list the agency under the government listings in the telephone book, while others do not. Any one of the agencies that works in conjunction with the child support enforcement agency should be able to direct you to the correct office. (A full listing of Child Support Enforcement Offices by state is in Appendix C.)

Child Support—You Owe It to Your Kids[5]

For several years Los Angeles County has conducted "Father's Day Sweeps" that have provided delinquent noncustodial parents with the opportunity to become current in their obligations. The amnesty program, announced on August 29, 1990, has been most successful. According to Carol Mentell, public inquiry coordinator of the Los Angeles County district attorney's office, Bureau of Family Support Operation, fifty thousand letters were mailed to delinquent child support obligors, providing them with a "window" from September 1 through October 31 to bring their child support obligations current and eliminate the criminal charges against them. Ms. Mentell reports that the huge response resulted in the district attorney's office having to extend the cutoff period for two or three days due to the large number of offenders standing in line with their checks. Through this program the Bureau of Family Support Operation collected in excess of $800,000 in child support arrearage and received more than twenty thousand calls from delinquent parents.

Working with the System

Every jurisdiction functions individually. While a minimal fee is required by some states, others have dispensed with it. In one Florida county a designated court commissioner prepares the cases for the local child support enforcement agency; in another county everything is channeled through the U. S. Department of Health and Human Services. There are a specified number of investigators and always enough cases. Depending on the person with whom you speak initially, you may be told to retain private counsel if you have the means.

\ Prior to the adoption of the 1984 Amendment there was a disparity in the Child Support Enforcement Agency between AFDC recipients and nonrecipients. While the federal government absorbed 75 percent of the administrative costs for both types of cases, "incentive payments" equal to 15 percent of all monies collected were paid to the state only for AFDC cases. The primary objective of the agency, therefore, was to encourage collection from nonpaying ex-spouses of AFDC recipients, and frequently the nonrecipient parent was encouraged to use private counsel or other means for enforcement. In *Carter v. Morrow*[6] it was found that such preferential treatment violated the Social Security Act. This case can be summarized as follows: Nonrecipients of Aid to Families with Dependent Children brought suit against the North Carolina Department of Human Resources for their failure to provide to them the same services they provided AFDC recipients. The district court held that the state's officials would be enjoined from further failure to accept applications from clients and from discriminating in any way against, or providing services of a different type or quality to, applicants based on welfare status.

The federal funding formulas have been changed through the 1984 Amendments. Today the federal government contributes 65 percent of the program's administrative costs but offers an incentive payment of 6 to 10 percent of all monies collected for all cases. While there has never been a shortage of cases and the caseload today is greater than it has ever been, it is nice to know that if you opt to take this route for enforcement, you will be treated equitably by the agency.

When working with an agency you follow the same procedure as with private counsel and supply your representative with accurate records of payments and your court order. The largest drawback in utilizing this service in most jurisdictions is time. You cannot expect your case to be brought to court as quickly as it would be through private counsel, nor should you assume that anyone in the agency is actively working on your case just because you have provided all the necessary paperwork. You must stay on top of the situation. In Los Angeles I was told repeatedly that those who keep following through with the district attorney's office achieve the best results. By knowing beforehand that the process may take between three and six months, you can understand the importance of commencing an action as soon as possible.

Donna J. Jones, serving as executive assistant to the director of the Maricopa County Human Resources Department, concluded that the family support system (meaning support cases that are handled by the Maricopa county attorney or the attorney general) "accomplishes too little because it frequently takes too long, is too weak, too costly, and is too dependent on parties."[7] Her report states that there is a 50 to 80 percent chance the custodial parent will not receive child support in the amount or on the date when ordered and that there were arrearages in over 14,700 of the 24,000 active cases handled by the county attorney. The reasons attributing to the lengthy time element were the following: difficulty in finding the absent parents, low success rate (47 percent) in process serving by the sheriff, and the forty-five days before the case can be presented to the judge.[8]

Due to the caseload of the attorneys who work in conjunction with the Child Support Enforcement Agency, it would be unrealistic to assume they could devote the amount of time to your case that you would expect from private counsel. When using an agency attorney you still have all the same collection remedies available that you have with private counsel: wage garnishment, writ of attachment, and so on. It will be up to you to acquaint your attorney with the status of your husband's employment and financial position, and any factual information you can provide to the agency can only strengthen your case. Several agency attorneys expressed their belief in employing any legal device available in order to effectuate collection, rather than always relying on a civil contempt procedure. Since the bottom line is collection, it is best to explore all possibilities with the attorney. Some of the enforcement remedies available are wage withholding, liens on real or personal property, and the interception of federal and, in some jurisdictions, state income tax refunds.

Since the procedure for enforcement of your child support order is primarily the same whether it is initiated by an agency or by private counsel, the outcome of the hearing is also frequently the same. Regardless of who represents you, it will always be up to you to initiate the process again if your ex-husband fails to comply with new or old court orders.

You can expect the outcome of a first hearing on contempt to be a strong admonition and a warning directed to your ex-husband by the judge. While nonpaying parents have been incarcerated the first time they have been found guilty of contempt, this is the exception. To take someone out of the work force and jeopardize his job or eliminate the possibility of his earning any income can be extremely counterproductive. If this initial hearing is successful, your ex-husband will realize the importance of making his child support payments and start acting responsibly.

The choice between using the services of the child support enforcement agency and private counsel will be based on the costs of retaining private counsel versus the free services provided by the agency and the consideration of the time factor involved in bringing an action.

Tax Intercepts

The enforcement tool of intercepting tax refunds can be instituted only through the Child Support Enforcement Agency, commonly referred to as the IV-D agency, so your attorney would have to prepare an affidavit of the amount of arrearage owed and direct you to the agency. While at one time the right to intercept a federal tax refund to offset outstanding child support obligations due to an ex-husband's failure to pay was available only to AFDC recipients, in 1985 it became an option for all obligees. In January 1991 the federal government set minimum requirements of child support refunds to intercept a tax refund at $150. It should be noted that there is no guarantee an agency will automatically attempt to intercept a tax refund on your behalf. Using the services of the agency alone for enforcement or in conjunction with private counsel is a viable option, however, and one well worth considering.

Many states are instituting tax intercepts on state income tax refunds due to delinquent obligors. Starting in 1979 the Franchise Tax Board in California initiated a program that enabled the Child Support Enforcement Agency to intercept obligor's refunds for AFDC recipients; in 1983 this method of enforcement was extended to nonrecipients as well. Some state tax intercept programs have been challenged in the courts. *McClelland v. Massinga*, a federal case, overturned a district court decision that struck down the Maryland tax reform program. The United States Court of Appeals for the Fourth District disagreed with the lower court's findings that the tax refund program denied delinquent parents a predeprivation hearing. The appeals court ruled that no hearing is required where a state withholds a tax refund for a taxpayer's failure to make court-ordered child support payments and held that the Maryland tax intercept program was constitutional.

CHAPTER 18

Parent Locator Service

"Congress has regularly considered the child support program and has encouraged the states to track down absent fathers."[1]

ACCORDING TO the Los Angeles County district attorney's office, some child support obligors will exit through bathroom windows if necessary to avoid prosecution. It is not surprising, then, that some obligors will leave the state to escape their child support responsibilities.

If your ex-husband has moved and you have no idea where he has gone or if you know which state your husband has moved to but do not have his address, you can seek the assistance of the Parent Locator Service. PLS came out of the Federal Child Support Enforcement Act, Title IV-D of the Social Security Act, adopted in 1975, and is an arm of the Department of Health, Education, and Welfare. (There are also state parent locator services in some states.) PLS serves as a clearinghouse for information on child support evaders when their whereabouts are unknown, and the state service provides assistance when the state in which the obligor has relocated is identified.

If you are receiving Aid to Dependent Children and therefore have filed the necessary forms with the state, the attempt to locate your husband is an automatic part of the process since one of the responsibilities of the agency is to attempt to obtain reimbursement for the aid you are receiving.

Many counties that previously required the non-AFDC recipient to pay approximately $25 for these services now waive the fee. The reason is that the federal government provides incentives to the counties for all obligees.

CHAPTER 19

Uniform Reciprocal Enforcement of Support Act

URESA IS the abbreviation for the Uniform Reciprocal Enforcement of Support Act. This body of legislation, recognized by all states, improved the enforcement of support obligations. Once dubbed the "Runaway Pappy Act," it allows you to file a petition in your own state that will result in a hearing to be held in the state where your ex-husband resides, generally without your being present. This can be accomplished if your ex-husband has left the state or if you have moved away from the state where you obtained your divorce. In the latter case you file a petition in your new state and the papers are sent to the state that retains jurisdiction over the matter—again without requiring your presence.

Filing a petition through URESA solves a variety of problems for the custodial parent. Consider Mary and Bill Green, who respectively live in California and Florida. Mary moved to California with their two children after obtaining a Florida divorce. Bill stops making his child support payments, and Mary wants to seek enforcement of the child support order. If Mary uses private counsel, she must retain a Florida attorney and incur the costs of traveling to Florida for the hearing. She will also have to consider various complications: long-distance communication with her attorney, a continuation of the hearing at a later date, Bill's failure to appear at the hearing, etc. If Mary brings the action through URESA, an attorney will represent her interests and a hearing will take place without her direct involvement.

Uniform Reciprocal Enforcement of Support Act 161

The initiation of action through URESA is done through the state or district attorney's office. You must bring your "divorce decree,"[1] which serves to establish the first required element—that your husband has a "duty to support." You will then fill out a petition, which is usually a preprinted form requesting all addresses of the obligor and the obligee. You will also be asked to provide your ex-husband's Social Security number, employer's name, aliases, if any, and any other information that might assist in locating him. The individual who does not have a divorce decree must provide additional data sufficient for the initiating court to determine that she is entitled to receive support and that the father of the child has a duty to provide support.

To file a URESA petition you must provide a record of payments received in order for the attorney to proceed. (This reinforces once again the importance of maintaining a diary.) The court in your jurisdiction that reviews the petition filed on your behalf is called the initiating court. In its review it determines that the petition states a claim upon which relief may be granted. The initiating court does not try the case. If it determines that there is a cause of action, then the petition is sent to the state or district attorney's office in the "responding state," that is, the state where your ex-husband resides.

If the respondent state cannot locate your ex-husband, it will inform the state where you filed the petition. If the state locates him, then the matter proceeds like any other civil case. A hearing is scheduled, and if the obligor fails to appear, the court enters a default judgment. If he does appear, the court orders payment of support. If he denies that he owes or should owe any support, the matter is continued to a date for a full hearing. At this hearing your ex-husband has the right to produce material evidence, confront adverse evidence, and have counsel present legitimate argument relating to the facts and the law. The prosecuting attorney will require you to introduce relevant evidence, either through your deposition or your appearance.

It is not uncommon for the nonpaying ex-spouse to raise or attempt to raise the argument of custody or visitation as a defense in cases that cross state lines. If you have been given sole custody of your child, then the issue of custody will not be an arguable defense. If you and your ex-husband have joint custody and he has left the state that has jurisdiction (the state in which you were divorced and the child support order was entered), he will probably be unable to base a defense for his failure to pay child support on the custody issue as well. If you and your ex-husband share joint custody and you have left the state of jurisdiction, the attorney handling your case will review the court documents before he files the petition and will advise you of potential problems regarding the custody provisions of your court order. Remember, you have an attorney representing you in this action, and you will have the opportunity to discuss any questions about your case with him before the petition is filed. While it is generally agreed that problems in the area of visitation should have nothing to do with the issue of child support, every judge, jurisdiction, and situation is different.

One of the primary objectives of URESA is to provide a means to seek enforcement of child support obligations at a minimum of expense to the obligee. While it is usually not necessary for you to travel to a sister state in order to be present at a hearing, in an exceptional situation the prosecuting attorney may prefer that you testify in court.

If your ex-husband doesn't deny that he has the duty to support your child, the responding court will enter a court order. This order may or may not be the same as the order you originally received when you first went to court. With proper proof, given in evidence, the court might raise or lower the amount of child support if it sees fit. In the case of a father who has moved out of the state, this action will establish jurisdiction over him in the state where he now lives, which will provide that court with the power to enforce child support payments in the future. The establishment of jurisdiction is the main thrust of the first hearing, as opposed to just attempting to collect the arrearage.

How quickly your case will be acted on depends on the level of commitment and the number of caseloads handled by those working on your behalf, both in your state and the responding state. Some states have a reputation for responding better than others. Your state or district attorney's office should be able to provide you with a reading on the sister state involved. The speediness with which your case is acted upon also depends on the county in which you reside. An analyst in the Child Support Operation Bureau of the California Department of Social Services informed me that one county in California is so backlogged that they are one year behind on their cases. Generally, he said, once the responding papers are received and returned to the county, a case is handled within six months.

URESA actions can be greatly hindered by these time lags. As one child support enforcement worker pointed out, you work so hard to locate the obligor, but months can go by before the caseworker can get around to the file and commence an action; meanwhile, if the obligor has moved across the street, you've lost him. This individual attributed the major problems of his agency to the fact that the agency is understaffed and that the bulk of their time is spent in compliance rather than enforcement because the federal government requires so much paperwork.

Once your case has been heard, however, you will be able to bring subsequent actions in the state where your ex-husband resides either through the state prosecutor's office or private counsel licensed to practice in that state. This is true as long as your husband does not relocate to a different state.

If the sister state recognizes the URESA registration process, there is a possibility that a hearing can be avoided. The registration process allows the court of the sister state to treat the support order as if it had been entered in that state. A certified copy of your support order is registered with the county clerk in the Registry of Foreign Support Orders. This gives your ex-husband twenty days to respond if he wishes to take issue with the court order. In no way does it preclude your ex-husband from being heard, nor does it empower the sister state to exercise power over him. If he wishes to modify the order, therefore, he must go to court; and if you want to attempt to enforce the order, the case must be heard. At the time of the hearing the court would determine if it has jurisdiction over your ex-husband and/or his property and the amount of arrearage.

In some states the URESA office also serves as the agency to administer the Federal Child Support Enforcement Act. Remember that the state is reimbursed through the successful collection efforts it makes on behalf of mothers receiving assistance. While the URESA office may proceed on your case as quickly as on an AFDC case, it is wise to follow up fervently on any action you initiate.

Criminal enforcement procedure through URESA is applicable if your jurisdiction permits you to bring criminal charges. This process is practically never used, however. If your ex-husband were constantly dodging court appearances and behaving in a manner that indicated total disregard for the court and the judicial process, a state attorney might be willing to bring a criminal action. This would necessitate extraditing your husband from the state where he resides. The governor of your state would have to write a letter to the governor of the state where your ex-husband resides requesting your ex-husband's extradition. The "threat of extradition"—the legal surrender of an alleged criminal to the jurisdiction of another state of government for trial—can be a very powerful tool.

CHAPTER 20

Wage Deduction

THE USE of a wage deduction as an enforcement technique for child support is available in practically every state. Some jurisdictions have created a special form that custodial parents use in order to obtain a wage deduction without having to go to the expense of a full court hearing. You can find out if a special form is available in your area by calling your local county clerk's office.

In South Dakota an administrative procedure falling under the auspices of the Department of Social Services enables the custodial parent to request a wage assignment without a court appearance and gives the respondent ten days to respond if he wishes to be heard. The matter is reviewed by a referee. If no papers are filed by the respondent, the request is given to the court for the order to be entered. The entire procedure costs between $5 and $15, and neither party has to be in attendance. If the respondent wishes to be heard, then a hearing is scheduled.

A wage garnishment is a process whereby an employer is instructed to withhold a specified amount from an employee's wages and send the check to whomever the court designates. A wage garnishment can sometimes be obtained as a result of a contempt hearing. Attorneys have been known to ask a nonpaying parent to agree voluntarily to a wage garnishment, as a show of good faith, prior to a contempt hearing. If he does not agree and is found guilty of contempt, the attorney can always direct this request to the presiding judge. Whether or not the request for the wage garnishment is granted lies within the discretion of the court.

An alternative to wage garnishment, income withholding, has

been used for some time and is considered an extremely effective tool. Also known as wage assignment or income deduction, income withholding, differs from wage garnishment in that "it is used to collect not only support arrearages but the regular monthly support obligation. "Traditional garnishment actions have been used for collection of arrearages only and must be refiled each time a new arrearage accumulates."[1] The use of the wage assignment not only provides a way for the nonpaying spouse to become current but also affords an automatic way for him to remain current on his child support obligations. A few states established effective practices some time ago whereby a custodial parent would be automatically entitled to obtain a withholding order if the nonpaying parent was, for example, twenty days late in his payment. In formulating the provisions for the Child Support Enforcement Amendments of 1984, Congress drew on the successful results of these states. The act requires that as of October 1, 1985, every support order issued or modified included "provision for withholding from wages in order to assure that withholding as a means of collecting child support is available if arrearages occur without necessity of filing application for services under this part."[2] While the act does not require that the states make this remedy available to private parties who are not clients of the IV-D agency, it has been argued that a denial would constitute unequal protection.

The following table lists the states that allow wage assignments or income deductions for child support as of 1987:[3]

It is important to remember that state statutes vary and are also frequently revised. In 1985, Nevada, through a statutory revision, amended its wage assignment provision to place the burden of requesting a hearing regarding a wage assignment on the obligor. Commencing July 1, 1987, all circuits in Wisconsin are required to issue assignments immediately upon entry of a support order. The income assignment is automatic unless the court commissioner wishes to make findings to justify a departure from the norm. In this case the findings are appealable by the custodial parent. The court issues a separate uniform income withholding order, a copy of which goes to the obligor's employer. This order is signed by the court, and the employer can be found in contempt if he fails to withhold the amount or percentage of the obligor's gross income as indicated in the order. Roger Rowan, who was project manager of Wisconsin's ten-county pilot program for evaluating income as-

TABLE XI
Enforcement of Support Orders

	A States with specific support long-arm statutes	B States with discretion to have payment made directly to court officer	C States which allow wage assignments or income deductions regarding support
Alabama			X
Alaska	X	X	X
Arizona		X	X
Arkansas	X	X	X
California		X	X
Colorado	X	X	X
Connecticut		X	X
Delaware	X	X	X
Florida	X	X	X
Georgia		X	X
Hawaii		X	X
Idaho		X	X
8Illinois	X	X	X
Indiana	X	X	X
Iowa		X	X
Kansas	X	X	X
Kentucky		X	X
Louisiana	X		X
Maine	X		X
Maryland	X	X	X
Massachusetts	X	X	X
Michigan		X	X
Minnesota		X	X
Mississippi	X		
Missouri	X	X	X
Montana		X	X
Nebraska			X
Nevada	X		X
New Hampshire		X	X
New Jersey			
New Mexico	X		X
New York	X		X
North Carolina	X	X	X
North Dakota		X	X
Ohio			X
Oklahoma	X		X
Oregon			X

TABLE XI (Continued)

	A States with specific support long-arm statutes	B States with discretion to have payment made directly to court officer	C States which allow wage assignments or income deductions regarding support
Pennsylvania		X	X
Rhode Island			X
South Carolina	X	X	
South Dakota	X	X	X
Tennessee	X	X	X
Texas	X	X	X
Utah	X		X
Vermont			X
Virginia	X	X	X
Washington		X	X
West Virginia			X
Wisconsin	X	X	X
Wyoming	X	X	X
Washington, D.C.	X	X	X
Puerto Rico			X
Virgin Islands			X

signments, told me that their use of income assignments for enforcement is extremely successful, and since the income assignment is automatic—it is issued to the employers of all noncustodial parents—there is no stigma attached to having a portion of one's wages withheld.

Some states provide for wage deduction orders after one or more defaults in maintenance and child support payments, *and* forbid an employer to discharge an employee whose wages are being garnisheed. Among the states providing for garnishment of wages for child support are Colorado, Delaware, Florida, Georgia, Hawaii, Kansas, Massachusetts, Michigan, Minnesota, Nebraska, Nevada, New Hampshire, New Jersey, New York, North Carolina, and Rhode Island.[4]

If your ex-husband has been with the same employer for some time and there are strong indications he intends to remain with the

Wage Deduction 169

company, then income withholding can be the perfect solution. By having the employer deduct the child support amount prior to issuing a paycheck, you will be assured of receiving the support as long as your husband continues to work for that firm. If your husband changes jobs, however, the withholding will no longer be effective. You would have to return to court to obtain a new order that could then be served on the new employer.

A wage attachment or garnishment can also be used to collect child support arrearage if your ex-husband is an independent contractor who performs works for a company as a "self-employed" individual. An attachment is often used after a pronouncement of judgment has been made. This can be accomplished in some jurisdictions by making an application to the court without the necessity of a hearing as long as there is an original court order. Other jurisdictions require a hearing to determine the amount of arrearage owed and to enter a judgment for that amount before any attachment can be made.

Some states have revised their statutes to require that wage assignment provisions be incorporated in the original support order. Arizona has revised its statute so that "an order for support shall provide for an assignment . . . to assure payment if an arrearage occurs in an amount equal to one month's child support or spousal maintenance."[5]

A New Hampshire statute revision requires that all orders for child support and separate maintenance have a provision for withholding of wages. This wage assignment statute can be used as soon as an obligor has fallen one month behind in his payments and provides that a percentage be applied to the arrearage.[6]

Your attorney must determine the appropriate procedure based on the nature of your ex-husband's employment. If he is an independent contractor, a one-time attachment may be the proper vehicle, but this is not always the case. My former husband was an independent contractor in Los Angeles and had a directorial contract with a commercial production company in which he was guaranteed a certain number of shooting days at a specified figure per year. He had entered into an arrangement with the production company whereby his annual guarantee was prorated over twenty-four equal bimonthly payments. My new attorney felt that a wage garnishment was the perfect vehicle for collecting my child support payments. By serving a wage garnishment on the production company I did receive payments directly from the company for a brief period of time, but when my ex-husband's working relationship with the production company terminated, so did the child support payments. My attorney and I had to go back to the drawing board.

With a judgment in hand, your attorney has the option of scheduling a debtor's examination whereby your ex-husband is required to respond to questions regarding his assets and employment. This can be very productive in discovering his source of funds or income in the near future.

FEDERAL EMPLOYEES

> "... as President of the United States of America, in order to provide for the enforcement of legal obligations to provide child support or make alimony payments incurred by employees of the Executive branch ..."
> —JIMMY CARTER, The White House, December 19, 1978

On August 21, 1980, a final rule went into effect regarding child support due from federal employees. As a result of Executive Order 12105, the U.S. Office of Personal Management was authorized to set forth regulations providing a uniform procedure for wage garnishment of federal employees to enforce child support and/or alimony obligations.

Part 581 of this ruling, entitled, "Processing garnishment orders for child support and/or alimony," specifically sets forth the manner in which a governmental agency must proceed in response to a garnishment order on one of its employees. It defines which funds are subject to garnishment and which are not. A copy of this rule can be obtained by writing or calling the Bureau of National Affairs, Inc., Washington, D.C. 20037. You should also be able to find it in the Law Library of your courthouse, in the *Family Law Reporter*, August 19, 1980, Volume 6, No. 40. Ask the librarian for "6FLR 3087."

There are two very significant matters to note in the analysis of this rule: (1) this rule does not mean that you can bring an action in Federal Court, nor does it mean that Congress has pre-empted state garnishment provisions, with the exception of a few areas, and (2) the law permits the garnishment of "all remuneration for employment," including salaries, retirement payments, Social Security benefits, and even compensation for work injuries.

Your attorney should be familiar with the requirements and rules governing garnishment in your jurisdiction and the procedure defined by this rule.

The wording of 581.102 Definitions (d) defines Child Support as follows: "Child Support means periodic payments of funds for the support and maintenance of a child or children and subject to and in accordance with state and local law includes, but is not limited to, payments to provide for health care, education, recreation, clothing, or to meet other specific needs of such a child or children; the term includes *attorney's fees, interest and court costs if they are expressly made recoverable under a decree, order, or judgment issued in accordance with applicable State or local law* by a court of competent jurisdiction."

I have purposely stressed the recoverability of fees in order that you may see that throughout the entire system the laws, rules, and procedure all lend themselves to fairness. As it is repeatedly stated, however, unless attorney's fees and the costs for bringing the action are requested *by your attorney*, granted, and made a part of the court order, you will not be reimbursed for these expenses.

One problem does exist with the remedy afforded through Rule 581, according to Beverly M. Jones, insurance system manager of the Office of Personal Management. If your state or jurisdiction has no applicable garnishment provisions, in most cases you will not be able to garnishee money due from the United States or the District of Columbia. What this means is that the collection of child support and the recovering of legal fees and costs through a wage garnishment under this rule is a viable option only if the state you reside in permits this form of garnishment. The table on page 167–68 lists the states that allow wage garnishment.

CHAPTER 21

Alternative Collection Devices

THE PRIMARY remedy utilized by domestic relations attorneys for enforcement of child support orders is the contempt proceeding. Depending on your attorney and where you live, your attorney may or may not be willing to represent you on a straight collection matter. Many attorneys in Beverly Hills will handle your divorce and file contempt actions for nonpayment but will not perform services that fall outside those realms. That means that if you have been unsuccessful in collecting and wish to proceed with a writ of execution and attachment, a domestic relations attorney may suggest that you seek the services of a collection attorney. On the other hand, many attorneys will handle all aspects of a divorce case including any collection work. Just as it is essential to select your divorce attorney based on his expertise, you must choose the attorney who will represent you for collection purposes for his expertise as well. Some aspects of collection can be very tricky. If an attorney suggests in any way that he may be lacking in that area, you would probably be wise to look elsewhere. The question you must face is where the domestic attorney's work ends and where the collection attorney's work commences.

If a court order must be reduced to a judgment before a writ can be issued in your jurisdiction, then someone must appear in court on your behalf to request that the judgment be entered. It is crucial to discuss this matter with counsel beforehand so you will know who you are going to have to pay and how much. Unfortunately, most collection attorneys base their fees on a percentage of recovery. It is acceptable in many places to pay as much as 40 percent of the amount recovered to a collection attorney who is working on a contingency fee arrangement. When it comes to child support arrearage, this percentage, which represents a very healthy cut for the custodial parent, is considered unethical by many practitioners. In some areas a collection attorney will not handle child support cases on a contingency fee basis because of the possibility that the court would rule against him by challenging him on the question of fees. Keep in mind that contingency fee arrangements vary from state to state as to whether and under what circumstances it can be used.

Of course the option to retain a collection attorney on a straight hourly basis is always available. Again, you must weight the amount of fees against the realistic possibility of recovering the fees and costs that your attorney requests for bringing the court action. All the options available to any creditor are available to you. Once he has obtained a judgment, your attorney should be able to effectuate an attachment if your ex-husband has any assets that can be attached—such as bank accounts, securities, or automobiles.

One of the most common devices used by a collection attorney is the judgment debtor's examination. This affords the opportunity to determine the amount of your ex-husband's assets and pinpoint their location. If there are assets, your ex-husband might decide that he would be wiser to enter into a real pay arrangement with you or clear up the debt rather than submit to an examination. If there are no assets, then an examination of this nature would be useless.

One legal remedy does not necessarily preclude another. If you have been successful in serving a wage garnishment on your ex-husband's employer, you know that you will be receiving child support payments on an ongoing basis for as long as your ex-husband remains in that employment or for the duration of the wage garnishment, whichever is shorter. If a substantial amount of arrearage has accumulated prior to the garnishment, you can pursue an additional collection remedy in order to satisfy the arrearage obligation. You would be precluded from moving forward on this basis, however, if the judge entered an order that prorates the arrearage to be paid over a specified period of time and bars you from obtaining a writ as long as your ex-husband complies with all the terms of the court order. For this reason it is very important that you discuss your ex-husband's assets with your attorney prior to commencing an action. This disclosure enables your attorney to make a knowledgeable determination as to procedure and to take all the potential ramifications into account.

When a judgment is filed it becomes part of the public records. This information is often picked up by credit reporting agencies. If your ex-husband's credit rating is important to him, he may realize that it is wiser to pay the debt than to have his credit negatively impacted. A judgment may also provide the means for you to collect arrearage if your husband owns any real property. A lien is a debt that the owner of the property must pay before it is sold. By filing a judgment lien against a piece of property owned by your ex-husband, the lien would show up against the title of the property. The amount of the lien would have to be paid to the lien holder when the property is sold. The amount of equity your husband has in the property determines the collectability on the lien. Other factors that come into play are whether or not this is your husband's primary residence and if there is a "homestead exemption" in the jurisdiction where the property is located. In their informational pamphlet, the Los Angeles Department of Consumer Affairs defines homestead exemption as follows: "A homestead exemption protects California homeowners who have had money judgments entered against them. It saves a certain amount of the value of the house for the homeowner if a creditor goes to court to force the sale of the house." The pamphlet states that "while a homestead offers protection, it does not protect against the forced sale of a house by a bank, savings and loan, or any other creditor holding a mortgage or deed of trust on the house, or against the enforcement of a valid mechanic's lien or *judgment for child or spousal support.*"[1] Your attorney can provide the answers to your questions about this.

Whether or not it is too late to collect arrearage owed to you can only be determined by the particular circumstances surrounding your case. Once again, your attorney should advise you in this matter.

An interesting case occurred in Ohio in 1984 (*Connin v. Bailey*) when a former wife presented a claim against the executor of her deceased ex-husband's estate for unpaid child support and alimony, and interest thereon, owing for thirty-five years.[2] The executor rejected her claim for $28,305.53, and she consequently filed a complaint. The amount of $28,305.53 was based on a judgment entry granting $3 per week for each of the two children and a lump sum alimony award of $100. Her reason for not having pursued this claim for so many years was that she had sought court enforcement of her child support and alimony rights on several occasions, but her attempts had been costly, yet fruitless. The trial court entered judgment for the estate, finding that the doctrine of *laches* was a complete bar to the action. In essence, laches is failure to assert a right for an unreasonable and unexplained period of time under circumstances that are prejudicial to the other party. She then appealed this decision of the court of common pleas: The court of appeals in Williams County, Ohio, reversed the lower court's decision, finding that the doctrine of laches did not bar suit because she had provided a reasonable explanation for the delay and there was no evidence that the decedent had been materially prejudiced by the delay. The former wife was awarded the amount she sought, and it was later affirmed by the supreme court of Ohio pursuant to a motion to certify the record. In their decision they called upon the rationale of the Smith court, from *Smith v. Smith*, an Ohio case heard in 1959:

> Defendant [father] was instrumental in bringing into the world the child for whom the benefit of the support money was intended, and he assumed, in addition to the natural duties of a parent, a statutory duty to support the child until emancipation or majority. The weekly support order merely put a price tag on the statutory duty already existent. The defendant knew of the existence of his obligation of support . . . and the extent of such obligation was fixed by . . . the judgment of divorce. The mere fact that he failed to meet such obligation does not mean that he was excused therefrom; it simply means that someone assumed his duty of support, for, in the absence of evidence to the contrary, the court will presume that the child was clothed, fed, and generally accorded the necessities of life, the payment for which the weekly support money was intended.[3]

In a different case, *Jasper v. Carter* (1982), in Washington, D. C., the superior court awarded a former wife $5,105 from her ex-husband's estate for child support obligations that had been ordered to commence twenty-four years prior. The executrix of the husband's estate appealed the decision, and the matter was heard in the District of Columbia Court of Appeals.[4] Once again the court found that the defense of laches did *not* bar the former wife from recovering the child support arrearage, but they found that the trial court should not have allowed the former wife to recover past-due payments that matured over twelve years before the suit was filed, making the payments unenforceable money judgments.

In this case the appeals court vacated the judgment and remanded the matter for a recalculation of the amount the former wife could collect. While a different procedure could have been used in the trial court, which may have resulted in a different outcome for the former wife, this case does bring home the importance of ensuring that you don't let too much time go by before taking appropriate action to keep a judgment enforceable.

CHAPTER 22

Bankruptcy and Support Enforcement

YOU MAY be wondering what you would do if your ex-husband were to file bankruptcy. Perhaps he has already threatened to do so. Bankruptcy law and procedures are extremely complex. Should your ex-husband file for this protection, you would definitely need an attorney's expertise. In the last decade, however, steps have been taken to safeguard your payments even if your husband does file for bankruptcy.

Certain acts and amendments have been enacted to establish a nondischargeability (meaning a person cannot be relieved of his obligations) of the following through bankruptcy: any debt to a spouse, former spouse, or child of a debtor for support in connection with separation agreements, divorce decrees, or property settlement agreements. This includes child support orders. The intent of these acts is clearly to establish that filing bankruptcy does not allow a debtor to discharge his marital and fatherly obligations. (To discharge a debt means that the debt does not have to be repaid. A nondischargeable debt is one that must be paid even though a bankruptcy has occurred.)

On August 13, 1981, Section 456(b) of the Social Security Act was amended to state: "A debt which is a child support obligation assigned to the state under Section 402(a)(26) is not released by a discharge in bankruptcy under Title 11, United States Code."[1]

Section 523(a)(5)(A) of the code was amended to state that a

177

discharge under Chapter 7 (bankruptcy of company), 11 (reorganization), or 13 (personal bankruptcy) does not relieve an individual debtor from any debt to a "spouse, former spouse, or child of a debtor for support in connection with a separation agreement, divorce decree, or property settlement agreement but not to the extent that such a debt is assigned to another entity, voluntarily, by operation of law or otherwise other than debts assigned pursuant to section 402(a)(26) of the Social Security Act."[2] The primary area of concern to you as the support creditor is Chapter 13, which constitutes most of the filings.

A technical amendment included in the Bankruptcy Amendments and Federal Judgeship Act of 1984, amending Section 523(a)(5)(A), states that claims "assigned to the federal government or to a state or any political subdivision of such state" are nondischargeable. This section is directed toward the noncustodial parent whose ex-spouse is receiving assistance through Aid to Families with Dependent Children.

The filing of a bankruptcy petition and obtaining an order for relief automatically stays (stops) collection activities on a support order obtained before the bankruptcy filing. Since violating the stay order is considered contempt of court and is therefore punishable, the stay must be lifted *before* you can proceed to collect support. Certain legal procedures must be followed to lift or "vacate" the stay regarding your ex-husband's child support payments, and you would have to retain an attorney. This type of proceeding or action "encompassed approximately two-thirds of all contested proceedings in the bankruptcy court in the Central District of California."[3]

John Replogle stated as follows: "The authorities are in agreement that the Chapter 13 debtor should maintain, either outside or inside the [bankruptcy] plan, post-petition alimony, maintenance, and support obligations on a current basis out of post-petition earnings or income and pursuant to Section 1322(b)(10) [the bankruptcy code] they can be included in the plan. As a practical matter, provisions to pay support and arrearages are routinely included in this plan."[4]

Several cases have upheld the debtor's obligation to pay current and past-due support inside or outside the plan. In 1980 an Oregon Chapter 13 case (Haag 3Bankr.649) required the debtor to pay past-due child support in full outside the plan while making reduced payments on unsecured claims. In 1979 a Missouri case (Curtis 2Bankr.43) required full payment on child support arrearage inside the plan while making partial payment to other unsecured creditors. What John Replogle stresses about these cases is that the child support obligee is not on the same par as other unsecured creditors; the child support obligation has a higher status in law than ordinary indebtedness. In other words, *you, the custodial parent, are not just another creditor.*

As is true with most case law, there are other cases that disagree. In one (Caswell, U.S.C.A. 4th, No. 84–1502, March 1985), the court found that child support enforcement lies in the realm of the state court, and the federal court should not interfere with state remedies. It was held that the right to collect child support should not be impaired by having to wait for a confirmation of a Chapter 13 plan. The court affirmed the bankruptcy court's finding that child support payments and debt from arrearage should not be included in the Chapter 13 plan for the following reasons: Inclusion of the arrearage in the plan would allow a federal court to change or modify the state court's decision regarding the payment of the overdue debt, and if the federal court assumed jurisdiction over the child support obligation, the debtor would be sheltered from making his child support payments when due.

An important decision came in 1981 (Adams 12B.R.540) when the court held that if a child support provision is included in the plan, a custodial parent could proceed to collect against the wages of the debtor if they exceeded the amount he is required to pay to the trustee under the bankruptcy plan. In addition, the court held that the support creditor could also go against any property of the debtor that was exempted from the plan. Other cases allowing this are Bernstein (Florida) CCH 68 825, Moore (Florida) CCH 68 833, and Sak 21B.R.305.

As was previously stated, bankruptcy law is extremely complex. If you need to go through the bankruptcy court, it is critical that you retain an attorney with expertise in bankruptcy proceedings. The bankruptcy court generally avoids incursion into family law matters. If a custodial parent seeks a modification of a child support order after the noncustodial parent files a bankruptcy petition, the matter will be decided by the same court that entered the original support order.

Following are three samples of forms that might be used if your

180 CHILD SUPPORT

ex-husband files for bankruptcy under Chapter 13: Motion for Relief from Automatic Stay, Complaint to Determine Dischargeability of a Debt, and Stipulation for Entry of Judgment of Nondischargeability. While these are samples of forms filed by a Child Support Enforcement Agency, a private attorney's motion, complaint, and stipulation would basically follow the same formats.

Family Support Bureau
291 Tenth Street
San Francisco, CA 94103

Telephone: (415) 553-4271

Attorney pursuant to W&I § 11475.1

UNITED STATES DISTRICT COURT FOR THE
NORTHERN DISTRICT OF CALIFORNIA

DA FP-	)	
In re	)	BANKRUPTCY No.
	)	
Debtor	)	(Chapter 13)
	)	
CITY & COUNTY OF SAN FRANCISCO	)	CONTESTED
	)	PROCEEDING
	)	No.
FAMILY SUPPORT BUREAU	)	
Plaintiff,	)	
vs.	)	
	)	
Defendant.	)	

MOTION FOR RELIEF FROM AUTOMATIC STAY

TO: The Honorable_____Bankruptcy Judge:

    COMES NOW THE CITY & COUNTY OF SAN FRANCISCO, FAMILY SUPPORT BUREAU and moves the Court for an Order for relief from the automatic stay order so that child support may be collected in State Court proceedings from earnings of the Debtor which are not property of the estate.

    THE CITY & COUNTY OF SAN FRANCISCO, FAMILY SUPPORT BUREAU RESPECTFULLY alleges, moves and requests:

I

    That the CITY & COUNTY OF SAN FRANCISCO, FAMILY SUPPORT BUREAU is a political subdivision organized and existing under the laws of the State of California.

II

    That on the_____day of_____, 198__, the above-entitled Debtor, filed a voluntary Petition in Bankruptcy in above-entitled Court and was adjudged a Bankrupt on or about the same date.

III

The Bankruptcy Court has jurisdiction over this proceeding pursuant to 11 U.S.C. § 362.

IV

That the Debtor's Chapter 13 plan was confirmed by the Court.

V

The plaintiff was listed as a creditor in the schedules of liabilities filed therein by said Bankrupt and was in fact an unsecured creditor of said Bankrupt at the date of the filing of said voluntary Petition in Bankruptcy in the amount of $ _____ .

VI

That the nature of said unsecured debt owing by Bankrupt to plaintiff is child support arising out of an order issued on _____ _____ by the Superior Court of the State of California in and for the City & County of San Francisco. By the terms of said judgment and order for child support the Bankrupt was to pay $ _____ per month for the support of the minor child(ren) commencing _____ .

VII

That Plaintiff, a Judgment Creditor of the Bankrupt debtor, having received a judgment on _____ 1984 as set forth in paragraph VI herein above plus interest thereon.

VIII

That the aforesaid Judgment and order is a judgment and order determining defendant Bankrupt debtor's obligation for present child support and past accrued reimbursement of child support and as such is non dischargeable by virtue of 11 U.S.C. § 523(a)(5)(A) as amended, 42 U.S.C. § 656(b) as amended, and 42 U.S.C. § 602(a)(26).

IX

That between _____ , 1984 and the date Bankrupt filed his voluntary Petition in Bankruptcy, the Bankrupt paid a total of $ _____ on account of his said on-going above-mentioned, child support obligation and nothing on account of said child support reimbursement arrearage obligation.

X

That between the date when the Bankrupt filed his voluntary Petition in Bankruptcy and the date of this motion, the Bankrupt has paid a total of $ _____ on account of his said on-going above-mentioned child support obligation and nothing on account of said child support reimbursement arrearage obligation.

XI

That was due and owing on the date of filing of the voluntary Petition in Bankruptcy by the Bankrupt the sum of $ _____ principal plus interest thereon from _____ , 1984 in child support reimbursement arrearages and the sum of $ _____ principal plus interest thereon from April 9, 1984 in child support reimbursement arrearages as of the date of this motion

XII

That the Chapter 13 plan of the Debtor makes no provision for child support and for $ _____monthly to be applied to the arrears as a general unsecured claim.

XIII

The Bankrupt has sufficient income to make the scheduled monthly payment of $_____to the Trustee on the arrearage and also pay said ongoing child support. Due to the automatic stay, plaintiff is unable to enforce the herein above-mentioned order for child support against the earnings and property of the Bankrupt which are not property of the estate.

It is therefore respectfully requested that Plaintiff's motion be granted and the stay order previously imposed be partially vacated insofar as it operates to prevent enforcement by plaintiff of the hereinabove referenced order for child support in the State court against earnings and other property of the debtor that are not property of the estate.

Date:

                        Respectfully submitted
                        ARLO SMITH
                        District Attorney:

                    By: _____
                        JOHN REPLOGLE
                        Assistant District Attorney

184 CHILD SUPPORT

DONALD N. STAHL
District Attorney
County of Stanislaus
Family Support Division
711 County Center No. 3 Court
Modesto, California 95355

Telephone: 526-6357

Attorney pursuant to W&I § 11475.1

UNITED STATES DISTRICT COURT FOR THE
EASTERN DISTRICT OF CALIFORNIA

In re Bankrupt's Name   )   BANKRUPTCY NO. F 80
                Bankrupt   )
THE COUNTY OF STANISLAUS,)
                Plaintiff,   )
    vs.   )
                Defendant.)

COMPLAINT TO DETERMINE DISCHARGEABILITY
OF A DEBT

TO: The Honorable J.W. HEDRICK, JR., Bankruptcy Judge:
    The Complaint of the County of Stanislaus respectfully represent:

I

That the plaintiff is a political subdivision organized and existing under the laws of the State of California.

II

That on the _____ day of _____, 19___ the above-entitled Bankrupt, filed a voluntary Petition in Bankruptcy in the above-entitled Court and was adjudged a Bankrupt on the same date.

III

That plaintiff was listed as a creditor in the schedules of liabilities filed therein by said Bankrupt and was in fact an unsecured creditor of said Bankrupt at the date of filing said Petition in Bankruptcy in the amount of $_____.

IV

That on the _____ day of_____, 19____, the Bankrupt executed in favor of plaintiff a Stipulation for Entry of Judgment and Order pursuant to California Welfare and Institution Code Section 11350 et seq.

V

By the terms of said Judgment and Order of Stipulation, the Bankrupt agreed to pay the sum of $_____ per month for support of his minor children and $_____, as reimbursement to the County of Stanislaus for its support of the minor children through Aid to Families with Dependent Children.

VI

That the aforesaid document was and is a stipulated Judgment determining defendant's obligation for child support and reimbursement of support and as such is nondischargeable by virtue of II USC § 523(a)(5)(A) as amended and 42 USC 656(b) as amended.

VII

That payment by the bankrupt as required by said Judgment and Order was made on the first and fifteenth days of 1978 and not since then and the bankrupt has failed and refused to make payments in accordance with said Judgment and Order. There was due and owing on the date of the filing of the petition in bankruptcy by the bankrupt the sum of $_____ and the further sum of $_____ has accrued since said date to $_____, no part of which has been paid. Should said debt be discharged in the above-entitled proceedings, plaintiff would be damaged in the sum of $_____ reason of the foregoing;

WHEREFORE, plaintiff prays as follows:

1. That an Order be made adjudging and determining that the debt of the bankrupt to plaintiff is excepted from the operation of discharge heretofore granted Bankrupt by this Court and is nondischargeable.

2. Adjudge that there is due and owing as of the date of the Bankrupt's petition in bankruptcy the sum of $_____.

3. That plaintiff recover from Bankrupt costs of suit herein.

4. Such other and further relief as the court may find proper.

DONALD N. STAHL
District Attorney

DATED:

By: _____
JOHN REPLOGLE
Deputy District Attorney

CHILD SUPPORT

DONALD N. STAHL
District Attorney
County of Stanislaus
Family Support Division
711 County Center #3 Court
Modesto, California 95355

Telephone: (209) 526-6357

Attorney pursuant to W&I § 11475.1

UNITED STATES DISTRICT COURT FOR THE EASTERN DISTRICT OF CALIFORNIA

In re   ) BANKRUPTCY NO. F80-
              Bankrupt   )
THE COUNTY OF STANISLAUS,)
              Plaintiff,)
    vs.   )
_____)
              Defendant.)

STIPULATION FOR ENTRY OF JUDGMENT OF NONDISCHARGEABILITY

    WHEREAS on _____, _____, filed a Voluntary Petition and was adjudged a Bankrupt by the above-entitled court.

    WHEREAS the Bankrupt listed the County of Stanislaus, Family Support Division, hereinafter called plaintiff as an unsecured creditor in the amount of $_____.

    WHEREAS on _____, plaintiff filed its Complaint asking the court to issue an Order declaring said debt to be nondischargeable under the Bankruptcy Act.

    IT IS, THEREFORE, STIPULATED AND AGREED by and between the parties hereto that all facts stated in plaintiff's Complaint are true and correct and that the court may enter its Judgment in favor of plaintiff by declaring said debt to be nondischargeable under the Bankruptcy Act and vacating all restraining orders concerning said debt.

Dated: _____   DONALD N. STAHL
                                    District Attorney

Dated: _____   _____
                                    JOHN REPLOGLE
                                    Deputy District Attorney

Dated: _____ ____   _____
                                   Bankrupt and Defendant

                                   _____
                                   Attorney for Bankrupt and
                                   Defendant

JUDGMENT AND ORDER

The Court having read and considered the Stipulation for Entry of Judgment of Nondischargeability of the parties herein, and good cause appearing therefore,

IT IS SO ORDERED, ADJUDGED, AND DECREED:

Dated: _____   _____
                              J.W. HEDRICK
                              UNITED STATES BANKRUPTCY JUDGE

PART FOUR

IN THE FUTURE

CHAPTER 23

Modification

THE RIGHT to seek modification of a child support order exists for both divorced parties. If your ex-husband wishes to reduce the amount that was originally ordered, his attorney will file for a modification downward. If you feel that your financial requirements for your child have increased and your ex-husband is able to provide for this additional expense, your attorney will file for a modification upward.

At one time in Los Angeles County, an ex-spouse behind in his child support payments who filed for a modification to have the obligation lowered would not prevail, but this is no longer true. An ex-spouse seeking a modification to lower child support payments can do so if he proves that there has been a change in his circumstances. If his salary was $40,000 when the order was entered and it is now only $20,000, the court must take his request into consideration. Assuming that you have been receiving an amount determined by his previous salary, there is a good chance that the support will be reduced.

In seeking a modification, all changes in circumstances should be brought to the attention of the court. If your ex-husband has remarried, for example, and his wife is earning a substantial salary, it is likely that her earnings are helping to offset their cost of living. Because he is sharing in that situation, even though he may be earning less, full disclosure of all financial benefit must be made.

In *Ewing v. May*,[1] a Kentucky case heard in 1986, the mother was attempting to obtain proof that her ex-husband's wife was earning an amount substantial enough to show the court that there was a change in circumstances warranting a modification of support upward. The court ruled that a custodial parent is entitled to obtain limited and reasonable discovery about a noncustodial parent's spouse's income for determining financial needs and resources when seeking an increase in child support.

Your attorney may be able to examine bank records, loan applications, and any other pertinent documents that relate to your ex-husband's finances. Just as the Internal Revenue Service performs an asset search to determine whether the taxpayer has declared all his earnings, your attorney can examine all the records to either confirm or challenge your husband's financial declaration provided to the court.

If you are seeking a modification upward, then you must prove either that the child's needs are greater and your ex-husband has the ability to pay more for support or that your ex-husband has an increased ability to pay and the existing child order is not adequate. In both cases there must be proof of a change in circumstances. Your attorney must be able to provide proof that your ex-husband's earnings have increased. As you know by now, the more information you are able to provide to your attorney in this situation (such as new purchases, new employer, and so forth), the fewer hours he will have to devote to your case. If your ex-husband is seeking a modification on the grounds that his monthly expenses have increased and it turns out that this change in circumstances occurred because he purchased a home with a $30,000 down payment and is obligated for large monthly payments, it is doubtful that a court would lower his child support obligation. It is important to remember that earnings consist of more than salary. Property, stocks, and other assets should be taken into consideration. If your husband's earnings have not increased and your child's needs have increased, there just may not be enough money, in the court's discretion, to justify an increase in support. Ultimately, the court's decision should revolve around a sense of fairness to all parties. A search at the county recorder's office should always be made before the court hearing.

In *Noddin v. Noddin*, a 1983 case appealed in New Hampshire,[2] a husband had obtained a modification of a support and alimony decree because of a change in his financial condition. He was earning $23,000 a year at the time of the divorce but was subsequently arrested for stealing trade secrets and was fired. Due to these circumstances, the husband was unable to obtain employment similar to the position he lost and was employed as a surveyor's helper at $5 per hour when he filed for a modification downward.

At the time of the divorce, however, the Noddins jointly owned a home that was awarded to the wife, with the provision that the husband would receive 25.1 percent of the proceeds on its sale on or before January 1, 1986. The wife moved the court to permit her to attach her ex-husband's interest in the house for the arrearage owed to her and future arrearages due to her ex-husband's nonpayment of support. The master who heard this case recommended that the arrearage of $2,671.31 be held in abeyance until the sale of the home and that the outstanding arrearage be deducted from the ex-husband's net proceeds, and this was approved by the trial court. The master, Earl J. Dearborn, held the hearing on the motion requesting alimony and support obligation be reduced and recommended the child support be reduced to $50 per week and the alimony payments be suspended. The master's recommendations were approved by the trial court (Nadeau, J.). The wife argued that the ex-husband's diminished income was due to his own criminal conduct, and it was an error to reduce his obligations especially since he had a tangible asset (the house). The New Hampshire Supreme Court agreed and found that the trial court had erred in modifying the support and alimony obligation, it reversed the trial court's decision and remanded the case back to the trial court, with the following finding: "Although unemployment or diminution of earnings is a common ground for modification, a petition for modification will be denied if the change in financial condition is due to fault or voluntary wastage or dissipation of one's talents and assets. 2A W. Nelson, Divorce and Annulment Section 17.16 at 87-88 (1961 rev.ed.).

The New Hampshire Supreme Court also found that "if the trial court had ordered the defendant's interest in the house held as security interest for future payments of the original support and alimony obligations, such action would not have been an abuse of discretion because any of the defendant's property may be applied to meet the support and alimony obligations. Id. citing *Dubois v. Dubois 121*, N.H. 664, 668–69, 433 A.sd 1277, 1279–80 (1981).

In another case the appeals court looked toward the assets despite the loss of income, and the Iowa Supreme Court ruled as follows:

We agree with the trial court that the petitioner's equity in the house should be charged for the support payments he is unable to meet during the period of his incarceration. The crucial thing is that, during petitioner's incarceration, it will continue to be necessary to care, feed, and provide for his children. He remains responsible for those expenses. It would not be equitable for his equity in the home to remain set off to him while his children were being supported by others.[3]

A child support obligor cannot simply quit his job and then seek a modification downward because of a change in circumstances. In *Gerber v. Gerber*, a 1985 Indiana case, the custodial father was awarded custody of the parties' two children and the mother was ordered to pay $40 per week child support. She remarried, quit her job, and then petitioned the court for a downward modification of the child support order. The trial court denied her petition and she appealed. The court of appeals affirmed the trial court's decision, holding that "a noncustodial parent under a support order cannot voluntarily terminate employment and then ask for modification of support."[4]

In researching for a modification case, you may well be the best investigative agent you know. While an attorney can hire or send someone from his firm to conduct a search of this nature, you can also do it yourself to keep your costs down. It is not difficult to search through the records at the county recorder's office. County office employees are available to help the public, and you needn't feel intimidated about not knowing what to do. Whenever a document is filed in the courthouse it becomes part of the public records. You are entitled to view and obtain a copy of any record that pertains to your ex-husband. Depending on where you live, these records are maintained in large volumes, on microfilm, or on microfiche. By inspecting the records you can determine if your ex-husband has bought or sold any property, obtained any mortgages, had any judgments filed against him, filed any judgments against another person or firm, or been involved in any other situation for which a document must be recorded.

One of the quickest methods available for researching ownership of property is through the tax rolls. If your ex-husband owns any real property, his name will be listed there. You can view the tax rolls in the tax assessor's office.

Information regarding corporations can be obtained by visiting a designated office or calling the state capitol. Public information includes the following:

UCC search UCC stands for Uniform Commercial Code. A UCC search provides you with any documents filed showing a secured interest in personal property. If your husband obtained a loan to purchase a computer, for example, there would be a UCC filing of the transaction. These records may be in the county recorder's office in your state.

Corporate record data These consist of all filings made on behalf of a firm incorporated in your state.

Registered agent search Every corporation must have a registered agent. If your husband is the registered agent for a corporation, this record is available through the Secretary of State's office.

Officer/director search You can determine if your husband is an officer or director of a firm incorporated in your state.

The Secretary of State's office conducts these searches by request. A fee is frequently charged for each search. The amount of time these searches take varies from state to state, but you should be able to obtain the information within a week. A company does not have to be incorporated in the state where it conducts business. If you believe your husband is an officer or director of a corporation but there is no record of this in your state, you may conduct searches in the four states most frequently used for incorporation: Delaware, New York, Texas, and Nevada.

The county office maintains records on all businesses (sole proprietorships and partnerships) other than corporations. If your husband is doing business under another name, commonly referred to as a "dba," there will be a record. This information is generally available for viewing in book format or on microfilm.

The department in your community where you register automobiles and boats maintains records of the vehicles registered in an individual's name. In some areas a fee is charged for this information, and it can take up to six weeks to obtain this information.

You are *not* entitled to examine your ex-husband's income tax return. You can obtain previously filed copies of joint returns by filling out the appropriate IRS form and mailing it in with a fee of approximately $4.00. It takes about six weeks to receive the return. If an accountant prepared the joint return, you can request a copy from him. Assuming that he is your husband's accountant, he would be hard pressed not to comply with such a request.

If your situation involves an ongoing series of conflicts over child support, it is prudent to keep abreast of any changes that could alter your ex-husband's financial picture by conducting a search periodically. The information you gather may also be important in executing a judgment or proving contempt in the future.

The statutes in most states place the obligation of child support on both parents. A change of circumstances therefore, on the part of either party provides a reason for considering a modification. Your ex-husband is entitled to seek a modification to reduce the amount of child support ordered due to a change in circumstances on your part. If, for example, you were not working and had no source of income when the two of you divorced but you have since obtained employment, there has been a change of circumstances. In a 1985 Colorado case, the custodial mother was going to school when she and her husband divorced. After graduation she went to work. Her ex-husband then sought a modification of the child support award. The appeals court, agreeing with the noncustodial parent, held that "a decrease in support is proper where the custodial parent, who is an unemployed student at the time of the decree, becomes capable of making substantial financial contributions toward the child support.[5]

The fact that you may have entered into an agreement with your ex-husband not to seek a modification of child support in the future does not automatically bar you from seeking a modification. Once again, every state has its own statutes and every court arrives at its own decisions. The following case illustrates one custodial parent's results in seeking a modification even though she had waived her right to do so.

Halum v. Halum, originally brought in the trial court in Indiana, was taken to the Indiana Court of Appeals in 1986. The original agreement between the parties contained a waiver of the custodial mother's rights to seek additional support, but the waiver was unenforceable. The trial court found that the only way the agreement could be disturbed was if it was absolutely necessary for the welfare of the children. The court of appeals disagreed and held that support orders based on agreements are "readily modifiable in light of changed circumstances."[6]

The courts are aware that people's lives change and that a change of circumstances in an individual's life justifies a reconsideration of previous court orders. The deciding factors in granting a modification always remain the same: what is equitable for all parties involved and what is in your child's best interests.

CHAPTER 24

Your Self-Esteem

WHEN YOU became a parent you received one of the dearest gifts of life. In return you have an obligation to nourish and provide stability and guidance so that your child may have all the opportunities to experience a rewarding life of his own.

The fact that so many parents simply turn their backs on their natural children is a national disgrace. It is equally sad that many people rationalize neglect by arguing that the majority of absent parents do not earn enough to support their children. Where is it written that the custodial parent will be able to meet the requirements for her contributive share of their child's support and also earn enough to make up for the deficit caused by the nonpaying parent? If your ex-husband fails to meet his financial obligations, however, finding more money yourself will be your only alternative *unless* you choose to fight for the rights of your child.

In fighting for these rights and attempting to obtain compliance with court orders, you may be exposed to various obstacles. You may discover that some attorneys on both sides and public officials don't treat this problem with the seriousness and importance it warrants. You may find that the term "child support" has been used so often its meaning has been lost. You may be accused of being money hungry and be characterized as a vengeful individual who will be happy only when your ex-husband has been put in jail. You may grow hoarse from reminding your attackers that you are attempting to enforce orders that were deemed just and necessary *by a court of law* and that the foundation for these orders can be traced back to a judgment made early in man's history, a judgment that a parent is obligated to care for his offspring.

Through it all you must never lose sight of the purpose. You will have to remind yourself constantly that your child has the right to the best quality of life that can be provided for him. You must maintain your dignity and remember that of all the roles you may be called upon to play in life, the role of being a parent will have the longest and most lasting effect. Your child has but one childhood in which to prepare himself for the rest of his life.

Until changes are made—overdue changes in the process of collecting child support, changes that will facilitate the job of making grownups behave in a mature, responsible manner—the burden of responsibility rests on you. To succeed you will need drive, energy, and stamina, but you *can* succeed. If it means your child will have a better place to live, a sufficient wardrobe, a better education, more nutritious food, the opportunity to spend more time with you, or, in the best of cases, all of these, then you have achieved a victory that was well worth the fight.

Appendix A

Obtaining Forms and Records

Court Forms

Court forms are available for a small fee from the clerk of the court. An information booth or directory can generally provide you with the appropriate room number. If you are in doubt as to which court hears family law matters, call the courthouse and inquire.

Birth Records

An official certificate of birth is generally on file in the locality where the event occurred. The county recorder's office can provide you with the correct street and/or mailing address. When you request a birth record, you must provide the following information: the full name of the person whose record you are requesting; the name of the father, the maiden name of the mother; the date of birth; the city, state, county, and name of the hospital, if available, where the birth occurred; the reason for requesting the record; and your relationship with the person whose record you are requesting. Fees vary from $2.00 to $11.00. If you are requesting the document through the mail, enclose a money order or cashier's check with your request. Personal checks are also accepted in some areas.

Each state also has a bureau of vital statistics, although the name of this bureau varies. Check your telephone directory under State Government Offices. Birth records as well as death, marriage, and divorce records can also be obtained through this source.

Marriage Records

When requesting a copy of a marriage certificate, include the following information: the full names of the bride and groom; the address(es) of the bride and groom at the time of the marriage; the date of the marriage; the date of birth for the bride and groom; the city, county, and state where the marriage took place; the reason for requesting the record; your relationship with the person whose record is being requested.

Divorce Records

When requesting a copy of a divorce record, include the following information: the full name of both husband and wife and their birth dates; the present resident addresses as well as the former addresses that appear in the court records; the date of the divorce; the place where the divorce occurred; the type of final decree; the purpose for which you are requesting the document; the relationship between those on the record and the person requesting it.

Appendix B

Child Support Advocacy Groups and State-Funded Groups*

Alabama
Association for Child Support Enforcement (ACES)
Judy Hayes, Regional Director
#2 Sherwood Forest
Duncanville, Alabama 35456
(205) 752-8760

Arizona
Organization for Protection of America's Children (OPAC)
April J. Skelton
18501 East Bay Road
Higley, Arizona 85236
(602) 988-3238

Kathy Gaddy
Chandler, Arizona
(602) 899-5056

California
Single Parent Action Network
Mary Drummond
10560 Colona Road
Rancho Cordova, California 95670
(916) 635-9176

* No active support groups have been found in states not listed.

Appendix B

Single Parents United "N" Kids (SPUNK)
Susan Speir
5823 Marna Street
Long Beach, California 90815
(213) 591-3381

Top Priority—Children
Teddy Kieley
P. O. Box 2161
Palm Springs, California 92263
(619) 323-1559

Gloria Allred, President
Stephanie, Contact
6380 Wilshire Boulevard, Suite 1404
Los Angeles, California 90048
(213) 653-8087

Colorado
Kids in Need Deserve Equal Rights (KINDER)
Mary Alice Chaffin
5420 Wild Lane
Loveland, Colorado 80537
(303) 663-0949

Fathers for Equal Rights
(303) 936-3257

Connecticut
Parents Enforcing Court Ordered Support (PECOS)
Patricia Caputo
23 Indian Run
Enfield, Connecticut 06082
(203) 749-0894

District of Columbia
National Congress of Men
Washington, D. C.
1-800-366-8786

Women's Legal Defense Fund
Amy Barrison (Child Support)
Suite 400
2000 P. Street, N.W.
Washington, D. C. 20036
(202) 887-0364

Florida
Association for Children for Enforcement of Support Inc. (ACES)
Southeast Region
Judy Hayes, Regional Director
(205) 752-8760

Georgia
Coalition to Help Enforce Child Support
Marianna Rich
3056-A Spring Hill Road
Smyrna, Georgia 30080
(404) 633-9503

Illinois
Organization for Child Support Action (OCSA)
Mary Wyse
P. O. Box 504
Villa Park, Illinois 60181
(708) 833-3427

Iowa
Association for Children for Enforcement of Support, Inc. (ACES)
702 Franklin Avenue
Council Bluffs, Iowa 51503

Coalition for Child Support Enforcement
631 42nd Street
Des Moines, Iowa 50312

Fathers for Equal Rights
3623 Douglas
Des Moines, Iowa 50310
(515) 277-8789

Parents for Child Support
1714 W. 15th Street
Sioux City, Iowa 51103

Maryland
Organization for the Enforcement of Child Support (OECS)
Elain and William Fromm
119 Nocodemus Road
Reistertown, Maryland 21136
(301) 833-2458

Michigan
ACES
Linda DeMare
815 S. Gargantua
Clawson, Michigan 48017
Unpublished Number

Fathers for Equal Rights
654 Forrest
East Lansing, Michigan
(517) 337-0333

Marge Johnson
P. O. Box 40563
Redford, Michigan 48240
(313) 357-0456

Karen Pattison
915 Lizzie Street
Sault Ste. Marie, Michigan 49783
(906) 632-6364

Missouri
Parents Unified for Lawful Support Enforcement (PULSE)
Pamela Burton, Director
3227 Greenwich
St. Charles, Missouri 63301
(314) 233-9125 Work
(314) 723-4659 Home

Association for Child Support Enforcement (ACES)
Jane Stout Van Winkle, President
P. O. Box 18314
Raytown, Missouri 64133

Child Health and Support Enforcement
Stephanie Maple
P. O. Box 10005
Springfield, Missouri 65808
(417) 836-1591 Work
(417) 831-8290 Home

Citizens Advocating Universal Support Enforcement
P. O. Box 32063
St. Louis, Missouri 63132

Nebraska
Child Support Collection Task Force
Nebraska Commission on the Status of Women
Betty Peterson
P. O. Box 6162
Lincoln, Nebraska 68106
(402) 471-2039

New Hampshire
Fathers United for Equal Justice
5 Harold Drive
Nashua, New Hampshire 03060
(603) 888-9389

Parents for Justice
3 Pleasant Street
Concord, New Hampshire 03301
(603) 224-4296

New Jersey
Camden County Probation Department
Mid Atlantic Bank Building, 2nd Floor
Broadway & Cooper Avenue
Camden, New Jersey 08002
(609) 756-0023

Judy Richter
P. O. Box 1401
Burlington, New Jersey 08016
(609) 586-6043

New Mexico
Dads Against Discrimination
Albuquerque, New Mexico
(505) 299-2673

New York
For Our Children and Us, Inc. (FOCUS)
Fran Mattera, Director
550 Old Country Road
Hicksville, New York 11801
(516) 433-6633

Helena Vitale
Brooklyn, New York 11204
(212) 232-6335

Office for Women
Mona Orange, Director
395 Oser Avenue
Hauppauge, New York 11788
(516) 348-5460

Ohio
Association for Children for Enforcement of Support, Inc. (ACES)
Ms. Jensen
723 Philips, Suite 216
Toledo, Ohio 43602
(419) 476-2511

Dayton Family Service Association
1714 West Third St.
Dayton, Ohio 45407
(513) 222-0381

Oklahoma
Association for Children for Enforcement of Support, Inc. (ACES)
Ms. Wright
(918) 492-7335

Oklahomans Organized for Child Support Enforcement
Debi Evans
3518 E. Virgin Place
Tulsa, Oklahoma 74115
(918) 832-1860

Oregon
Child Deserve Support
Gail Esters
150 Kingwood Avenue, NW
Salem, Oregon 97304
(503) 378-7526
(502) 393-2344

Pennsylvania
New Jersey Council for Children's Rights (NJCCR)
Ms. Seidel
P. O. Box A
Glenside, Pennsylvania 19038

South Dakota
Linda Lea M. Viken, Attorney
Member of the House of Representatives
P. O. Box 3299
Rapid City, South Dakota 57709
(605) 341-4400

Tennessee
Gail Forsythe
Forsythe Road
Route 3, Box 42A
Selmer, Tennessee 38375
(901) 645-6387

Parents For Equal Rights
227 Music Square East, Suite 272
Nashville, Tennessee 37203
(615) 327-8667

Texas
Organization for Child Support Action (OCSA)
Deborah Seitzer
24163 Boerne Stage Road
San Antonio, Texas 78255
(513) 698-3354

Women's Advocacy Project
1-800-777-FAIR

Vermont
Legal Aid
151 Elm Street
Montpelier, Vermont
(802) 223-6377

Vermont for Kids
103 S. Main
Waterbury, Vermont 05676
1-800-645-5437 (in Vermont)
(802) 341-2740

Virginia
For Our Children's Unpaid Support (FOCUS)
Bettiane Walsh
P. O. Box 842
Vienna, Virginia 22180
(703) 860-1123

Washington
POPS
Michael Carrell
10210 Lake Louise Drive, S.W.
Tacoma, Washington 98498
(206) 581-2859

Appendix C

STATE CHILD SUPPORT ENFORCEMENT OFFICES

Alabama

Bureau of Public Assistance
Child Support Division
State Department of Pensions and Security
50 Riple Street
Montgomery, Alabama 36130
(205) 242-9300

Alaska

Child Support Enforcement Agency
Department of Revenue
500 W. 7th Street, Suite 410
Anchorage, Alaska 99501
(907) 276-3441

Arizona

Child Support Enforcement
Department of Economic Security
P. O. Box 40458
Phoenix, Arizona 85067
or
2222 W. Encanto
Phoenix, Arizona 85009
(602) 252-0236
1-800-543-7383 (in Arizona)

Arkansas

Office of Child Support Enforcement
105 Main Street
Little Rock, Arkansas 72203
(501) 377-6130

California

Child Support Program Management Branch
Department of Social Services
744 P Street
Sacramento, California 95814
(916) 323-8994

Colorado

Division of Child Support Enforcement
Department of Social Services
1575 Sherman Street, 2nd Floor
Denver, Colorado 80203
(303) 866-5994

Connecticut

Child Support Division
Department of Human Resources
149 Asylum Avenue
Hartford, Connecticut 06105
(203) 566-3053

Delaware

Division of Child Support Enforcement
Department of Health and Social Services
P. O. Box 904
New Castle, Delaware 19720
(302) 421-8328

District of Columbia

Office of Paternity and Child Support
Department of Human Services
425 I Street, N.W., 3rd Floor
Washington, D. C. 20001
(202) 724-5610

Florida
Office of Child Support Enforcement
Department of Health and Rehabilitative Services
1317 Winewood Boulevard
Tallahassee, Florida 32301
(904) 488-9900

Georgia
Office of Child Support Recovery
State Department of Human Resources
P. O. Box 80000
Atlanta, Georgia 30357
(414) 894-4996

Guam
Department of Public Health and Social Services
Government of Guam
P. O. Box 2816
Agana, Guam 96910
(671) 777-8928

Hawaii
Child Support Enforcement Agency
Intake Section
628 Cook Street
Honolulu, Hawaii 96813
(808) 548-5326

Idaho
Bureau of Child Support Enforcement
Department of Health and Welfare
Statehouse Mail
450 W. State Street, 5th Floor
Boise, Idaho 83720
(208) 334-5710

Illinois
Bureau of Child Support
Department of Public Aid
201 S. Grand Avenue East
Springfield, Illinois 62705
(217) 782-1366

Indiana

Child Support Enforcement Division
State Department of Public Welfare
141 S. Meridian Street, 4th Floor
Indianapolis, Indiana 46225
(317) 232-4894

Iowa

Child Support Recovery Unit
Iowa Department of Social Services
Hoover Building, 5th Floor
Des Moines, Iowa 50319
(515) 281-5580

Kansas

Child Support Enforcement Program
Department of Social and Rehabilitation Services
300 S.W. Oakley
1st Floor, Perry Building
Topeka, Kansas 66606
(913) 296-3237

2701 North 11th Street
Garden City, Kansas 67846
(316) 275-0271

Kentucky

Division of Child Support Enforcement
Department of Social Insurance
Cabinet for Human Resources
First City Complex
102 Athletic Drive
Frankfort, Kentucky 40621
(502) 564-2285

(Mailing Address)
Division of Child Support Enforcement
Department of Social Insurance
Cabinet for Human Resources
275 East Main Street, 6th Floor
Frankfort, Kentucky, 40621

Appendix C   215

Louisiana
Office of Family Support
Support Enforcement Services
P. O. Box 94065
Baton Rouge, Louisiana 70804-4065
(504) 342-4780

Maine
Support Enforcement and Location Unit
Bureau of Social Welfare
Department of Human Services
Division of Child Support
State House, Station 11
Augusta, Maine 04333
(207) 289-2886

Maryland
Child Support Enforcement Administration
Department of Human Resources
300 W. Preston Street
Baltimore, Maryland 21201

City Office:
110 N. Utah
Baltimore, Maryland 21201
(301) 333-6500

Massachusetts
Division of Revenue
Child Support Enforcement Unit
Department of Public Welfare
600 Washington Street
Boston, Massachusetts 02111
(617) 621-4444

Michigan
Office of Child Support
235 S. Grand Avenue, Suite 1400
Lansing, Michigan 48909
(517) 373-7570

(Mailing Address)
Office of Child Support
P. O. Box 3007
Lansing, Michigan 48909

Minnesota
Office of Child Support
Department of Human Services
Space Center Building
444 Lafayette Road
St. Paul, Minnesota 55101
(612) 296-2499

Mississippi
Child Support Division
State Department of Public Welfare
515 E. Amite Street
Jackson, Mississippi 39205
(601) 354-0341

Missouri
Division of Child Support Enforcement
Department of Social Services
P. O. Box 1527
Jefferson City, Missouri 65102-1527
(314) 751-4301

Montana
Child Support Enforcement
Department of Social Rehabilitation
P. O. Box 5955
Helena, Montana 59604
(406) 444-2848

Nebraska
Child Support Enforcement Office
Department of Social Services
P. O. Box 95026
Lincoln, Nebraska 68509
(402) 471-9355

Nevada
Child Support Enforcement
Nevada State Welfare Division
Department of Human Resources
2527 N. Carson
Carson City, Nevada 89710
(702) 885-4744

New Hampshire
Office of Support Enforcement Services
Division of Welfare
Health and Welfare Building
Hazen Drive
Concord, New Hampshire 03301
(603) 271-4426

New Jersey
Child Support and Paternity Unit
Department of Human Services
612 S. Broad
Trenton, New Jersey 08650
(609) 989-6250

New Mexico
Child Support Enforcement Bureau
Department of Human Services
2009 S. Pachel
Santa Fe, New Mexico 87503
(505) 827-7200

(Mailing Address)
Child Support Enforcement Bureau
Department of Human Services
P. O. Box 25109
Santa Fe, New Mexico 87504

New York
Office of Child Support Enforcement
New York Department of Social Services
P. O. Box 14, 1 Commerce Plaza
Albany, New York 12260
(518) 474-9081

North Carolina
Child Support Enforcement Section
Division of Social Services
Department of Human Resources
160 E. Six Forks Road
Raleigh, North Carolina 27609-7750
(919) 571-4120

Appendix C

North Dakota
Child Support Enforcement Agency
North Dakota Department of Human Services
600 E. Boulevard, Judicial Wing
Bismarck, North Dakota 58505-0254
(701) 224-3582

Ohio
Bureau of Child Support
Ohio Department of Human Services
State Office Tower
30 E. Broad Street, 27th Floor
Columbus, Ohio 43266-0423
(614) 466-3233

Oklahoma
Division of Child Support
2409 N. Kelly
Oklahoma City, Oklahoma 73125
(405) 424-5871

(Mailing Address)
Division of Child Support
P. O. Box 25352
Oklahoma City, Oklahoma 73125

Oregon
Department of Justice
1535 Edgewater
Salem, Oregon 97310
(503) 378-7300

(Mailing Address)
Department of Justice
P. O. Box 14506
Salem, Oregon 97309

Pennsylvania
Child Support Office of Enforcement
Bureau of Claim Settlement
Department of Public Welfare
P. O. Box 8018
Harrisburg, Pennsylvania 17105
(717) 783-1779

Appendix C 219

Puerto Rico
Child Support Enforcement Program
Department of Social Services
P. O. Box 11398, Fernandez Juncos Station
Santurce, Puerto Rico 00910
(809) 722-7400 (Social Services)
(809) 758-1519 (Department of Justice)

Rhode Island
Bureau of Family Support
Department of Social and Rehabilitative Services
77 Dorrance
Providence, Rhode Island 02903
(401) 277-2409

South Carolina
Office of Child Support
Public Assistance Division
Bureau of Public Assistance and Field Operations
3150 Harding Street Extension
Columbia, South Carolina 29203
(803) 737-5875

(Mailing Address)
Office of Child Support
Public Assistance Division
Bureau of Public Assistance and Field Operations
P. O. Box 1469
Columbia, South Carolina 29202

South Dakota
Office of Child Support Enforcement
Department of Social Services
700 Governors Drive
Pierre, South Dakota 57501
(605) 773-3641

Tennessee
Child Support Services
Tennessee Department of Human Services
Citizen Plaza Building, 12th Floor
400 Beaderick
Nashville, Tennessee 37219
(615) 741-1820

Texas
Child Support Enforcement Branch
Texas Department of Human Resources
P. O. Box 12548
Austin, Texas 78711-2548
(512) 929-7350 or (512) 444-5463
1-800-252-9330 (in Texas)

Utah
Office of Recovery Services
Department of Social Services
120 N. 200 West
Salt Lake City, Utah 84103
(801) 538-4400
1-800-662-8525 (in Utah)
1-800-257-9165 (out of state)

(Mailing Address)
Office of Recovery Services
Department of Social Services
P. O. Box 45011
Salt Lake City, Utah 84145

Vermont
Child Support Division
Department of Social Welfare
103 S. Main Street
Waterbury, Vermont 05676
(802) 241-2319
1-800-786-3124

Virgin Islands
Paternity and Child Support Program
Department of Law
P. O. Box 1074
Christiansted, St. Croix, Virgin Islands 00820
(809) 773-8240

Virginia
Division of Child Support Enforcement
Department of Social Services
8004 Franklin Farm Drive
Richmond, Virginia 23299
(804) 756-6400 (Central)
(804) 662-9629 (District)

Washington
Office of Support Enforcement/Mail Stop HJ-31
Department of Social and Health Services
P. O. Box 9162
Olympia, Washington 98504
(206) 586-6111

West Virginia
Office of Child Support Enforcement
Department of Health and Human Services
Capito Complex, Building 6
Charleston, West Virginia 25305
(304) 348-3780

Wisconsin
Bureau of Child Support
Divison of Health and Social Services
1 W. Wilson Street, Room 382
Madison, Wisconsin 53707-7935
(608) 266-9909

Wyoming
Child Support Enforcement Section
Division of Public Assistance and Social Services
State Department of Health and Social Services
Hathaway Building
Cheyenne, Wyoming 82002
(307) 777-6948

Appendix D

Helpful Studies and Reports

TITLE: *Handbook on Child Support Enforcement*
AUTHOR: Department of Health and Human Services
PRICE: Free

This publication addresses the problems of enforcement and provides suggestions.

To order, request GPO Order Number 501T from S. James, Consumer Information Center-E, P. O. Box 100, Pueblo, Colorado 81002.

TITLE: *Money Matters*
AUTHOR: Federal Trade Commission
PRICE: $.50

This booklet offers methods for selecting the best attorney, a financial planner, an income tax preparer, and a real estate broker, and advises you on how to obtain their help at the price agreed upon.

To order, request GPO Order Number 432T from R. Woods, Consumer Information Center-E, P. O. Box 100, Pueblo, Colorado 81002.

TITLE: *A Consumer's Guide to Life Insurance*
AUTHOR: Department of Agriculture
PRICE: Free

This publication provides a glossary of commonly used insurance terms. It describes various types of policies, coverage, and costs.

To order, request GPO Order Number 514P from S. James, Consumer Information Center-E, P. O. Box 100, Pueblo, Colorado 81002

TITLE: *Student Guide—Five Federal Financial Aid Programs*
AUTHOR: Department of Education
PRICE: Free

Information on five grant and loan programs for students who want to attend college or a vocational or technical school. This booklet provides the requirements for eligibility and instructions on how to apply.

To order, request GPO Number 511T from Superintendent of Documents, U. S. Government Printing Office, Washington, D. C. 20402.

TITLE: *Children Today*
AUTHOR: Department of Health and Human Services
PRICE: $16.00 per year; $2.50 per single copy

This is a bimonthly publication that provides information regarding federal, state, and local services for children, child development, health and welfare laws, and additional news concerning child welfare.

To order a single copy, request GPO Number S/N 717-006-00000-3. To order a subscription, ask for GPO Number CT and Superintendent of Documents Number HE 23.1209: (v. nos. & nos.). Mail requests to Superintendent of Documents, U. S. Government Printing Office, Washington, D. C. 20402.

Government Printing Office publications can also be ordered by telephone if you are paying with a MasterCard or Visa credit card. The telephone number is (202) 783-3238.

When ordering by mail, make your check or money order payable to the Superintendent of Documents. You must provide your name, address, and telephone number; the date; and the quantity, stock number, title, and price of each publication. Orders are shipped by nonpriority mail and should be received within six weeks, although expedited shipping is available. You may call (202) 783-3238 for applicable rate information.

There are government bookstores in several states throughout the country. These stores have a variety of publications, and if you want a publication that is not currently in stock, they will special order it for you.

The Office of Child Support Enforcement frequently has reports, studies, and periodicals authored by the U. S. Department of Health and Human Services. You may request these from your local Child Support Enforcement Agency.

Appendix E

FORMS

These California Family forms are included on the following pages for reference only:

1. Petition for Dissolution of Marriage
2. Response
3. Income and Expense Declaration
4. Minimum Child Support Worksheet
5. Stipulation to Establish or Modify Child or Family Support Order
6. Notice of Motion
7. Order to Show Cause
8. Notice of Request to Change Support Order
9. Application for Order and Supporting Declaration
10. Ex Parte Application for Wage Assignment for Child Support

Appendix E 225

ATTORNEY OR PARTY WITHOUT ATTORNEY *(Name and Address)*	TELEPHONE NO.	**FOR COURT USE ONLY**
ATTORNEY FOR *(Name)*		

SUPERIOR COURT OF CALIFORNIA, COUNTY OF
STREET ADDRESS:
MAILING ADDRESS:
CITY AND ZIP CODE:
BRANCH NAME:

MARRIAGE OF
PETITIONER:

RESPONDENT:

PETITION FOR	CASE NUMBER:
☐ Dissolution of Marriage ☐ And Declaration Under Uniform	
☐ Legal Separation Child Custody Jurisdiction Act	
☐ Nullity of Marriage	

1. RESIDENCE (Dissolution only) ☐ Petitioner ☐ Respondent has been a resident of this state for at least six months and of this county for at least three months immediately preceding the filing of this Petition for Dissolution of Marriage.

2. STATISTICAL FACTS
   a. Date of marriage: b. Date of separation:
   c. Period between marriage and separation   d. Petitioner's Social Security No.:
      Years: Months: e. Respondent's Social Security No.:

3. DECLARATION REGARDING MINOR CHILDREN OF THIS MARRIAGE
   a. ☐ There are no minor children.   b. ☐ The minor children are:

   <u>Child's name</u>   <u>Birthdate</u>   <u>Age</u>   <u>Sex</u>

   c. IF THERE ARE MINOR CHILDREN, COMPLETE EITHER (1) OR (2)
      (1) ☐ Each child named in 3b is presently living with ☐ petitioner ☐ respondent
            at *(address)*:

            and during the last five years has lived in no state other than California and with no person other than petitioner or respondent or both. Petitioner has not participated in any capacity in any litigation or proceeding in any state concerning custody of any minor child of this marriage. Petitioner has no information of any pending custody proceeding or of any person not a party to this proceeding who has physical custody or claims to have custody or visitation rights concerning any minor child of this marriage.
      (2) ☐ A completed Declaration Under Uniform Custody of Minors Act is attached.

4. ☐ **Petitioner requests** confirmation as separate assets and obligations the items listed
      ☐ in Attachment 4   ☐ below:
      <u>Item</u>   <u>Confirm to</u>

(Continued on reverse)

Form Adopted by Rule 1281
Judicial Council of California
1281 [Rev. July 1, 1990]
RD 011/R 1-90
76P307A

PETITION
(Family Law)

Civil Code, § 4503
Cal. Rules of Court, rule 1215

1281

226 Appendix E

MARRIAGE OF *(last name, first name of parties)*:	CASE NUMBER

5. DECLARATION REGARDING COMMUNITY AND QUASI-COMMUNITY ASSETS AND OBLIGATIONS AS PRESENTLY KNOWN
   a. ☐ There are no such assets or obligations subject to disposition by the court in this proceeding.
   b. ☐ All such assets and obligations have been disposed of by written agreement.
   c. ☐ All such assets and obligations are listed ☐ in Attachment 5 ☐ below:

6. **Petitioner requests**
   a. ☐ Dissolution of the marriage based on
      (1) ☐ irreconcilable differences. CC 4506(1)
      (2) ☐ incurable insanity. CC 4506(2)
   b. ☐ Legal separation of the parties based on
      (1) ☐ irreconcilable differences. CC 4506(1)
      (2) ☐ incurable insanity. CC 4506(2)
   c. ☐ Nullity of void marriage based on
      (1) ☐ incestuous marriage. CC 4400
      (2) ☐ bigamous marriage. CC 4401
   d. ☐ Nullity of voidable marriage based on
      (1) ☐ petitioner's age at time of marriage. CC 4425(a)
      (2) ☐ prior existing marriage. CC 4425(b)
      (3) ☐ unsound mind. CC 4425(c)
      (4) ☐ fraud. CC 4425(d)
      (5) ☐ force. CC 4425(e)
      (6) ☐ physical incapacity. CC 4425(f)

7. **Petitioner requests** the court grant the above relief and make injunctive (including restraining) and other orders as follows:

	Petitioner	Respondent	Joint	Other
a. Legal custody of children to	☐	☐	☐	☐
b. Physical custody of children to	☐	☐	☐	☐
c. Child visitation be granted to	☐	☐	☐	☐
☐ supervised as to *(specify)*:				
d. Child support payable by (wage assignment will be issued)	☐	☐	☐	☐
e. Spousal support payable by (wage assignment will be issued)	☐	☐		
f. Attorney fees and costs payable by	☐	☐		

   g. ☐ Terminate the court's jurisdiction (ability) to award spousal support to respondent.
   h. ☐ Property rights be determined.
   i. ☐ Wife's former name be restored *(specify)*:
   j. ☐ Other *(specify)*:

8. I have read the restraining orders on the back of the Summons, and I understand that they apply to me when this petition is filed.

I declare under penalty of perjury under the laws of the State of California that the foregoing is true and correct.

Date: ▶ _____
(SIGNATURE OF PETITIONER)

▶ _____
(TYPE OR PRINT NAME OF ATTORNEY)   (SIGNATURE OF ATTORNEY FOR PETITIONER)

1281 [Rev. July 1, 1990]   **PETITION**
(Family Law)

Appendix E 227

ATTORNEY OR PARTY WITHOUT ATTORNEY *(Name and Address)*:	TELEPHONE NO.:	FOR COURT USE ONLY
ATTORNEY FOR *(Name)*:		

SUPERIOR COURT OF CALIFORNIA, COUNTY OF
STREET ADDRESS:
MAILING ADDRESS:
CITY AND ZIP CODE:
BRANCH NAME:

MARRIAGE OF
PETITIONER:

RESPONDENT:

RESPONSE ☐ REQUEST FOR:	CASE NUMBER:
☐ Dissolution of Marriage ☐ And Declaration Under Uniform Child Custody Jurisdiction Act	
☐ Legal Separation	
☐ Nullity of Marriage	

1. RESIDENCE (Dissolution only) ☐ Petitioner ☐ Respondent has been a resident of this state for at least six months and of this county for at least three months immediately preceding the filing of this Petition for Dissolution.

2. STATISTICAL FACTS
   a. Date of marriage:
   b. Date of separation:
   c. Period between marriage and separation
      Years: Months:

3. DECLARATION REGARDING MINOR CHILDREN OF THIS MARRIAGE
   a. ☐ There are no minor children.
   b. ☐ The minor children are:

Name	Birthdate	Age	Sex

   c. IF THERE ARE MINOR CHILDREN, COMPLETE EITHER (1) *or* (2)
      (1) ☐ Each child named in 3b is presently living with ☐ petitioner ☐ respondent at *(address)*:

      and during the last five years has lived in no state other than California and with no person other than petitioner or respondent or both.

      Respondent has not participated in any capacity in any litigation or proceeding in any state concerning custody of any minor child of this marriage.

      Respondent has no information of any pending custody proceeding or of any person not a party to this proceeding who has physical custody or claims to have custody or visitation rights concerning any minor child of this marriage.

      (2) ☐ A completed Declaration Under Uniform Custody of Minors Act is attached.

4. ☐ Respondent requests confirmation of the following as separate assets and obligations:
   Item   Confirm to

(Continued on reverse)

Form Adopted by Rule 1282
Judicial Council of California **1282**
1282 [Rev. January 1, 1983]

**RESPONSE
(FAMILY LAW)**

76R447B (Rev. 1-83) 11-83
RD016

CC 4355; CRC 1215

Appendix E

MARRIAGE OF (last name—first names of parties):	CASE NUMBER:

RESPONSE (FAMILY LAW)

1282 [Rev. January 1, 1983]
Page two

5. DECLARATION REGARDING COMMUNITY AND QUASI-COMMUNITY ASSETS AND OBLIGATIONS AS PRESENTLY KNOWN
   a. ☐ There are no such assets or obligations subject to disposition by the court in this proceeding.
   b. ☐ All such assets and obligations have been disposed of by written agreement.
   c. ☐ All such assets and obligations are listed in the property declaration to be filed with this response.
   d. ☐ All such assets and obligations are listed below:

6. ☐ Respondent contends there is a reasonable possibility of reconciliation.

7. ☐ Respondent denies the grounds set forth in item 6 of the petition.

8. ☐ Respondent requests
   a. ☐ Dissolution of the marriage based on
      (1) ☐ irreconcilable differences. CC 4506(1)
      (2) ☐ incurable insanity. CC 4506(2)
   b. ☐ Legal separation of the parties based on
      (1) ☐ irreconcilable differences. CC 4506(1)
      (2) ☐ incurable insanity. CC 4506(2)
   c. ☐ Nullity of void marriage based on
      (1) ☐ incestuous marriage. CC 4400
      (2) ☐ bigamous marriage. CC 4401
   d. ☐ Nullity of voidable marriage based on
      (1) ☐ respondent's age at time of marriage. CC 4425(a)
      (2) ☐ prior existing marriage. CC 4425(b)
      (3) ☐ unsound mind. CC 4425(c)
      (4) ☐ fraud. CC 4425(d)
      (5) ☐ force. CC 4425(e)
      (6) ☐ physical incapacity. CC 4425(f)

9. Respondent requests that the court grant the relief or judgment specified in item 8, make injunctive and other orders as may be proper, and that
   a. ☐ Child custody be awarded
      (1) Legal custody
         (a) ☐ Joint to petitioner and respondent
         (b) ☐ Sole to ☐ petitioner ☐ respondent ☐ other (specify):
      (2) Physical custody
         (a) ☐ Joint to petitioner and respondent
         (b) ☐ Sole to ☐ petitioner ☐ respondent ☐ other (specify):
   b. ☐ Child visitation rights be granted (specify):
   c. ☐ Child support be awarded ☐ petitioner ☐ respondent
   d. ☐ Spousal support be awarded ☐ petitioner ☐ respondent
   e. ☐ Property rights be determined.
   f. ☐ Attorney's fees and costs be awarded ☐ petitioner ☐ respondent
   g. ☐ Wife's former name be restored (specify):

I declare under penalty of perjury under the laws of the State of California that the foregoing is true and correct and that this declaration is executed on
(date):

_____
(SIGNATURE OF RESPONDENT)

_____
(TYPE OR PRINT NAME OF ATTORNEY)

_____
(SIGNATURE OF ATTORNEY FOR RESPONDENT)

Appendix E 229

ATTORNEY OR PARTY WITHOUT ATTORNEY *(Name and Address)*:	TELEPHONE NO.:	*FOR COURT USE ONLY*
ATTORNEY FOR *(Name)*:		

SUPERIOR COURT OF CALIFORNIA, COUNTY OF
STREET ADDRESS:
MAILING ADDRESS:
CITY AND ZIP CODE:
BRANCH NAME:
PETITIONER/PLAINTIFF:
RESPONDENT/DEFENDANT:

INCOME AND EXPENSE DECLARATION

CASE NUMBER:

Step 1 — Attachments to this summary
a. ☐ I have attached completed Income Information and Expense Information forms.
 *You must complete and attach the Expense Information form **and** Income Information form unless b is checked.*
b. ☐ My only income is AFDC, so I have attached an Expense Information form only.

Step 2 — Answer all questions that apply to you
1. Are you receiving or have you applied for or do you intend to apply for welfare or AFDC?
 ☐ Receiving ☐ Applied for ☐ Intend to apply for ☐ No.
2. What is your date of birth (month/day/year)? ....
3. What is your occupation? _____
4. Mark the highest year of education completed:
 | Primary | High School | College | Postgraduate |
 | 1 2 3 4 5 6 7 8 | 9 10 11 12 | 13 14 15 16 | 17 18 19 20 |
5. Are you presently employed? ☐ Yes ☐ No
 a. If yes: (1) Where do you work? (name and address): _____
  (2) When did you start work there (month/year)? ....
 b. If no: (1) When did you last work (month/year)? ....
  (2) What were your gross monthly earnings? ....
6. What is your social security number:
7. What is the total number of minor children you are legally obligated to support? ....

Step 3 — Monthly income information
8. Net monthly disposable income (from line 13 of Income Information): .... $ _____
9. Current net monthly disposable income *(if different from line 8, explain below or on Attachment 9)*: $ _____

Step 4 — Deductions and adjustments
10. ☐ Hardship deductions are requested in the total amount of (item 21 of Expense Information): $ _____
11. ☐ Child support should be adjusted because of shared custody (item 22 of Expense Information).

Step 5 — Expense information
12. Total monthly expenses from line 17 of Expense Information: .... $ _____
13. Amount of these expenses paid by others: .... $ _____

Step 6 — Other party's income
14. My estimate of the other party's gross monthly income is: ☐ unknown .... $ _____

Step 7 — Date and sign this form
I declare under penalty of perjury under the laws of the State of California that the foregoing and the attached information forms are true and correct.
Date:

▶

....
(TYPE OR PRINT NAME OF DECLARANT)

_____
(SIGNATURE OF DECLARANT)
☐ Petitioner ☐ Respondent

Form Adopted by Rule 1285.50
Judicial Council of California
1285.50 (Rev. January 1, 1986)

1285.50

INCOME AND EXPENSE DECLARATION
(Family Law)

761101 — RD041 — 1/86

page one of four
Civil Code, § 4721

Appendix E

PETITIONER/PLAINTIFF:	CASE NUMBER:
RESPONDENT/DEFENDANT:	
INCOME INFORMATION OF *(name)*:	

Step 1
Figure your total gross annual income
If your income is irregular, show the total for the past 12 months and indicate that your income is irregular

1. Total gross salary or wages, including commissions, bonuses, and overtime paid during last 12 months: .... 1. $ _____
2. All other money received during last 12 months **except welfare, AFDC, spousal support from this marriage, or any child support.**   *Specify sources below:*
   Include pensions, social security, disability, unemployment, military basic allowance for quarters (BAQ), spousal support from a different marriage, dividends, interest or royalty, trust income, and annuities.
   Include income from a business and rental properties. Prepare and attach a schedule showing gross receipts less cash expenses for each business or rental property.
   _____ 2a. $ _____
   _____ 2b. $ _____
   _____ 2c. $ _____
   _____ 2d. $ _____
3. Add lines 1 through 2d .... 3. $ _____

Step 2 Gross monthly income

4. Divide the amount on line 3 by 12 months   **total gross monthly income**   4. $ _____

Step 3 Figure the deductions from income each month

5. State income tax withheld: .... 5. $ _____
6. Federal income tax withheld: .... 6. $ _____
   a. Number of exemptions claimed on W-4 form: _____
   b. Number of exemptions claimed on last federal income tax return: _____
7. FICA (Social Security) or self employment tax or an amount not greater for persons not subject to FICA, if the amount is used to secure retirement or disability benefits: 7. $ _____
8. Health insurance: .... 8. $ _____
8a. State disability insurance: .... 8a. $ _____
9. Mandatory union dues: .... 9. $ _____
10. Mandatory retirement and pension fund contributions: .... 10. $ _____
    Do not include any deduction claimed in item 7.
11. Court ordered child or spousal support **actually being paid for a relationship other than that involved in this proceeding:** .... 11. $ _____
12. Add lines 5 through 11   **total monthly deductions**   12. $ _____

Step 4 Net income

13. Subtract line 12 from line 4   **net monthly disposable income**   13. $ _____

Step 5 Other income and deduction information

14a. Current gross monthly salary or wages: .... 14a. $ _____
14b. Current gross monthly **other** income: .... 14b. $ _____
15. AFDC, welfare, spousal support from this marriage, and child support from other relationships received each month: .... 15. $ _____
16. Monthly costs of child care to permit your work or education: .... 16. $ _____

Step 6 Other property owned

17. Cash and checking accounts: .... 17. $ _____
18. Savings, credit union, certificates of deposit, and money market accounts: .... 18. $ _____
19. Stocks, bonds, and other liquid assets: .... 19. $ _____
20. All other property, real or personal *(specify below)*: .... 20. $ _____

Form Adopted by Rule 1285.50a
Judicial Council of California
1285.50a (Rev. January 1, 1986) **1285.50A**

INCOME INFORMATION
(Family Law)

761119 — RDQ86 — 1-86

Civil Code, § 4721

Appendix E 231

PETITIONER/PLAINTIFF:		CASE NUMBER:
RESPONDENT/DEFENDANT:		
EXPENSE INFORMATION OF *(name)*:		

1.
a. List all persons living in your home **whose expenses are included below** and their income: ☐ Continued on Attachment 1a.	name 1. 2. 3. 4.	age	relationship	gross monthly income
b. List all other persons living in your home and their income: ☐ Continued on Attachment 1b.	1. 2. 3.			

MONTHLY EXPENSES
2. Residence payments
   a. Rent or mortgage .... $ _____

   b. Taxes & insurance .... $ _____

   c. Maintenance .... $ _____

3. Food at home and household supplies .. $ _____

4. Food eating out .... $ _____

5. Utilities .... $ _____

6. Telephone .... $ _____

7. Laundry & cleaning .... $ _____

8. Clothing .... $ _____

9. Medical & dental .... $ _____

10. Insurance *(life, accident, etc. Do not include auto, home, or health insurance)* $ _____

11. Child care .... $ _____

12. Education *(specify)*:
                                                                                                    $ _____

13. Entertainment .... $ _____

14. Transportation & auto expenses (insurance, gas, oil, repair) .... $ _____

15. Installment payments (insert total and itemize below at 18) .... $ _____

16. Incidentals.................... $ _____
   a. Other *(specify)*:

   b. Other *(amount)*: .... $ _____

17. TOTAL MONTHLY EXPENSES ...... $ _____

18. ITEMIZATION OF INSTALLMENT PAYMENTS OR OTHER DEBTS ☐ Continued on Attachment 18.

CREDITOR'S NAME	PAYMENT FOR	MONTHLY PAYMENT	BALANCE	DATE LAST PAYMENT MADE

19. ATTORNEY FEES
   a. I have paid my attorney for fees and costs: $ _____   The source of this money was:
   b. I have incurred to date the following fees and costs:
   c. My arrangement for attorney fees and costs is:
   d. ☐ Attorney fees have been requested.
       I confirm this information and fee arrangement. _____
                                                                                         (SIGNATURE OF ATTORNEY)

_____   _____
(SIGNATURE OF DECLARANT)   (TYPE OR PRINT NAME OF ATTORNEY)

1285.50B

(Continued on reverse)

Form Adopted by Rule 1285.50b
Judicial Council of California
1285.50b (Rev. January 1, 1986)

EXPENSE INFORMATION
(Family Law)

76E896 — RD087 — 1/86

Civil Code, § 4721

Appendix E

PETITIONER/PLAINTIFF:	CASE NUMBER:
RESPONDENT/DEFENDANT:	
EXPENSE INFORMATION OF *(name)*:	

This question must be completed if there are minor children

20. Health insurance for my children ☐ is ☐ is not available through my employer.
    Monthly cost paid by me for the health insurance for the children only is: $ _____
    Do not include the amount paid or payable by your employer or others.

Complete section this if you claim expenses that have caused extreme financial hardship. Enter them here, check item 10 on the Income and Expense Declaration, and enter total on line 10 of that form

21. ☐ The court is requested to allow the deductions identified below, which are justifiable expenses that have caused an extreme financial hardship.

	Amount paid per month	How many months will you need to make these payments
a. ☐ Extraordinary health care expenses *(specify and attach any supporting documents)*:	$ _____	_____
b. ☐ Uninsured catastrophic losses *(specify and attach supporting documents)*:	$ _____	_____
c. ☐ Minimum basic living expenses of dependent minor children from other marriages or relationships *(specify names and ages of these children)*:	$ _____	_____
d. ☐ Other *(specify and attach supporting documents)*:	$ _____	_____
e. Total hardship deductions requested *(add lines a-d)*:	$ _____	

Complete this section if there are minor children of this relationship

22. Describe the custody arrangement you have or hope to have with the children.

Child's name	Arrangement

If each parent has physical custody of any of the children 110 days or more, check item 11 on the Income and Expense Declaration.

EXPENSE INFORMATION
(Family Law)

Appendix E   233

PETITIONER/PLAINTIFF:	FOR COURT USE ONLY
RESPONDENT/DEFENDANT:	

TABLE (Effective July 1, 1988)*

Number of Minor Children (From line 12)	AFDC Minimum (Enter on line 15)	Percentage	(Multiplier) (Enter on line 13)
1	$ 326	18%	(.18)
2	$ 535	27%	(.27)
3	$ 663	36%	(.36)
4	$ 788	40%	(.40)
5	$ 899	44%	(.44)
6	$ 1010	48%	(.48)
7	$ 1109	52%	(.52)
8	$ 1209	56%	(.56)
9	$ 1311	60%	(.60)
10	$ 1423	64%	(.64)

*Caution: The amounts in this table and the amount on line 20 are subject to yearly change, normally occurring about July 1.

CASE NUMBER:

MINIMUM CHILD SUPPORT WORKSHEET

	Noncustodial	Custodial
Gross monthly income (from line 4 of Income Information)	1) $	6) $ ....
Monthly deductions (from line 12 of Income Information)	2) $ −	7) $ − ....
Subtract line 2 from line 1 and enter result on line 3. Subtract line 7 from line 6 and enter result on line 8	3) $	8) $ ....
Monthly extraordinary hardship expenses (from line 10 of Income and Expense Declaration)	4) $ −	9) $ − ....
MONTHLY NET DISPOSABLE INCOME (subtract line 4 from line 3 and enter result on line 5. Subtract line 9 from line 8 and enter result on line 10)	5) $	10) $ ....

To determine the Minimum Child Support Award, you may use the tables (Appendix A to the Instruction Booklet) if neither parent's monthly net disposable income is more than $2,050. Otherwise, you must use the rest of this worksheet.

11. Total Monthly Net Disposable Income of both parents (add lines 5 and 10) .... 11) $ ....
12. Number of minor children of this relationship .... 12) ....
13. Applicable multiplier (from table above) .... 13) ....
14. Multiply line 11 by line 13 and enter on line 14 .... 14) $ ....
15. AFDC Minimum (from table above) .... 15) $ ....
16. Enter line 14 or line 15 whichever is less .... 16) $ ....
17. Figure percentage of child support to be paid by noncustodial parent.
    Divide line 5 by line 11 and enter result on line 17 .... 17) .... %
18. Multiply line 16 by line 17 and enter result on line 18 .... 18) $ ....
19. Enter amount from line 5 .... 19) $ ....
                                                                 20) $ − 3 2 6 . 0 0
21. Subtract line 20 from line 19 and enter result on line 21; if less than zero, enter zero .... 21) $ ....
22. Enter line 18 or line 21, whichever is less (**Minimum Child Support Award**) .... 22) $ ....
    (This amount is the minimum to be paid by the noncustodial parent to the custodial parent for child support. The court may award a higher amount.)

Prepared by: ☐ Petitioner ☐ Respondent ☐ Court

_____
(SIGNATURE OF JUDGE OR PARTY)

Form Approved by Rule 1285.25
Judicial Council of California
1285.25 (Rev. July 1, 1988)

1285.25

MINIMUM CHILD SUPPORT WORKSHEET
(Family Law)

76M214W
Civil Code, §§ 4720-4732

Appendix E

ATTORNEY OR PARTY WITHOUT ATTORNEY (Name and Address):	TELEPHONE NO.:	FOR COURT USE ONLY
ATTORNEY FOR (Name):		

SUPERIOR COURT OF CALIFORNIA, COUNTY OF
STREET ADDRESS:
MAILING ADDRESS:
CITY AND ZIP CODE:
BRANCH NAME:

PETITIONER/PLAINTIFF:

RESPONDENT/DEFENDANT:

STIPULATION TO ESTABLISH OR MODIFY CHILD OR FAMILY SUPPORT AND ORDER	CASE NUMBER:

1. We agree that we are fully informed of our rights under the Minimum Child Support Standards Act.
2. We make this agreement freely without threat or duress **and** the needs of our children will be adequately met under this agreement.
3. *Complete a, b, or c.*
   a. ☐ The right to support has not been assigned to any county and no application for public assistance is pending.
   b. ☐ The right to support has been assigned to *(county name)*:
   c. ☐ An application for public assistance is pending in *(county name)*:
   If you checked b or c, a district attorney of the county named must sign below before the court will accept your stipulation.
   Date:

   _____   _____
   (TYPE OR PRINT NAME)   (SIGNATURE OF DISTRICT ATTORNEY)

4. Petitioner's net monthly income: $ _____   Respondent's net monthly income: $ _____
5. Check one.
   a. ☐ We agree that child or family support will be ordered in a sum which **is equal to or greater than the current AFDC payment** for the number of children we have. The AFDC payment is: $ _____
   b. ☐ We agree that child or family support will be ordered in a sum **less than the current AFDC payment** for the number of children we have. The AFDC payment is: $ _____
   c. ☐ We agree that child or family support will be ordered in a sum less than that provided by the Minimum Child Support Standards Act and no change of circumstances need be demonstrated for a modification.
6. We agree that ☐ child ☐ family support will be payable as follows beginning on *(date)*: _____

Name of child	Monthly amount	Payable by	Payable to	Payable on (dates)
a.	$			
b.	$			
c.	$			
d.	$			
e. Family support	$			

_____   _____
(SIGNATURE OF PETITIONER/PLAINTIFF)   (SIGNATURE OF RESPONDENT/DEFENDANT)

ORDER

7. a. ☐ Child support is ordered payable as set forth in item 6. All provisions of previous orders relating to the child or children remain in effect unless specifically modified by this order. Child support payments shall continue until further order of the court or until the child marries, dies, is emancipated, reaches 19, or reaches 18 and is not a full-time high school student residing with a parent, whichever occurs first.
   b. ☐ Family support is ordered payable as set forth in item 6e. The payments shall continue until the death of the recipient or until further order of the court.

Date: _____   _____
                                       JUDGE OF THE SUPERIOR COURT

Form Approved by Rule 1285.27
Judicial Council of California
1285.27 (Rev. January 1, 1986)

1285.27

STIPULATION TO ESTABLISH OR MODIFY CHILD OR
FAMILY SUPPORT AND ORDER
(Family Law)

76S693 – RD084 – 1/86
Civil Code, § 4728

Appendix E 235

ATTORNEY OR PARTY WITHOUT ATTORNEY *(Name and Address)*	TELEPHONE NO.	FOR COURT USE ONLY
ATTORNEY FOR *(Name)*		

SUPERIOR COURT OF CALIFORNIA, COUNTY OF
STREET ADDRESS
MAILING ADDRESS
CITY AND ZIP CODE
BRANCH NAME

PETITIONER/PLAINTIFF:

RESPONDENT/DEFENDANT:

NOTICE OF MOTION ☐ MODIFICATION ☐ Child Custody* ☐ Visitation* ☐ Injunctive Order ☐ Child Support ☐ Spousal Support ☐ Other (specify): ☐ Attorney Fees and Costs	CASE NUMBER

1. TO *(name)*:
2. A hearing on this motion for the relief requested in the attached application will be held as follows:
   If child custody or visitation is an issue in this proceeding, Civil Code section 4607 requires mediation before or concurrently with the hearing above.

   a. date: time: in ☐ dept.:   ☐ rm.:
   b. Address of court   ☐ same as noted above   ☐ other *(specify)*:

***PLEASE NOTE:** If this petition involves a dispute over custody or visitation, you must contact the Conciliation Court in the district in which you are filing for dissolution for an appointment for mediation prior to any hearing of the custody matter pursuant to Civil Code 4607. If you have any questions, call the Conciliation Court, (213) 974-5524.*

3. Supporting attachments
   a. Completed Application for Order and Supporting Declaration and a **blank** Responsive Declaration
   b. ☐ Completed Income and Expense Declaration and a **blank** Income and Expense Declaration
   c. ☐ Completed Property Declaration and a **blank** Property Declaration
   d. ☐ Points and authorities
   e. ☐ Other *(specify)*:

Date:

.... ▶ ....
(TYPE OR PRINT NAME)   (SIGNATURE)

ORDER SHORTENING TIME

4. ☐ Time for ☐ service ☐ hearing is shortened. Service shall be on or before *(date)*:

Date: _____
                              JUDGE OF THE SUPERIOR COURT

NOTICE: If you have children from this relationship, the court is required to order payment of child support based on the income of both parents. The amount of child support can be large. It normally continues until the child is 18. You should supply the court with information about your finances. Otherwise the child support order will be based on the information supplied by the other parent.
   You do not have to pay any fee to file responsive declarations in response to this order to show cause (including a completed Income and Expense Declaration that will show your finances). The original of the responsive declarations must be filed with the court and a copy served on the other party at least five court days before the hearing date.

1285.10   (See reverse for Proof of Service by Mail)
Form Adopted by Rule 1285.10
Judicial Council of California   **NOTICE OF MOTION**
1285.10 (Rev. July 1, 1985)   **(Family Law)**
76N642NM—RD 085/R3-89   Gov. Code § 26826

236 *Appendix E*

PETITIONER/PLAINTIFF:	CASE NUMBER
RESPONDENT/DEFENDANT:	

PROOF OF SERVICE BY MAIL

a. I am over the age of 18, not a party to this cause, a resident or employed in the county where the mailing took place, and my residence or business address is:

b. I served copies of the following papers by enclosing them in a sealed envelope with postage fully prepaid, depositing them in the United States mail as follows:

  (1) Papers served:
    (a) A completed Application for Order and Supporting Declaration and a **blank** Responsive Declaration
    (b) ☐ Completed Income and Expense Declaration and a **blank** Income and Expense Declaration
    (c) ☐ Completed Property Declaration and a **blank** Property Declaration
    (d) ☐ Points and authorities
    (e) ☐ Other *(specify)*:

  (2) Manner of service:
    (a) Date of deposit:
    (b) Place of deposit (city and state):
    (c) Addressed as follows:

c. I declare under penalty of perjury under the laws of the State of California that the foregoing is true and correct.

Date:

.... ▶ ....
(TYPE OR PRINT NAME)   (SIGNATURE OF DECLARANT)

NOTICE OF MOTION
(Family Law)

Appendix E 237

ATTORNEY OR PARTY WITHOUT ATTORNEY *(Name and Address)*	TELEPHONE NO.	FOR COURT USE ONLY
ATTORNEY FOR *(Name)*		

SUPERIOR COURT OF CALIFORNIA, COUNTY OF
STREET ADDRESS
MAILING ADDRESS
CITY AND ZIP CODE
BRANCH NAME

PETITIONER/PLAINTIFF:

RESPONDENT/DEFENDANT:

ORDER TO SHOW CAUSE FOR ☐ MODIFICATION ☐ Child Custody* ☐ Visitation* ☐ Injunctive Order ☐ Child Support ☐ Spousal Support ☐ Other (specify): ☐ Attorney Fees and Costs	CASE NUMBER

1. TO *(name)*:
2. YOU ARE ORDERED TO APPEAR IN THIS COURT AS FOLLOWS TO GIVE ANY LEGAL REASON WHY THE RELIEF SOUGHT IN THE ATTACHED APPLICATION SHOULD NOT BE GRANTED. *If child custody or visitation is an issue in this proceeding, Civil Code section 4607 requires mediation before or concurrently with the hearing below.*

   a. date: time: in ☐ dept.:   ☐ rm.:
   b. Address of court ☐ same as noted above ☐ other *(specify)*:

PLEASE NOTE: If this petition involves a dispute over custody or visitation, you must contact the Conciliation Court in the district in which you are filing for dissolution for an appointment for mediation prior to any hearing of the custody matter pursuant to Civil Code 4607. If you have any questions, call the Conciliation Court, (213) 974-5524.

3. IT IS FURTHER ORDERED that a completed Application for Order and Supporting Declaration, a **blank** Responsive Declaration, and the following documents shall be served with this order:
   (1) Completed Income and Expense Declaration and a **blank** Income and Expense Declaration
   (2) ☐ Completed Property Declaration and a **blank** Property Declaration
   (3) ☐ Points and authorities
   (4) ☐ Other *(specify)*:
   a. ☐ Time for ☐ service ☐ hearing is shortened. Service shall be on or before *(date)*:
   b. ☐ You are ordered to comply with the temporary orders attached.
   c. ☐ Other *(specify)*:

Date: _____

JUDGE OF THE SUPERIOR COURT

NOTICE: If you have children from this relationship, the court is required to order payment of child support based on the income of both parents. The amount of child support can be large. It normally continues until the child is 18. You should supply the court with information about your finances. Otherwise the child support order will be based on the information supplied by the other parent.

You do not have to pay any fee to file responsive declarations in response to this order to show cause (including a completed Income and Expense Declaration that will show your finances). The original of the responsive declarations must be filed with the court and a copy served on the other party at least five court days before the hearing date.

1285
Form Adopted by Rule 1285
Judicial Council of California
1285 (Rev. July 1, 1985)
760745—RD 005/R3-89

ORDER TO SHOW CAUSE
(Family Law)

Gov. Code § 26826
Civil Code §§ 4359, 4370, 4455,
4801, 4809

238   Appendix E

ATTORNEY OR PARTY WITHOUT ATTORNEY *(Name and Address)*:	TELEPHONE NO.	**FOR COURT USE ONLY**
ATTORNEY FOR *(Name)*:		

SUPERIOR COURT OF CALIFORNIA, COUNTY OF
STREET ADDRESS:
MAILING ADDRESS:
CITY AND ZIP CODE:
BRANCH NAME:

PETITIONER/PLAINTIFF:

RESPONDENT/DEFENDANT:

NOTICE OF REQUEST TO CHANGE ☐ CHILD SUPPORT ORDER (Civil Code, § 4700.1) ☐ SPOUSAL SUPPORT ORDER (Civil Code, § 4801.9)	CASE NUMBER:

To *(name)*:

1. I am requesting the court to change
   a. ☐ **child support** from the present total of *(specify current amount)*: $ _____ to *(specify requested total amount)*: $ _____ per month.
   b. ☐ **spousal support** from the present amount of *(specify current amount)*: $ _____ to *(specify requested amount)*: $ _____ per month.

2. *(Check a or b or both)*
   a. ☐ At least one year has passed since the last order for support was entered on *(date)*:
      and the amount of
      (1) ☐ the change in child support sought does not exceed 10 percent of the previous order for each year since it was made.
      (2) ☐ the increase in spousal support sought does not exceed the increase in the California All Consumer Price Index since it was made.
   b. ☐ This request is based on a significant decrease in my income as shown on the attached Income and Expense Declaration.

---

3. **IF YOU OBJECT TO THIS REQUEST, YOU MUST FILE A WRITTEN OBJECTION AND ASK FOR A COURT HEARING WITHIN 30 DAYS.** Instructions and the necessary forms (Notice of Hearing and Notice of Opposition to Request to Change Support Order, Income and Expense Declaration, and Proof of Service (Simplified Support Modification)) are attached.
   a. If you have this matter set for hearing, you must bring a copy of your most recent federal and state income tax returns (whether individual or joint) to the hearing. See the Information Sheet for instructions if you don't have a copy of your tax return.
   b. You may be represented in court by an attorney. If you hire an attorney, the court will proceed under Civil Code section 4700 (if child support) or Civil Code section 4801 (if spousal support), and
      (1) You must check box 8b in your Notice of Hearing and Notice of Opposition to Request to Change Support Order.
      (2) I may hire an attorney and ask the court to order you to pay my attorney.
      (3) I may ask the court to award an amount of child or spousal support different from the amount sought in this request.

---

4. a. ☐ **Child support**
      I understand that I must file a court-stamped copy of this notice with the district attorney of the county where this proceeding was filed within five working days after I file this notice with the court.
   b. ☐ **Spousal support** *(check one)*
      (1) ☐ The district attorney has previously sought to enforce the spousal support involved. I understand that I must file a court-stamped copy of this notice with the district attorney of the county where this proceeding was filed within five working days after I file this notice with the court.
      (2) ☐ The district attorney has not previously sought to enforce the spousal support involved.

(Continued on reverse)

Form Adopted by Rule 1285.30
Judicial Council of California
1285.30 (Rev. July 1, 1990)
RD 062/R1-90
76N778R

NOTICE OF REQUEST TO CHANGE SUPPORT ORDER
(Civil Code, § 4700.1 or § 4801.9)
(Family Law)

1285.30

Appendix E   239

PETITIONER/PLAINTIFF:	CASE NUMBER
RESPONDENT/DEFENDANT:	

5. I am requesting issuance of a wage assignment showing the new amount to be withheld.

6. ☐ **Child support** *(check one)*
   a. ☐ I am receiving **public assistance** for the child or children listed in the proposed order.
   b. ☐ I am not receiving **public assistance** for the child or children listed in the proposed order.
   c. ☐ I intend to apply for **public assistance** for the child or children listed in the proposed order.

I declare under penalty of perjury under the laws of the State of California that the foregoing is true and correct.

Date:

_____   ▶ _____
(TYPE OR PRINT NAME)   (SIGNATURE)

—IMPORTANT WARNING—
Unless you file a written objection and ask the court for a hearing **within 30 calendar days** from the date of service of this form on you, this request to change the support order will **automatically** become a court order.

1285.30 (Rev. July 1, 1990)   **NOTICE OF REQUEST TO CHANGE SUPPORT ORDER**   Page two
(Civil Code, § 4700.1 or § 4801.9)
(Family Law)

240 *Appendix E*

MARRIAGE OF *(last name, first name of parties)*:	CASE NUMBER:

(THIS IS NOT AN ORDER)

☐ Petitioner ☐ Respondent ☐ Claimant requests the following orders be made:

1. ☐ CHILD CUSTODY   ☐ **To be ordered pending the hearing**
   a. Child *(name and age)*   b. Request custody to *(name)*   c. ☐ Modify existing order
                                                                             (1) filed on *(date)*:
                                                                             (2) ordering *(specify)*:

   d. ☐ Petitioner ☐ Respondent shall have the temporary physical custody of the minor children.

2. ☐ CHILD VISITATION   ☐ **To be ordered pending the hearing**
   a. ☐ Reasonable   d. ☐ Modify existing order
   b. ☐ Other *(specify)*:   (1) filed on *(date)*:
   c. ☐ Neither party shall remove the minor child or children of the parties   (2) ordering *(specify)*:

      (1) ☐ from the State of California. (2) ☐ other *(specify)*:

3. ☐ CHILD SUPPORT *(If support is awarded, a wage assignment order will be issued.)*
   a. Child   b. Support request   c. ☐ Modify existing order
      Name and age   Monthly amount   (1) filed on *(date)*:
                                    $ (2) ordering *(specify)*:

4. ☐ SPOUSAL SUPPORT *(If support is awarded, a wage assignment order will be issued.)*
   a. ☐ Amount requested *(monthly)*: $ b. ☐ Modify existing order
   c. ☐ Terminate existing order   (1) filed on *(date)*:
      (1) filed on *(date)*:   (2) ordering *(specify)*:
      (2) ordering *(specify)*:

5. ☐ ATTORNEY FEES AND COSTS   a. ☐ Fees: $ b. ☐ Costs: $
6. ☐ RESIDENCE EXCLUSION AND RELATED ORDERS   ☐ **To be ordered pending the hearing**
      ☐ Petitioner ☐ Respondent must move out immediately and must not return to the family dwelling at *(address)*:
      ☐ taking only clothing and personal effects needed until the hearing.

7. ☐ STAY-AWAY ORDERS   ☐ **To be ordered pending the hearing**
   a. ☐ Petitioner ☐ Respondent must stay at least . . . . . yards away from applicant and the following places:
      (1) ☐ applicant's residence *(address optional)*:
      (2) ☐ applicant's place of work *(address optional)*:
      (3) ☐ the children's school *(address optional)*:
      (4) ☐ other *(specify)*:

   b. ☐ Contacts relating to pickup and delivery of children pursuant to a court order or a stipulation of the parties arrived at during mediation shall be permitted.

8. ☐ RESTRAINT ON PERSONAL CONDUCT   ☐ **To be ordered pending the hearing**
      ☐ Petitioner ☐ Respondent
      a. ☐ shall not molest, attack, strike, threaten, sexually assault, or otherwise disturb the peace of the other party ☐ **and** any person under the care, custody, and control of the other party.

      b. ☐ shall not contact or telephone the other party.
      c. ☐ **except** that peaceful contacts relating to minor children of the parties shall be permitted.

(Continued on reverse)

Form Adopted by Rule 1285.20
Judicial Council of California
1285.20 (Rev. July 1, 1990)
RD 054/R1-90
76A166

**APPLICATION FOR ORDER
AND SUPPORTING DECLARATION
(Family Law)**

Civil Code, § 4359

1285.20

Appendix E 241

MARRIAGE OF (last name, first name of parties):	CASE NUMBER:

9. [ ] PROPERTY RESTRAINT [ ] To be ordered pending the hearing
   a. The [ ] petitioner [ ] respondent [ ] claimant be restrained from transferring, encumbering, hypothecating, concealing, or in any way disposing of any property, real or personal, whether community, quasi-community, or separate, except in the usual course of business or for the necessities of life.
   [ ] and applicant be notified at least five business days before any proposed extraordinary expenditures and an accounting of such be made to the court.
   b. [ ] Both parties are restrained and enjoined from cashing, borrowing against, canceling, transferring, disposing of, or changing the beneficiaries of any insurance or other coverage including life, health, automobile, and disability held for the benefit of the parties or their minor children.
   c. [ ] Neither party shall incur any debts or liabilities for which the other may be held responsible, other than in the ordinary course of business or for the necessities of life.

10. [ ] PROPERTY CONTROL [ ] To be ordered pending the hearing
    a. [ ] Petitioner [ ] Respondent be given the exclusive temporary use, possession, and control of the following property we own or are buying *(specify)*:

    b. [ ] Petitioner [ ] Respondent be ordered to make the following payments on liens and encumbrances coming due while the order is in effect:

    Debt   Amount of payment   Pay to

11. [ ] LAW ENFORCEMENT AGENCIES I request that copies of orders be given to the following law enforcement agencies having jurisdiction over the locations where violence is likely to occur:

    Law enforcement agency   Address

12. [ ] **I request** that time for service of the Order to Show Cause and accompanying papers be shortened so that they may be served no less than *(specify number)*: .... days before the time set for the hearing. I need to have the order shortening time because of the facts specified in the attached declaration.

13. [ ] OTHER RELIEF *(specify)*:

14. [ ] FACTS IN SUPPORT of relief requested and change of circumstances for any modification are *(specify)*:
    [ ] contained in the attached declaration.

I declare under penalty of perjury under the laws of the State of California that the foregoing is true and correct.
Date:

▸

_____   _____
(TYPE OR PRINT NAME)   (SIGNATURE OF APPLICANT)

1285.20 [Rev. July 1, 1990]

**APPLICATION FOR ORDER
AND SUPPORTING DECLARATION
(Family Law)**

242 Appendix E

ATTORNEY OR PARTY WITHOUT ATTORNEY *(Name and Address)*:	TELEPHONE NO.:	FOR COURT USE ONLY
ATTORNEY FOR *(Name)*:		

SUPERIOR COURT OF CALIFORNIA, COUNTY OF
STREET ADDRESS:
MAILING ADDRESS:
CITY AND ZIP CODE:
BRANCH NAME:
PETITIONER/PLAINTIFF:

RESPONDENT/DEFENDANT:

EX PARTE APPLICATION FOR WAGE ASSIGNMENT FOR SUPPORT ORDERED BEFORE JULY 1, 1990	CASE NUMBER:

APPLICANT DECLARES

1. ☐ **Child support** was ordered as follows:
   a. Date of order:
   b. Payable by ☐ petitioner ☐ respondent
   c. Payable to ☐ petitioner ☐ respondent ☐ other *(specify)*:
   d. Total amount unpaid is at least: $ _____ as of *(date)*:

2. ☐ **Spousal support** ☐ **family support** was ordered as follows:
   a. Date of order:
   b. Payable by ☐ petitioner ☐ respondent
   c. Payable to ☐ petitioner ☐ respondent ☐ other *(specify)*:
   d. Total amount unpaid is at least: $ _____ as of *(date)*:

3. Payment of ☐ child support ☐ spousal support is overdue in the sum of at least one month's payment. Written notice of my intent to seek a wage assignment was
   a. ☐ given at least 15 days prior to the date of filing this application
      (1) ☐ by first class mail.
      (2) ☐ by personal service.
      (3) ☐ contained in the support order described in item 1 or 2.
      (4) ☐ other:

   b. ☐ waived *(explain)*:

4. The amount of arrears stated in items 1(d) and 2(d) ☐ do ☐ do not include interest at the legal rate. *(If interest is included, attach calculation.)*

5. **I request** an order directing the employer of the person ordered to pay support to deduct each month from the wages or salary due the employee, until further order of the court, the following:
   a. ☐ Child support: $
   b. ☐ Spousal support ☐ family support: $
   c. ☐ Arrears (child, family, and spousal): $

(Continued on reverse)

Form Adopted by Rule 1285.65
Judicial Council of California
1285.65 (Rev. July 1, 1990)
RD 061/R1-90
78E653

EX PARTE APPLICATION FOR WAGE ASSIGNMENT FOR SUPPORT ORDERED BEFORE JULY 1, 1990
(Family Law)

Civil Code, § 4390.5

1285.65

Appendix E 243

PETITIONER/PLAINTIFF:	CASE NUMBER:
RESPONDENT/DEFENDANT:	

6. ☐ The ☐ petitioner ☐ respondent has the ability to pay reasonable attorney fees.
   I request an order directing the employer to deduct and pay attorney fees for the preparation of this form as follows:

   a. Total amount to be paid: .... $

   b. Monthly amount to be paid: .... $

I declare under penalty of perjury under the laws of the State of California that the foregoing is true and correct.

Date:

_____   ▶ _____
(TYPE OR PRINT NAME)   (SIGNATURE OF APPLICANT)

**EX PARTE APPLICATION FOR WAGE ASSIGNMENT
FOR SUPPORT ORDERED BEFORE JULY 1, 1990**
(Family Law)

Appendix F

1. State of Delaware Child Support Calculation
2. State of Wisconsin Formula

Appendix F   **245**

Form 509 (Rev. 11/90)

The Family Court of the State of Delaware

Case Name:_____ Period Covered:_____
File Number:_____

CHILD SUPPORT CALCULATION

	Father___	Mother___	Total
	(filing status)	(filing status)	

Net Income Derived From (__) Tax Return (__) Tax Table
1 A-Monthly Gross Earned Income $_____ $_____
    B-Monthly Gross Other Income (type) _____   +_____   +_____
    C-Total Monthly Gross Income (Line 1A + Line 1B) =$_____ =$_____
2 Total Tax   Fed   + FICA   + State   + City   + Other =
    -Father _____ _____ _____ _____ _____   -_____
    -Mother _____ _____ _____ _____ _____   -_____
3 Allowable Insurance: _____ -_____ -_____
4 Allowable Deductions
        Support Order + Req. Pension + Union Dues   + Other =
    -Father   _____   _____   _____   _____   -_____
    -Mother   _____   _____   _____   _____   -_____
5 Monthly Net Income (Line 1C - Lines (2+3+4))   =$_____ =$_____

Net Income Available for Primary Support
6 Parent's Self Support Allowance   -$ 550   -$ 550
7 Net Income Available for Primary Support (Line 5 - Line 6) =$[____] =$[____] $[____]
8 Share of Total Available Net Income (Line 7 + Line 7 Total)   ____%   ____%

Child(ren's) Primary Support Need
9 Number of Children Due Support in this Support Action
10 Primary Support Allowance (from table below) $_____ $_____ $_____
11 A-Monthly Child Care Expenses of Working Custodial Parent _____   _____   +_____
     B-Other_____   _____   _____   +_____
12 Total Primary Need (Line 10 + Line 11A + Line 11B)   =$_____
13 A-Primary Support Obligation (Line 8 x Line 12 Total) $[____] $[____]
     B-Primary Support for Other Dependents (fr. Suppl. Wksheet) +_____   +_____
     C-Total Primary Support Obligation (Line 13A + Line 13B) =$_____   =$_____

Standard of Living Adjustment (SOLA)
14 Amount Available for SOLA (Line 7 - Line 13C) $_____ $_____
15 SOLA Percentage (from table below)   ____%   ____%
16 A-SOLA Amount (Line 14 x Line 15) $[____] +$[____] = $[____]
     B-SOLA Amount Per Child (Line 16A + Line 9) $_____
                                                                                        (per child)

Total Monthly Support Amount
17 Total Monthly Child Support Obligation (Line 13A + Line 16)$[____] $[____]
18 Amount Retained by Custodial Parent   _____   _____
19 Total Monthly Ordered Child Support (Line 17 - Line 18) =$_____ =$_____
20 Pay Period Amount: Weekly___ Bi-Weekly___ Semi-Monthly___ =$_____ =$_____

# of Children	Primary Support Allowance	SOLA%
1	$220	18%
2	$385	27%
3	$550	35%
each additional child	+$110	+5%

246   Appendix F

Form 509 S
(Rev. 11/90)   **The Family Court of the State of Delaware**

Case Name: _____   Period Covered: _____

File Number: _____

SUPPLEMENTAL WORKSHEET for
PRIMARY SUPPORT of OTHER DEPENDENTS

	Parent (filing status)	Spouse (filing status)	Total

Net Income Derived From ( ) Tax Return ( ) Tax Table
S1 A-Monthly Gross Earned Income $ _____ $ _____
    B-Monthly Gross Other Income (type) _____   + _____   + _____
    C-Total Monthly Gross Income (Line S1 A + Line S1 B)   = $ _____   = $ _____
S2 Total Tax   Fed   + FICA   + State   + City   + Other =
   -Parent _____ _____ _____ _____ _____   - _____
   -Spouse _____ _____ _____ _____ _____   - _____
S3 Allowable Insurance: _____   - _____   - _____
S4 Allowable Deductions
        Support Order + Req. Pension + Union Dues + Other =
   -Parent   _____   _____   _____   _____   - _____
   -Spouse   _____   _____   _____   _____   - _____
S5 Monthly Net Income (Line S1 C - Lines (S2+S3+S4))   = $ _____   = $ _____

Net Income Available for Primary Support
S6 Parent's Self Support Allowance   -$ 550   -$ 550
S7 Net Income After Self Support (Line S5 - Line S6)   = $ _____   = $ _____
S8 Other Child(ren)'s Primary Support (Line 13 A other worksheet)-
S9 Net Income Available for Support (Line S7 - Line S8)   = $ [___]   = $ [___] $ [___]
S10 Parent's Share Net Income Available (Line S9 + Line S9 Total)   _____%

Child(ren's) Primary Support Need
S11 Number of Children Due Support in this Union
S12 Primary Support Allowance (from table below) $ _____
S13 A-Monthly Child Care Expenses   + _____
    B-Other _____   + _____
S14 Total Primary Need (Line S12 + Line S13 A + Line S13 B)   = $ _____
S15 Primary Support Obligation (Line S10 x Line S14 Total) $ [_____]

Number of Children	Primary Support Allowance
1	$220
2	$385
3	$550
each additional child	+$110

Form 509 S Instructions (Rev. 4/90)

INSTRUCTIONS for SUPPLEMENTAL WORKSHEET for PRIMARY SUPPORT of OTHER DEPENDENTS

This worksheet is part of the Delaware Child Support Formula established by the Family Court under Civil Rule 52(c). It serves as a supplement to the "Child Support Calculation" worksheet in cases where a parent supports a child(ren) living in his/her household that are not part of the child support action. The parent referred to in the worksheet is the parent involved in the child support action. The spouse is that parent's current spouse or person with whom he/she cohabitates in the relationship of husband and wife 13 Delaware Code §1512(g).

NET INCOME

Determine the net monthly income available to the parent and spouse. Figure net income by taking monthly gross income and subtracting allowable payroll deductions. Monthly gross income and allowable deductions are defined in lines 1 through 5 in the "Instructions for Child Support Calculation."

Note: all figures for this section and other sections must be made in monthly amounts. If figures are given in weekly amounts then multiply the amount by 52 and then divide by 12 to get the correct monthly amount. If figures are for bi-weekly amounts then multiply the amount by 26 and then divide by 12.

Lines S1-S5--Net Income: These lines are calculated the same way as the first five lines of the "Child Support Calculation" worksheet. Information concerning the parent of the children for whom child support is being sought should be placed in the column under "Parent." Information concerning his/her spouse should be placed in the column under "Spouse".

NET INCOME AVAILABLE FOR PRIMARY SUPPORT

Determine how much income the parent and spouse have available for the child(ren)'s primary support. After subtracting the parent and spouse's self support allowance, and the amount of primary support the parent owes in the support action the total income available to support the child(ren) is derived. Then calculate the parent's share of the total income.

Line S6--Parent's Self Support Allowance: Each Parent's Self Support Allowance equals $550. This amount is already entered.

Line S7--Other Child(ren)'s Primary Support: Enter the parent's Primary Support Obligation (line 13 A) in the "Child Support Calculation" worksheet.

Line S8--Net Income Available for Support: Subtract the Parent's Self Support Allowance ($550) (line S6) and the Other Child(ren)'s Primary Support (line S7) from the parent and spouse's Monthly Net Income (line S5). Enter the result for the parent and spouse. Add the figure for the parent and spouse to get the total available income. Enter the result in the total column.

Line S9--Parent's Share of Net Income Available: Divide the Net Income Available for Support for the parent (line S8) by the Total Net Income Available for Support (line S8).

to Families with Dependent Children (AFDC), Supplemental Security Income (SSI) if it goes to the parents, and Food Stamps (FS). SSI for a child will be included in the child's income.

Imputed Income: When a support obligor is not working full time or is working below full earning capacity, determine why there is a limitation on earnings. See, e.g. DCSE v. James Barrows, Del. Supr., No 147, 1989 Holland, J. (February 21, 1990); R.T. v. R.T. Del. Supr., 494 A.2d 150 (1985); Dolgas v. Dolgas, Del. Fam., No. 1974-85, Gallagher, J. (December 9, 1988). If the obligor has voluntarily chosen to earn less than his/her capacity the Court will impute income. First, look at the obligor's previous earning history to see what type of earnings potential he/she has. If no earnings history is present look at the obligors employment qualifications. Determine what someone with comparable qualifications would earn in the local job market. If income is imputed in either of these two fashions use withholding tables to determine the appropriate withholding. Base withholding on the maximum number of allowable exemptions. The minimum amount that can be imputed under any of these circumstances is a net monthly income figure of $607. If the minimum amount is imputed skip lines 1-4 for the obligor concerned and put $607 in line 5.

C--Total Monthly Gross Income: Total Monthly Gross Income is the sum of Monthly Gross Earned Income (Line 1 A) and Monthly Gross Other Income (Line 1 B).

Line 2--Total Tax: Determine the amount of tax withheld in a month. Base withholding on the maximum number of allowable exemptions the parent can claim. Look up the amount of withholding on the withholding tables. Enter the amount for each parent for each of the separate taxes identified. Add these taxes across the line and enter the result in the appropriate column. The number of exemptions claimed by a parent and the amount of withholding shown on the Form 16a may differ from the amount used for this calculation.

Line 3--Allowable Insurance: On the line for medical, enter the cost of monthly medical insurance if the policy covers the child(ren). Normally health insurance should be provided by the parent that can obtain the most comprehensive coverage through an employer at least cost. If the coverage is provided through an employer, only the employee portion should be deducted. Include the cost of the parent's coverage if the parent is covered with the children under a family policy. Enter the monthly cost of life or any other insurance that benefits the child(ren). Enter the appropriate sum of insurance expenditures under the respective column for Father and Mother.

Line 4--Allowable Deductions: Enter the total amount of allowable deductions. These deductions would include: court ordered child support payments; payments required by an employer, such as retirement benefits; and payments of union dues. Under the other column, enter the monthly amount of any court ordered alimony payments or allowable business expenses if the person is self-employed or required by his/her employer to purchase supplies etc. Add these deductions across the line and enter the result in the appropriate column. Deductions for payments on credit union debts or car payments are not allowed except to the extent that such debts are incurred for indispensable items in use by the dependents or necessary health care.

Line 5--Monthly Net Income: Calculate the Monthly Net Income by taking the Total Monthly Gross Income in line 1 C and subtracting the amounts in lines 2 through 4.

NET INCOME AVAILABLE FOR PRIMARY SUPPORT

The Court has established an absolute minimum amount of income that a parent must retain to function at maximum productivity. Subtract each parent's self support allowance from their net income and calculate the net total income available to support the child(ren). Then, figure each parent's share of the total income.

Line 6--Parent's Self Support Allowance: Each Parent's Self Support Allowance equals $550. This

Appendix F **249**

Form 509 Instructions (Rev. 4/90)

INSTRUCTIONS FOR CHILD SUPPORT CALCULATION

PREFACE

The Family Court of the State of Delaware has established the Delaware Child Support Formula under Civil Rule 52(c). This formula outlines the procedure for determining child support awards in the state of Delaware. The formula is based on the following principles:

- Each parent is entitled to keep a minimum amount of income for their basic needs.
- The child(ren)'s basic needs are taken care of before the parents may retain any additional income.
- If income is available after the primary needs of the parents and child(ren) are taken care of, the child(ren) is (are) entitled to share in any additional income of the parents.

In determining each parent's child support obligation the Court considers each parent's ability to pay. Ability to pay includes: the health, income and financial circumstances, and earning capacity of the parties, including the children. The manner of living to which the parties have been accustomed when they were living under the same roof and the general equities inherent in the situation are also considered. See 13 Delaware Code §514.

USE OF THE DELAWARE CHILD SUPPORT FORMULA

The Delaware Child Support Guideline serves as a rebuttable presumption for establishing all child support awards in the state of Delaware. The Court will use the formula in setting support unless it finds that the results would not be in the best interest of the child(ren) or would be inequitable to the parties involved. See, e.g. Dalton v. Clanton, Del. Supr. 55 A.2d 1197 (1989).

NET INCOME

Net income is used for calculating the child support amount under the Delaware Child Support Formula. Figure net income by taking monthly gross income and subtracting allowable payroll deductions. Monthly gross income and allowable deductions are defined below.

Note: all figures for this section and other sections must be made in monthly amounts. If figures are given in weekly amounts then multiply the amount by 52 and then divide by 12 to get the correct monthly amount. If figures are for bi-weekly amounts then multiply the amount by 26 and then divide by 12.

Line 1

    A--Monthly Gross Earned Income: Monthly Gross Earned Income includes income from salaries, wages, commissions, and bonuses. **Document all earned income with the most recent tax return, W-2 Form and the three most recent pay stubs.** See, e.g. Kane v. Kane, Del. Fam., No. 341-87 Gallagher, J., (April 4, 1989).

    B--Monthly Gross Other Income: Monthly Gross Other Income includes but is not limited to dividends, severance pay, pensions, interest, trust income, annuities, capital gains, social security benefits, veteran's benefits, workers' compensation benefits, unemployment insurance benefits, disability insurance benefits, gifts, prizes, and alimony or maintenance received.

    Expense reimbursements or in-kind payments received by a parent in the course of employment, self-employment, or operation of a business should be counted as other income if they are significant and reduce personal living expenses. Such payments might include a company car, free housing, or reimbursed meals. Also, any social security benefits paid on behalf of or directly to a minor child (included in this support action) should be counted as income of the custodial parent or the parent receiving the benefits on behalf of the child(ren). Social Security benefits of children who are not included in the child support order will not be included.

    Income from the following means tested programs will be **excluded** from gross other income: Aid

Appendix F

CHILD(REN)'S PRIMARY SUPPORT NEED

Determine the primary support needs of the child(ren) and the parent's contribution to that need. The child(ren)'s primary need is based on the sum of the primary support allowance and monthly child care expenses. The portion that the parent owes of this primary need is based on his/her share of net income available.

Line S10--Number of Children Due Support in this Union: Enter the number of children living in the household from the union of the parent and spouse.

Line S11--Primary Support Allowance: Enter the Primary Support Allowance that matches the number of children in line 11 (see table below for Primary Support Allowance).

Line S12--Monthly Child Care Expenses: Enter the Monthly Child Care Expenses if both parents work. Document these expenses with receipts from payments for care. The documentation must be attached to the Form 16a.

Line S13--Total Primary Need: To arrive at the Total Primary Need add the Primary Support Allowance (line S11) and the Child Care Expenses (line S12).

Line S14--Primary Support Obligation: Multiply the Parent's Share of Net Income Available (line S9) by the Total Primary Need (line S13). This number will be entered on Line 13 B on the "Child Support Calculation" worksheet for the parent concerned.

Number of Children	Primary Support Allowance
1	$220
2	$385
3	$550
each additional child	+$110

amount has already been entered on the form.

Line 7--Net Income Available for Primary Support: Subtract the Parent's Self Support Allowance ($550) (line 6) from each of the parent's Monthly Net Income (line 5). Enter the result for each parent. Add the figure for the father and mother to get the total available income. Enter the result in the total column.

Line 8--Share of Total Income Available: Divide the Net Income Available for Primary Support for each parent (line 7) by the Total Net Income Available for Primary Support (line 7). Enter the result for each parent.

CHILD(REN)'S PRIMARY SUPPORT NEED

The Court has established minimum levels of income needed to support one or more children. This primary support allowance is added to any work related child care expenses. Each parent's share of the child(ren)'s primary support need is based on each parents share of net income available.

Line 9--Number of Children Due Support in this Support Action: Enter the number of children due support in this support action under the parent's household where they live. Add the number in the father's and mother's column and enter the result in the total column. Do not include children from other families. They are considered in another part of the support formula.

Line 10--Primary Support Allowance: Enter the Primary Support Allowance that matches the number of children in line 9 for each household (see table below for Primary Support Allowance). Add the number in each column and enter the result in the total column.

Line 11--Monthly Child Care Expenses: Enter the Monthly Child Care Expenses that are the result of a parent working. Document these expenses with receipts from payments for care. This documentation must be attached to the Form 16a.

Line 12--Total Primary Need: To arrive at the Total Primary Need add the Primary Support Allowance (line 10) and the Child Care Expenses (line 11).

Line 13

    A--Primary Support Obligation: Multiply the Share of Total Income Available to each parent (line 8) by the Total Primary Need (line 12). Enter the result for each parent.

    B--Primary Support for Other Dependents: If this case involves a parent that supports a child(ren) living in his/her household that are not part of this child support action stop here and complete the "Supplemental Worksheet for Primary Support of Other Dependents." After completing the supplemental worksheet, enter the amount on line S14.[1]

    C--Total Primary Support Obligation: Enter the sum of the Primary Support Obligation (line 13 A)

---

[1] 13 Del.C. § 505 states:

    "(a) The duties of support specified in § 501 and § 504 of this title shall be performed according to the following order or priority:
      (1) Duty to support one's own minor child;
      (2) Duty to support a spouse;
      (3) Duty to support a woman pregnant with child conceived out of wedlock;
      (4) Duty to support a step-child or the child of a person with whom the obligor cohabits in the relationship of husband and wife;
      (5) Duty to support a poor person."

Number of Children:	Primary Support Allowance	SOLA%
1	$220	18%
2	$385	27%
3	$550	35%
each additional child	+$110	+5%

STANDARD OF LIVING ADJUSTMENT (SOLA)

When there is income available after each parent has met their own and any of their dependents primary support needs the SOLA adjustment is made. SOLA is designed to give the child(ren) a share in each parents economic well being similar to what the child(ren) would have received if the parents had remained together. See, e.g. Shuba v. DCSE/Reese, Del., Supr. 564 A.2d 1084 (1989); Flaherty v. Fidance, Del. Fam., No. B-2900, James, J. (January 8, 1980); I.B. v. R.S.W.B., Del. Fam., No. A-3000 Melson, J. (November 10, 1977).

Line 14--Amount Available for SOLA: Subtract the Total Primary Support Obligation (line 13 C) from the Net Income Available for Primary Support (line 7) for each parent. Enter the result for each parent.

Line 15--SOLA Percentage: Enter the SOLA percentage, from the table above, that corresponds to the Number of Children Due Support in this Support Action (line 9 Total). If there are more than three children add five percent for each additional child up to 50 percent. The SOLA percentage shall not exceed 50 percent unless there is a prior finding of a specific need.

Line 16--SOLA Amount: Multiply the Amount Available for SOLA (line 14) by the SOLA Percentage (line 15). Enter the result for each parent. Add the amounts for each parent and divide by the Total Number of Children Due Support in this Action (Line 9 Total) to get the per child SOLA: enter in the total column.

TOTAL MONTHLY SUPPORT AMOUNT

The total monthly support amount is based on the primary support obligation of each parent plus the SOLA obligation. The amount of monthly child support owed depends on the custody arrangement for the child(ren) and the child support obligation of each parent. This formula contemplates normal visitation arrangements. Some adjustment may result if visitation is significantly beyond the norm.

Line 17--Total Monthly Child Support Obligation: Add the Primary Support Obligation (line 13 A) for each parent to the SOLA Amount (line 16). Enter the result for each parent.

Line 18--Amount Retained by Custodial Parent: Enter the Total Monthly Child Support Obligation (line 17) where the parent is the custodian of the child(ren). Enter zero where the parent is not the custodian. Where there is a split custody arrangement, enter the amount of support required for the child(ren) in each parent's household. The SOLA amount for each child would be the per child SOLA which is calculated in the total column of Line 16.

Line 19--Total Monthly Ordered Child Support: Subtract the Amount Retained by Custodial Parent (line 18) from the Total Monthly Child Support Obligation (line 17). Enter the result for each parent. This is the Total Monthly Ordered Child Support. The minimum order allowed is $50 per child per month.

Line 20--Pay Period Amount: If the support amount is to be paid at intervals other than monthly check that appropriate period and determine the amount owed for the period based on the monthly support obligation. If the period is weekly, multiply the monthly amount (Line 19) by 12 and then divide by 52. If the period is bi-weekly, multiply the monthly amount by 12 and then divide by 26. If the period is semi-monthly, divide the monthly amount by 2.

Appendix F

DEPARTMENT OF HEALTH AND SOCIAL SERVICES

Chapter HSS 80

CHILD SUPPORT PERCENTAGE OF INCOME STANDARD

HSS 80.01 Introduction
HSS 80.02 Definitions
HSS 80.03 Support orders
HSS 80.04 Determining the child support obligation in special cases
HSS 80.05 Determining imputed income for child support

PREFACE

Section 46.25 (9) (a), Stats., requires the department to adopt and publish a standard to be used by courts in determining child support obligations. The standard is to be based on a percentage of the gross income and assets of either or both parents.

The percentage standard established in this chapter is based on an analysis of national studies, including a study done by Jacques Van der Gaag as part of the Child Support Project of the Institute for Research on Poverty, University of Wisconsin, Madison, entitled "On Measuring the Cost of Children," which disclose the amount of income and disposable assets that parents use to raise their children. The standard is based on the principle that a child's standard of living should, to the degree possible, not be adversely affected because his or her parents are not living together. It determines the percentage of a parent's income and potential income from assets that parents should contribute toward the support of children if the family does not remain together. The standard determines the minimum amount each parent is expected to contribute to the support of their children. It expects that the custodial parent shares his or her income directly with their children. It also presumes that the basic needs of the children are being met. This latter presumption may be rebutted by clear and convincing evidence that the needs of the children are not being met.

The rules also prescribe procedures for determining equitable child support obligations under a variety of financial and family circumstances.

HSS 80.01 Introduction. (1) AUTHORITY AND PURPOSE. This chapter is promulgated under the authority of s. 46.25 (9) (a), Stats., for the purpose of establishing a standard to be used in determining child support under ss. 767.02, 767.08, 767.10, 767.23, 767.25, and 767.51, Stats.

(2) APPLICABILITY. This chapter applies to the party that petitions for and the party that responds to a petition for a temporary or final order for child support of a marital or nonmarital child in an action affecting a family under s. 767.02, Stats., and includes stipulated child support settlements under s. 767.10, Stats. At the court's discretion, upon a finding of a substantial change of circumstances, this chapter may also apply to revisions of judgment under s. 767.32, Stats.

History: Cr. Register, January, 1987, No. 373, eff. 2-1-87; r. (2) (b) to (d), Register, August, 1987, No. 380, eff. 9-1-87.

HSS 80.02 Definitions. In this chapter:

(1) "Adjusted base" means the monthly income at which the child support obligation is determined for serial family payers, which is the payer's base less the amount of any existing child support obligation.

(2) "Assets" means all real and personal property, including automobiles and other vehicles, real estate, profit-sharing, pension and retirement accounts, life insurance, cash and deposit accounts, stocks and bonds and business interests.

(3) "Base" means the monthly income at which the child support obligation is determined, which is calculated by adding together the payer's

gross income adjusted for child support and the payer's imputed income for child support, and dividing by 12.

(4) "Child" means the natural or adopted child of the payer.

(5) "Child support" or "child support obligation" means an amount of money that a person is legally obligated to pay toward the expense of raising a child or children in an intact family or pursuant to the order of a Wisconsin court under ch. 767, Stats., or the order of a court of competent jurisdiction in another state.

(6) "Court" means a circuit court judge or family court commissioner.

(7) "Current 6-month treasury bill rate" means the yield of a U.S. government security with a term of 6 months.

(8) "Department" means the Wisconsin department of health and social services.

(9) "Dependent household member" means a person for whom a taxpayer is entitled to an exemption for the taxable year under 26 USC 151 (e).

(10) "Family support" means an amount which a person is legally obligated to pay pursuant to an order under s. 767.261, Stats., as a substitute for child support under s. 767.25, Stats., and maintenance payments under s. 767.26, Stats.

(11) "Federal dependency exemption" means the deduction allowed in computing taxable income pursuant to 26 USC 151 (e) for a child of the taxpayer who has not attained the age of 19 or who is a student.

(12) "Gross income" means all income as defined under 26 CFR 1.61-1 that is derived from any source and realized in any form, whether money, property or services, and whether reported as total income on the payer's federal tax return or exempt from being taxed under federal law.

(13) "Gross income adjusted for child support" means gross income adjusted by adding wages paid to dependent household members, the business assets depreciation allowance under 26 USC 179 and the excess of accelerated depreciation as determined under 26 USC 167, and 26 USC 168 over straight-line depreciation allowable under 26 USC 167 and subtracting public assistance and child and spousal support received from previous marriages.

(14) "Imputed income for child support" means the amount of income ascribed to assets which are unproductive or to which income has been diverted to avoid paying child support or from which income is necessary to maintain the child or children at the economic level they would enjoy if they were living with their parents, and which exceeds the actual earnings of the assets.

(15) "Marital child" means a child determined to be a marital child under s. 767.60, Stats.

(16) "Parent" means the natural or adopted parent of the child.

(17) "Payee" means the parent who is the recipient of child support as a result of a court order.

DEPARTMENT OF HEALTH AND SOCIAL SERVICES

(18) "Payer" means the parent who incurs a child support obligation as a result of a court order.

(19) "Primary custodian" means the parent having physical custody of the child more than 182 days a year or the parent designated by the court as primary custodian when the parents share the child-caring responsibility equally.

(20) "Self-employed payer" means a payer determined by the court to be self-employed for the purpose of determining child support.

(21) "Serial family payer" means a payer with an existing child support obligation who incurs an additional child support obligation in a subsequent family or as a result of a paternity judgment.

(22) "Shared-time payer" means a payer who is not the primary custodian but who provides overnight child care beyond the threshold and assumes all variable child care costs in proportion to the number of days he or she cares for the child under the shared-time arrangement.

(23) "Split custody payer" means a payer who has 2 or more children and who has physical custody of one or mnore but not all of the children.

(24) "Standard" or "percentage standard" means the percentage of income standard under s. HSS 80.03 (1) which, multiplied by the payer's base or adjusted base, results in the payer's child support obligation.

Note: The standard is based on national studies of the percentage of income used to support a child or children with adjustment downward of those percentages to reflect costs incurred by the payer for visitation and to maintain health insurance for the child or children.

(25) "Threshold" means 30% of a year or 109.5 out of every 365 days.

Note: The threshold was derived by taking 30% of a 365 day year.

(26) "Total annual income for child support" means gross income adjusted for child support plus imputed income for child support.

(27) "Unemployed payer" means a payer not employed at the time child support is ordered, but who may be employed in the future.

(28) "Variable costs" means costs that include payment for food, clothing, school, extracurricular activities and recreation.

(29) "Worksheet" means the department's percentage standard worksheet, printed as Appendix B to this chapter.

History: Cr. Register, January, 1987, No. 373, eff. 2-1-87; r. (2) (b) to (d), r. and recr. (12) to (14), renum. (26) to (28) to be (27) to (29) and am. (29), cr. (26), Register, August, 1987, No. 380, eff. 9-1-87.

HSS 80.03 Support orders. (1) DETERMINING CHILD SUPPORT USING THE PERCENTAGE STANDARD. The payer's base shall be determined by adding together the payer's gross income adjusted for child support and the payer's imputed income for child support and dividing by 12. This may be done by completing the worksheet in Appendix B, although use of the worksheet for this purpose is not required. The percentage of the payer's base or adjusted base that constitutes the child support obligation shall be:

(a) 17% for one child;

(b) 25% for 2 children;

316-4 WISCONSIN ADMINISTRATIVE CODE
HSS 80

(c) 29% for 3 children;

(d) 31% for 4 children; and

(e) 34% for 5 or more children.

Note: See Appendix A which indicates the amount of child support at various levels of income using the percentage standard.

(2) CALCULATION OF FAMILY SUPPORT. When the standard under sub. (1) is used to calculate support under s. 767.261, Stats., the amount determined shall be increased by the amount necessary to provide a net family support payment, after state and federal income taxes are paid, of at least the amount of a child support payment under the standard.

(3) EXPRESSION OF ORDERED SUPPORT. In temporary and final support orders, the ordered support may be expressed either as a percentage of the base or adjusted base, or as a fixed sum, as permitted under ss. 767.23 (1), 767.25 (1) and 767.51 (4), Stats.

(4) DEPENDENCY EXEMPTION. The court may order the payee to waive the federal dependency exemption provided that the payee's execution of the exemption waiver is made contingent on the receipt of child support payments.

History: Cr. Register, January, 1987, No. 373, eff. 2-1-87; am. (1) (intro.), Register, August, 1987, No. 380, eff. 9-1-87.

HSS 80.04 Determining the child support obligation in special circumstances. Child support may be determined under special circumstances as follows:

(1) DETERMINING THE CHILD SUPPORT OBLIGATION OF A SERIAL FAMILY PAYER. For a serial family payer the child support obligation may be determined as follows:

(a) Determine the payer's base in accordance with s. HSS 80.03 (1) (intro.);

(b) Determine the payer's adjusted base by applying one of the following methods, as appropriate:

1. When the payer is subject to an existing support order, subtract the amount of the court-ordered support, if it is being paid, from the base to get the adjusted base; or

2. When the payer has other children legally under his or her care who are not subject to a court order, multiply the appropriate percentage for the number of children legally under the payer's care by the base as determined on the worksheet. Subtract this amount from the base to determine the adjusted base; and

(c) Multiply the appropriate percentage for the number of children subject to the new order by the adjusted base determined in either par. (b) 1 or 2 to determine the child support obligation.

Note 1: The following example shows how the child support obligation is determined for a serial family payer whose additional child support obligation has been incurred for a subsequent family:

Appendix F 257

DEPARTMENT OF HEALTH AND SOCIAL SERVICES
HSS 80

Assumptions:

The payer's base is $2,000;

The payer's existing monthly support order for 2 children is $500; and

The payer is getting divorced from her second husband with whom she has one child.

Calculation:

Base		$2,000
Existing court order	−	500
Adjusting base for determining child support		1,500
Percentage standard for 1 child	×	.17
Monthly child support order		$ 255

Note 2: The following example shows how the child support obligation is determined for a serial family payer whose additional child support obligation has been incurred as a result of a paternity judgment.

Assumptions

The payer's base is $2,000;

The payer and his wife have 2 children of their own; and

The payer has been adjudicated the father of another child in a paternity judgment.

Calculation:

Base		$2,000
Standard for 2 children under the payer's care (25% × $2,000)	−	500
Adjusted base		$1,500
Standard for one child as a result of paternity judgment	×	.17
Monthly child support order		$ 255

(2) DETERMINING THE CHILD SUPPORT OBLIGATION OF A SHARED-TIME PAYER. The child support obligation for a parent who the court determines is a shared-time payer may be calculated as follows:

(a) Determine the payer's base in accordance with s. HSS 80.03 (1) (intro.);

(b) Multiply the appropriate percentage under s. HSS 80.03 (1) by the payer's total annual income for child support to establish the payer's original annual level of child support;

(c) Divide the payer's original annual level of child support in par. (b) by 365 to determine the payer's original daily child support obligation;

(d) Determine the number of days a year the payer will care for the child overnight;

(e) Determine the number of days a year above the threshold and less than 183 that the payer will care for the child overnight;

(f) Multiply the number of days a year above the threshold the payer will care for the child overnight in par. (e) by the payer's original daily child support level in par. (c) to determine the amount by which the payer's annual support obligation is to be reduced;

Appendix F

HSS 80

(g) Subtract the amount by which the payer's annual support obligation is to be reduced in par. (f) from the payer's original annual level of child support as identified in par. (b) to determine the payer's final annual child support obligation;

(h) Divide the amount determined under par. (g) by 12 to determine the payer's monthly level of child support; and

(i) Express the shared-time payer's monthly child support obligation either as a fixed sum or as a percentage of the payer's base.

Note: The following example shows how to calculate the amount of child support for a shared-time payer:

Assumptions:

The payer is divorced and has one child;

The payer assumes 40% of child-caring responsibility, or 146 days;

The payer's monthly gross income is $3,000; and

The payer has available assets.

Calculation:

The payer's total annual income for child support = $36,000.

The payer's original annual child support obligation = 17% × $36,000 = $6,120.

The payer's original daily child support obligation = $6,120 ÷ 365 = $16.77.

The payer provides overnight child care 146 days a year.

The payer provides overnight child care 36.5 days a year above the threshold (146 − 109.5 days = 36.5 days).

The payer's child support obligation is reduced by $611.38 (36.5 × $16.77).

The annual child support obligation of the shared time payer is $6,120 − $611.38 = $5,508.62.

The monthly child support obligation of the shared-time payer is $5,508.60 ÷ 12 = $459.05.

(3) DETERMINING THE CHILD SUPPORT OBLIGATION OF A SPLIT-CUSTODY PAYER. (intro.) For a split-custody payer, the child support obligation may be determined as follows:

(a) Determine the payer's base in accordance with s. HSS 80.03 (1) (intro.) for calculating the amount of child support.

(b) Multiply the payer's base established under par. (a) by the appropriate percentage under s. HSS 80.03 (1) for the number of children in the payee's custody to determine the payer's child support obligation in dollars.

(c) Determine the payee's base in accordance with s. HSS 80.03 (1) (intro.) for calculating the amount of child support.

(d) Multiply the payee's base established under par. (c) by the appropriate percentage under s. HSS 80.03 (1) for the number of children in the payer's custody to determine the payee's child support obligation.

DEPARTMENT OF HEALTH AND SOCIAL SERVICES
HSS 80

(e) Subtract the smaller child support obligation from the larger to determine the reduced amount of child support owed by the parent with the larger child support obligation.

Note: The following example shows how to calculate the amount of child support for a split-custody payer:

Assumptions:

The payer is divorced and has 3 children;

The payer has custody of one child;

The payer's monthly gross income is $3,000;

The payee has custody of 2 children; and

The payee's monthly gross income is $1,500.

Calculation:

The payer's base $3,000	
The payer's original child support obligation (25% x $3,000)	750
The payee's base	1,500
The payee's original child support obligation (17% x $1500)	255
The payer owes the payee (750 - 255)	$495

History: Cr. Register, January, 1987, No. 373, eff. 2-1-87; am. (1) (a), (b) (intro.) and 1., (3) (intro.), (a) and (c), r. and recr. (2), Register, August, 1987, No. 380, eff. 9-1-87.

HSS 80.05 Determining imputed income for child support. For a payer with assets, a reasonable earning potential may be attributed to the assets as follows:

(1) Determine the payer's gross income;

(2) If the court finds that the payer has underproductive assets or has diverted income into assets to avoid paying child support or that income from the payer's assets is necessary to maintain the child or children at the economic level they would enjoy if they and their parents were living together, identifying those assets and then impute income to them by multiplying the total net value of the assets by the current 6-month treasury bill rate or any other rate that the court determines is reasonable; and

(3) Subtract the actual earnings of the assets from the imputed income from the assets to determine the imputed income for child support.

History: Cr. Register, January, 1987, No. 373, eff. 2-1-87; r. and recr. Register, August, 1987, No. 380, eff. 9-1-87.

Appendix F

316-8 WISCONSIN ADMINISTRATIVE CODE
HSS 80

Appendix A
CHILD SUPPORT PERCENTAGE CONVERSION TABLE

BASE	ONE CHILD 0.17	TWO CHILDREN 0.25	THREE CHILDREN 0.29	FOUR CHILDREN 0.31	FIVE OR MORE CHILDREN 0.34
10.00	2.00	3.00	3.00	3.00	3.00
20.00	3.00	5.00	6.00	6.00	7.00
30.00	5.00	8.00	9.00	9.00	10.00
40.00	7.00	10.00	12.00	12.00	14.00
50.00	9.00	13.00	15.00	16.00	17.00
60.00	10.00	15.00	17.00	19.00	20.00
70.00	12.00	18.00	20.00	22.00	24.00
80.00	14.00	20.00	23.00	25.00	27.00
90.00	15.00	23.00	26.00	28.00	31.00
100.00	17.00	25.00	29.00	31.00	34.00
110.00	19.00	28.00	32.00	34.00	37.00
120.00	20.00	30.00	35.00	37.00	41.00
130.00	22.00	33.00	38.00	40.00	44.00
140.00	24.00	35.00	41.00	43.00	48.00
150.00	26.00	38.00	44.00	47.00	51.00
160.00	27.00	40.00	46.00	50.00	54.00
170.00	29.00	43.00	49.00	53.00	58.00
180.00	31.00	45.00	52.00	56.00	61.00
190.00	32.00	48.00	55.00	59.00	65.00
200.00	34.00	50.00	58.00	62.00	68.00
210.00	36.00	53.00	61.00	65.00	71.00
220.00	37.00	55.00	64.00	68.00	75.00
230.00	39.00	58.00	67.00	71.00	78.00
240.00	41.00	60.00	70.00	74.00	82.00
250.00	43.00	63.00	73.00	78.00	85.00
260.00	44.00	65.00	75.00	81.00	88.00
270.00	46.00	68.00	78.00	84.00	92.00
280.00	48.00	70.00	81.00	87.00	95.00
290.00	49.00	73.00	84.00	90.00	99.00
300.00	51.00	75.00	87.00	93.00	102.00
310.00	53.00	78.00	90.00	96.00	105.00
320.00	54.00	80.00	93.00	99.00	109.00
330.00	56.00	83.00	96.00	102.00	112.00
340.00	58.00	85.00	99.00	105.00	116.00
350.00	60.00	88.00	102.00	109.00	119.00
360.00	61.00	90.00	104.00	112.00	122.00
370.00	63.00	93.00	107.00	115.00	126.00
380.00	65.00	95.00	110.00	118.00	129.00
390.00	66.00	98.00	113.00	121.00	133.00
400.00	68.00	100.00	116.00	124.00	136.00
410.00	70.00	103.00	119.00	127.00	139.00
420.00	71.00	105.00	122.00	130.00	143.00
430.00	73.00	108.00	125.00	133.00	146.00
440.00	75.00	110.00	128.00	136.00	150.00
450.00	77.00	113.00	131.00	140.00	153.00
460.00	78.00	115.00	133.00	143.00	156.00
470.00	80.00	118.00	136.00	146.00	160.00
480.00	82.00	120.00	139.00	149.00	163.00
490.00	83.00	123.00	142.00	152.00	167.00
500.00	85.00	125.00	145.00	155.00	170.00
510.00	87.00	128.00	148.00	158.00	173.00
520.00	88.00	130.00	151.00	161.00	177.00
530.00	90.00	133.00	154.00	164.00	180.00
540.00	92.00	135.00	157.00	167.00	184.00
550.00	94.00	138.00	160.00	171.00	187.00
560.00	95.00	140.00	162.00	174.00	190.00
570.00	97.00	143.00	165.00	177.00	194.00
580.00	99.00	145.00	168.00	180.00	197.00
590.00	100.00	148.00	171.00	183.00	201.00
600.00	102.00	150.00	174.00	186.00	204.00
610.00	104.00	153.00	177.00	189.00	207.00
620.00	105.00	155.00	180.00	192.00	211.00

Appendix F 261

DEPARTMENT OF HEALTH AND SOCIAL SERVICES 316-9
HSS 80

BASE	ONE CHILD 0.17	TWO CHILDREN 0.25	THREE CHILDREN 0.29	FOUR CHILDREN 0.31	FIVE OR MORE CHILDREN 0.34
630.00	107.00	158.00	183.00	195.00	214.00
640.00	109.00	160.00	186.00	198.00	218.00
650.00	111.00	163.00	189.00	202.00	221.00
660.00	112.00	165.00	191.00	205.00	224.00
670.00	114.00	168.00	194.00	208.00	228.00
680.00	116.00	170.00	197.00	211.00	231.00
690.00	117.00	173.00	200.00	214.00	235.00
700.00	119.00	175.00	203.00	217.00	238.00
710.00	121.00	178.00	206.00	220.00	241.00
720.00	122.00	180.00	209.00	223.00	245.00
730.00	124.00	183.00	212.00	226.00	248.00
740.00	126.00	185.00	215.00	229.00	252.00
750.00	128.00	188.00	218.00	233.00	255.00
760.00	128.00	188.00	218.00	233.00	255.00
760.00	129.00	190.00	220.00	236.00	258.00
770.00	131.00	193.00	223.00	239.00	262.00
780.00	133.00	195.00	226.00	242.00	265.00
790.00	134.00	198.00	229.00	245.00	269.00
800.00	136.00	200.00	232.00	248.00	272.00
810.00	138.00	203.00	235.00	251.00	275.00
820.00	139.00	205.00	238.00	254.00	279.00
830.00	141.00	208.00	241.00	257.00	282.00
840.00	143.00	210.00	244.00	260.00	286.00
850.00	145.00	213.00	247.00	264.00	289.00
860.00	146.00	215.00	249.00	267.00	292.00
870.00	148.00	218.00	252.00	270.00	296.00
880.00	150.00	220.00	255.00	273.00	299.00
890.00	151.00	223.00	258.00	276.00	303.00
900.00	153.00	225.00	261.00	279.00	306.00
910.00	155.00	228.00	264.00	282.00	309.00
920.00	156.00	230.00	267.00	285.00	313.00
930.00	158.00	233.00	270.00	288.00	316.00
940.00	162.00	238.00	276.00	295.00	323.00
960.00	163.00	240.00	278.00	298.00	326.00
970.00	165.00	243.00	281.00	301.00	330.00
980.00	167.00	245.00	284.00	304.00	333.00
990.00	168.00	248.00	287.00	307.00	337.00
1000.00	170.00	250.00	290.00	310.00	340.00
1010.00	172.00	253.00	293.00	313.00	343.00
1020.00	173.00	255.00	196.00	316.00	347.00
1030.00	175.00	258.00	299.00	319.00	350.00
1040.00	177.00	260.00	302.00	322.00	354.00
1050.00	179.00	263.00	305.00	326.00	357.00
1060.00	180.00	265.00	307.00	329.00	360.00
1070.00	182.00	268.00	310.00	332.00	364.00
1080.00	184.00	270.00	313.00	335.00	367.00
1090.00	185.00	273.00	316.00	338.00	371.00
1100.00	187.00	275.00	319.00	341.00	374.00
1110.00	189.00	278.00	322.00	344.00	377.00
1120.00	190.00	280.00	325.00	347.00	381.00
1130.00	192.00	283.00	328.00	350.00	384.00
1140.00	194.00	285.00	331.00	353.00	388.00
1150.00	196.00	288.00	334.00	357.00	391.00
1160.00	197.00	290.00	336.00	360.00	394.00
1170.00	199.00	293.00	339.00	363.00	398.00
1180.00	201.00	295.00	342.00	366.00	401.00
1190.00	202.00	298.00	345.00	369.00	405.00
1200.00	204.00	300.00	348.00	372.00	408.00
1210.00	206.00	303.00	351.00	375.00	411.00
1220.00	207.00	305.00	354.00	378.00	415.00
1230.00	209.00	308.00	357.00	381.00	418.00
1240.00	211.00	310.00	360.00	384.00	422.00
1250.00	213.00	313.00	363.00	388.00	425.00
1260.00	214.00	315.00	365.00	391.00	428.00
1270.00	216.00	318.00	368.00	394.00	432.00
1280.00	218.00	320.00	371.00	397.00	435.00

Register, August, 1987, No. 380

Appendix F

316-10 WISCONSIN ADMINISTRATIVE CODE
HSS 80

BASE	ONE CHILD 0.17	TWO CHILDREN 0.25	THREE CHILDREN 0.29	FOUR CHILDREN 0.31	FIVE OR MORE CHILDREN 0.34
1290.00	219.00	323.00	374.00	400.00	439.00
1300.00	221.00	325.00	377.00	403.00	442.00
1310.00	223.00	328.00	380.00	406.00	445.00
1320.00	224.00	330.00	383.00	409.00	449.00
1330.00	226.00	333.00	386.00	412.00	452.00
1340.00	228.00	335.00	389.00	415.00	456.00
1350.00	230.00	338.00	392.00	419.00	459.00
1360.00	231.00	340.00	394.00	422.00	462.00
1370.00	233.00	343.00	397.00	425.00	466.00
1380.00	235.00	345.00	400.00	428.00	469.00
1390.00	236.00	348.00	403.00	431.00	473.00
1400.00	238.00	350.00	406.00	434.00	476.00
1410.00	240.00	353.00	409.00	437.00	479.00
1420.00	241.00	355.00	412.00	440.00	483.00
1430.00	243.00	358.00	415.00	443.00	486.00
1440.00	245.00	360.00	418.00	446.00	490.00
1450.00	247.00	363.00	421.00	450.00	493.00
1460.00	248.00	365.00	423.00	453.00	496.00
1470.00	250.00	368.00	426.00	456.00	500.00
1480.00	252.00	370.00	429.00	459.00	503.00
1490.00	253.00	373.00	432.00	462.00	507.00
1500.00	255.00	375.00	435.00	465.00	510.00
1510.00	257.00	378.00	438.00	468.00	513.00
1520.00	258.00	380.00	441.00	471.00	517.00
1530.00	260.00	383.00	444.00	474.00	520.00
1540.00	262.00	385.00	447.00	477.00	524.00
1550.00	264.00	388.00	450.00	481.00	527.00
1560.00	265.00	390.00	452.00	484.00	530.00
1570.00	267.00	393.00	455.00	487.00	534.00
1580.00	269.00	395.00	458.00	490.00	537.00
1590.00	270.00	398.00	461.00	493.00	541.00
1600.00	272.00	400.00	464.00	496.00	544.00
1610.00	274.00	403.00	467.00	499.00	547.00
1620.00	275.00	405.00	470.00	502.00	551.00
1630.00	277.00	408.00	473.00	505.00	554.00
1640.00	279.00	410.00	476.00	508.00	558.00
1650.00	281.00	413.00	479.00	512.00	561.00
1660.00	282.00	415.00	481.00	515.00	564.00
1670.00	284.00	418.00	484.00	518.00	568.00
1680.00	286.00	420.00	487.00	521.00	571.00
1690.00	287.00	423.00	490.00	524.00	575.00
1700.00	289.00	425.00	493.00	527.00	578.00
1710.00	291.00	428.00	496.00	530.00	581.00
1720.00	292.00	430.00	499.00	533.00	585.00
1730.00	294.00	433.00	502.00	536.00	588.00
1740.00	296.00	435.00	505.00	539.00	592.00
1750.00	298.00	438.00	508.00	543.00	595.00
1760.00	299.00	440.00	510.00	546.00	598.00
1770.00	301.00	443.00	513.00	549.00	602.00
1780.00	303.00	445.00	516.00	552.00	605.00
1790.00	304.00	448.00	519.00	555.00	609.00
1800.00	306.00	450.00	522.00	558.00	612.00
1810.00	308.00	453.00	525.00	561.00	615.00
1820.00	309.00	455.00	528.00	564.00	619.00
1830.00	311.00	458.00	531.00	567.00	622.00
1840.00	313.00	460.00	534.00	570.00	626.00
1850.00	315.00	463.00	537.00	574.00	629.00
1860.00	316.00	465.00	539.00	577.00	632.00
1870.00	318.00	468.00	542.00	580.00	636.00
1880.00	320.00	470.00	545.00	583.00	639.00
1890.00	321.00	473.00	548.00	586.00	543.00
1900.00	323.00	475.00	551.00	589.00	646.00
1910.00	325.00	478.00	554.00	592.00	649.00

DEPARTMENT OF HEALTH AND SOCIAL SERVICES 316-11
HSS 80

BASE	ONE CHILD 0.17	TWO CHILDREN 0.25	THREE CHILDREN 0.29	FOUR CHILDREN 0.31	FIVE OR MORE CHILDREN 0.34
1920.00	326.00	480.00	557.00	595.00	653.00
1930.00	328.00	483.00	560.00	598.00	656.00
1940.00	330.00	485.00	563.00	601.00	660.00
1950.00	332.00	488.00	566.00	605.00	663.00
1960.00	333.00	490.00	568.00	608.00	666.00
1970.00	335.00	493.00	571.00	611.00	670.00
1980.00	337.00	495.00	574.00	614.00	673.00
1990.00	338.00	498.00	577.00	617.00	677.00
2000.00	340.00	500.00	580.00	620.00	680.00

Appendix F

WISCONSIN ADMINISTRATIVE CODE
HSS 80

WISCONSIN

Wisconsin-DHSS
Division of Community Services
DCS-3144 (Issued 5/87)

APPENDIX B

Check one
☐ Temporary
☐ Final

Judge

CHILD SUPPORT PERCENTAGE STANDARD WORKSHEET

This form may be used to calculate a child support obligation in accordance with Chapter HSS 80, Wisconsin Administrative Code.
USE OF THIS FORM BY THE COURT IS OPTIONAL

Branch

Case name		Case number
	☐ Mother ☐ Father	

This worksheet makes use of the financial information provided to the court under Wisconsin Statutes, S. 767.27. Calculation of child support on this form requires, at a minimum, knowing the payer's gross income. Show the net value of any assets which are underproductive or to which income has been diverted to avoid paying child support, or from which income is necessary to maintain the child or children at the economic level they would enjoy if they or their parents were living together in order to impute income to those assets. The amount by which the imputed income from assets exceeds the actual earnings of those assets is added to the gross income adjusted for child support. Imputation of income to assets is done at the temporary hearing only to the extent that information is available to the court or family court commissioner.

SECTION I - COMPUTATION OF THE BASE AMOUNT FOR CALCULATING SUPPORT
A. Calculation of gross income adjusted for child support
   INSTRUCTIONS: Determine the payer's annual gross income using the total disclosed to the court on the standard financial disclosure form and reported on the taxpayer's individual income tax return as total income.

1. Annual gross income ....

   INSTRUCTIONS: Add the following amounts to annual gross income:

2. Wages paid to dependent household members ....

3. The excess of accelerated over straight-line depreciation
   (IRS Form 4562) ....

4. Section 179, Expense Deduction (IRS Form 4562) ....

5. SUBTOTAL ....

   INSTRUCTIONS: Subtract the following amounts from annual gross income:

6. Public assistance ....

7. Child and spousal support received from previous marriages ....

8. SUBTOTAL ....

   INSTRUCTIONS: Add the amounts in lines 1 and 4, and subtract the amount in line 8 to determine the payer's gross income adjusted for child support.

9. Line 1 ....

10. Line 5 + ...

11. Line 8 − ....

12. Gross income adjusted for child support : ....

Appendix F

DEPARTMENT OF HEALTH AND SOCIAL SERVICES 316-13
HSS 80

C. Determination of total monthly support obligation
INSTRUCTIONS: Add the amount in Part A, line 12 and final amount in Part B to determine the total annual income for child support.

1. Part A, line 12 (gross income adjusted for child support) ---------------

2. Part B (imputed income for child support) ---------------

3. TOTAL ANNUAL INCOME FOR COMPUTING CHILD SUPPORT ---------------

---

INSTRUCTIONS: Divide the amount in line 3 by 12 to determine the BASE for calculating support.

5. ------------------------------ ÷ 12 = ---------------------------------
   (total annual income for child support)   (BASE)

INSTRUCTIONS: Multiply BASE (Part C, line 5) by the appropriate percentage.

6. a. One child........................17%
   b. Two children.....................25%
   c. Three children...................29%   x BASE = -------------------------------
   d. Four children....................31%   (TOTAL MONTHLY SUPPORT OBLIGATION)
   e. Five children or more children...34%

SECTION II – COMPUTATION OF THE ADJUSTED MONTHLY SUPPORT OBLIGATION FOR SERIAL FAMILY PAYERS

A. When the <u>payer</u> is subject to an existing support order:

1. Determine the BASE under SECTION I, C. 5 ---------------

2. Adjust the BASE by subtracting the amount(s) of any existing support order(s) ---------------

3. Adjusted BASE ---------------

4. Multiply adjusted BASE by the percentage for the appropriate family size (I, C. 6) to determine the Adjusted Monthly Support Obligation ---------------

---

B. When the payer has other children legally under his/her care, not subject to an existing support order:

1. Determine the BASE under Section I, C. 5. ---------------

2. Apply the standard (___%) (I, C.) for the appropriate family size to the children legally under the payer's care ---------------

3. Subtract line 2 from line 1 to determine the Adjusted BASE ---------------

4. Determine appropriate percentage (I, C.) for children to be covered under new order ---------------

5. Multiply line 3 (Adjusted BASE) by line 4 to determine ADJUSTED MONTHLY SUPPORT OBLIGATION ---------------

WISCONSIN ADMINISTRATIVE CODE
HSS 80

B. Calculation of imputed income for child support

INSTRUCTIONS: Indicate the netvalue and actual earnings of each asset from the financial disclosure form (Wisconsin Statutes, S 767.27) which is underproductive or to which income has been diverted to avoid paying child support, or from which income is necessary to maintain the child or children at the economic level they would enjoy if they and their parents were all living together.

Property description	Net value	Actual earnings
1.	$	$
2.		
3.		
4.		
5.		
6.		
7.		
8.		
9.		
10. TOTAL		

INSTRUCTIONS: Multiply the total net value of assets listed above by the current six (6) month Treasury bill rate or by any other rate the court considers to be reasonable to determine the imputed income from assets.

_____ x _____ = _____
(total net value of assets)   (rate)   (imputed income from assets)

INSTRUCTIONS: Subtract the actual earnings of the assets from the imputed income from assets to determine the imputed income for child support.

_____ - _____ = _____
(imputed income from assets) (actual earnings from assets) (imputed income for child support)

Notes

Foreword
1. Lenore Weitzman, *The Divorce Revolution* (New York: The Free Press, 1985), pp. 400–401.
2. Ibid., p. 401.

Introduction
1. Robert M. Horowitz, "Congress Gets Tough," *Family Advocate*, vol. 8, no. 1, p. 3.
2. Robert L. Gottsfield, "The Child Support Problem: Credible Threat and Use of Incarceration Works," *Arizona Bar Journal*, vol. 19, p. 14.
3. U.S. Bureau of the Census, Current Population Reports, Series P-23, no. 167, *Child Support and Alimony: 1987*, U.S. Government Printing Office, Washington, D.C., p. 1.
4. Continuing efforts are being made through federal and state legislatures to improve support guidelines and support enforcement. For a discussion of states' response to federal legislation, see, for example, *The New York Times* 4/8/91, p. A8.
5. Diane J. Vogt, "Civil Versus Criminal Contempt," *Creighton Law Review*, vol. 22, 1988, p. 175.
6. Joseph I. Lieberman, *Child Support in America*, New Haven: Yale University Press, 1986, p. 15.
7. Robert L. Gottsfield, "The Child Support Problem: Credible Threat and Use of Incarceration Works," *Arizona Bar Journal*, vol. 19, p. 12.
8. Philip Hager, "Lawyer-Client Sex May Be Banned by State Bar," *Los Angeles Times*, January 21, 1991, p. A3.
9. Lucy Marsh Yee, "What Really Happens in Child Support Award Cases: An Empirical Study of Establishment and Enforcement of Child Support Orders in the Denver District Court," *Denver Law Journal*, vol. 57, no. 1, 1979, pp. 38–42.

1: The Starting Point

1. Robert G. Williams, *Development of Guidelines for Establishing and Updating Child Support Orders: Interim Report,* Institute for Court Management of the National Center for State Courts, U.S. Department of Health And Human Services, Office of Child Support Enforcement, Denver, Colorado, 1985, p. 17.
2. Ibid, p. 17.
3. Using the Consumer Price Index alone to calculate increased costs doesn't take into account the decrease in the value of the dollar. In reality, the increase in the cost of raising a child is greater than that reflected here.

3: Your Child's Expenses

1. Robert L. Gottsfield, "The Child Support Problem: Credible Threat and Use of Incarceration Works," *Arizona Bar Journal,* vol. 19, p. 14.

4: Evaluating Special Needs

1. While the age of majority may be eighteen, in New York and some other states the obligation to support continues until twenty-one. The obligation to support a disabled child beyond the statutory age does not yet exist in New York and most states. This is a developing area of the law.
2. Edward Fishbein, *The Threatened Dream: The Economic Squeeze on California Middle Class,* Report to the California Commission for Economic Development, Office of Lieutenant Governor, Sacramento, California, October 1988, p. 25.
3. Doris Freed and Timothy Walker, "Family Law in the Fifty States," *Family Law Quarterly,* ABA Section of Family Law, Chicago, Illinois, vol. 20, p. 557. *In re Marriage of Plummer,* 703 P.2d 657 (Colorado App. 1985).
4. Ibid., pp. 553–54. *Martin v. Martin,* 487 N.E. 2d 1321 (Indiana App. 1986).
5. Ibid., p. 558. *Jackman v. Jackman,* 696 P. 2d 1191 (Utah 1985).
6. "Family Law in the Fifty States," *Family Law Quarterly,* ABA Section of Family Law, Chicago, Illinois, vol. 20, p. 150. New Hampshire Rev. Stat Ann 458:35-c.

5: Inflation

1. *Monthly Labor Review,* "Consumer Prices in the 1980's" Bureau of Labor Statistics of the U.S. Department of Labor, Washington D.C., August 1990, p. 20.
2. Richard Wurman, Alan Siegel, Kenneth Morris, *The Wall Street Journal*

Guide to Understanding Money & Markets, Access Press Ltd., Siegel & Gale Inc. & Prentice Hall Press, a division of Simon & Schuster Inc., 1989, p. 110.
3. Robert G. Williams, *Development of Guidelines for Establishing and Updating Child Support Orders: Interim Report*, Institute for Court Management of the National Center for State Courts, U.S. Department of Health and Human Services, Office of Child Support Enforcement, Denver, Colorado, 1985, p. 29.
4. Ibid., p. 9.
5. Ibid.
6. Doris Freed and Timothy Walker, "Family Law in the Fifty States," *Family Law Quarterly*, ABA Section of Family Law, Chicago, Illinois, vol. 20, p. 557. *Fossum v. Fossum*, 374 N.W. 2d 132 (South Dakota, 1985).

6: Insurance

1. Arizona Rev. Stat Ann 25–320.
2. "Family Law in the Fifty States," *Family Law Quarterly*, ABA Section of Family Law, Chicago, Illinois, vol. 20, p. 554. *Clements v. Young*, 481 So.2d 263 (Mississippi 1985).
3. U.S. Bureau of the Census, Current Population Reports, Series P-23, no. 167, *Child Support and Alimony: 1987*, U.S. Government Printing Office, Washington, D.C., p. 9.

7: The Education Trust

1. Larry Gordon, "40% Fee Increase Sought for UC," *Los Angeles Times*, February 14, 1991, p. A3.
2. *1987–88 Edition College Costs*, Life Insurance Marketing and Research Association, Inc., Hartford, Connecticut, 1989.
3. Lee A. Daniels, "College Tuition To Be 5% to 9% Higher This Fall, *The New York Times*, August 10, 1989.
4. *1990–91 Edition College Costs*, Life Insurance Marketing and Research Association, Inc., Hartford, Connecticut, 1989, p.i.
5. Prepared by John Hancock Financial Services, a subsidiary of John Hancock Life Insurance Company, Boston, Massachusetts (1991).
6. Savings Account and Certificate of Deposit rates provided by Home Savings of America, Beverly Hills, California; T-bill rates provided by Bear Stearns & Co. Inc., Century City, California; Money Market rate for Dreyfus Corporation provided by Bear Stearns General Money Market Fund, Bear Stearns & Co. Inc., Century City, California.

8: Evaluating Your Spouse

1. Diane J. Vogt, "Civil Versus Criminal Contempt," *Creighton Law Review*, vol. 22, 1988, p. 175.

9: Selecting an Attorney

1. California Supreme Court Order Pursuant to Statutes, September 1987 Business and Professions Code 6155.
2. Pacific Bell, SMART Yellow Pages, Greater Los Angeles, August 1989–90.
3. To obtain a list of members who practice in your area, write to the American Academy of Matrimonial Lawyers, 300 Garden City Plaza, Garden City, New York, 11530.
4. Katherine A. Klos, "The Merit Systems Protection Board's Application of the Community Rate Principle in Its Awards of Reasonable Attorney Fees," *Labor Law Journal*, vol. 39, pp. 81–90.

10: The Attorney-Client Relationship

1. Associated Press, "Clients and Sex Don't Mix, State Bar Panel Warns Attorneys," *Los Angeles Daily Journal*, April 5, 1988, p. 2.
2. "No Sex Please, We're Lawyers," *Capitol Insider, California Lawyer*, vol. 9, pp. 26–27.
3. Philip Hager, "Lawyer-Client Sex May Be Banned by State Bar," *Los Angeles Times*, January 21, 1991, p. A3.
4. The AAML has recently deemed sexual relations between lawyers and clients unethical. However, a New York State Court recently declared that sanctions against an attorney who was having sexual relations with his client were imposed improperly because no law was being broken. There is a lot of activity regarding recommended conduct between clients and lawyers.
5. U.S. Bureau of the Census, Current Population Reports, Series P-23, no. 167, *Child Support and Alimony: 1987*, U.S. Government Printing Office, Washington, D.C., p. 4.

11: Your Day in Court

1. Stipulation to Establish or Modify Child or Family Support Order Form used in superior court of California. Adopted by rule 1285.27 of the Judicial Council of California

15: Visitation

1. If you and your ex-husband have agreed to joint custody of your child, the agreement will set forth when your child is to be with whom.
2. Diane J. Vogt, "Civil Versus Criminal Contempt," *Creighton Law Review*, vol. 22, 1988, p. 183.
3. "Family Law in the Fifty States," *Family Law Quarterly*, ABA Section of Family Law, Chicago, Illinois, vol. 20, p. 555. *Appert v. Appert*, 80 North Carolina App. 27, 341 S.E. 2d 342 (1986).
4. *Biamby v. Biamby*, 114 A.D. 2d 830, 494 N.Y.S. 2d 741 (1985).

16: Contempt Proceedings

1. The Children's Foundation, *An Overview of the Child Support Enforcement Problem 1*, September 1983.
2. *Utah State Department of Social Services v. Toledo*, 699 P. 2d 710 (Utah 1985).
3. California and several other states consider contempt actions as "quasi-criminal," meaning they are similar enough to ordinary criminal proceedings that the respondent receives most of the due process protections allowed criminal defendants. The respondent is only afforded the right to take the Fifth Amendment in a criminal or quasi-criminal action.
4. Robert L. Gottsfield, "The Child Support Problem: Credible Threat and Use of Incarceration Works," *Arizona Bar Journal*, vol. 19, p. 14. *Niemyjski v. Niemyjski*, 98 N.M. 176, 66 P. 2d 1240 (1982).
5. Diane J. Vogt, "Civil Versus Criminal Contempt," *Creighton Law Review*, vol. 22, 1988, p. 174.
6. Joseph I. Lieberman, *Child Support in America*, New Haven: Yale University Press, 1986.
7. Robert L. Gottsfield, "The Child Support Problem: Credible Threat and Use of Incarceration Works," *Arizona Bar Journal*, vol. 19, p. 14.
8. Ibid., pp. 14–15. Judge Gottsfield's references are to David Chambers, law professor and author of *Making Fathers Pay: The Enforcement of Child Support*, University of Chicago Press, Chicago, Illinois, 1979, and Robert H. Mnookin, legal scholar and author of "Review: Using Jail for Child Support Enforcement," 48 U. Chi. L. Rev. 338 (1981), a review of Chambers's book.
9. Ibid., p. 12.

17: Child Support Enforcement Agency

1. U.S. Bureau of the Census, Current Population Reports, Series P-23, no. 167, *Child Support and Alimony: 1987*, U.S. Government Printing Office, Washington, D.C., p. 1.
2. U.S. Department of Health and Human Services, Office of Child Support Enforcement, *A Judge's Guide to Child Support Enforcement*, 1982.
3. Robert L. Gottsfield, "The Child Support Problem: Credible Threat and Use of Incarceration Works," *Arizona Bar Journal*, vol. 19, p. 13–14.
4. H. R. 1720, Public Law 100-485, *One Hundredth Congress of the United States of America*, 1988, p. 1.
5. Slogan used on buses, billboards, and benches by the Los Angeles County district attorney's office, Bureau of Family Support Operation, under District Attorney Ira Reiner, seeking child support enforcement in 1990.
6. 562 Federal Supplement 311. *Carter v. Morrow*, United States District Court, W.D., (North Carolina, April 15, 1983).

7. Discussed in Robert L. Gottsfield, "The Child Support Problem: Credible Threat and Use of Incarceration Works," *Arizona Bar Journal*, vol. 19, p. 19.
8. *McClelland v. Massinga*, 786 Federal 2d 1205, U. S. Court of Appeals, Fourth District, 1986.

18: Parent Locator Service
1. J. Cassety, *The Parent-Child Support Obligation 4*, 1982.

19: Uniform Reciprocal Enforcement of Support Act
1. In some states this document is called a Decree for Dissolution of Marriage.

20: Wage Deduction
1. Diane Dodson, "Wage Withholding Gets Tougher," *Family Advocate*, vol. 8, no. 1.
2. Child Support Enforcement Amendments of 1984 (CSEA). Public Law 98-378. 50 Fed. Reg. 19,608 et. seq. 19,658 (May 9, 1985).
3. "Family Law in the Fifty States," *Family Law Quarterly*, ABA Section of Family Law, Chicago, Illinois, vol. 20, pp. 561–62.
4. Ibid., pp. 560–62.
5. Ibid., p. 552.
6. New Hampshire Rev. State. Ann. 458:35-c. The only defense is mistake of fact.

21: Alternative Collection Devices
1. *Homestead Exemptions, What You Need to Know*, Los Angeles, California, Department of Consumer Affairs, 1988.
2. *Connin v. Bailey*, 472 N.E. 2d 328 (Ohio 1984).
3. *Smith v. Smith*, 168 Ohio St. 456–57, 156 N.E. 2d 113 (1959).
4. *Jasper v. Carter*, D.C. App., 451 A2d 46 (1982).

22: Bankruptcy and Support Enforcement
1. Public Law 97-35, Section 2334.
2. John Replogle, *Bankruptcy and Support Enforcement, How to Make Sure It Stays Owed to the Kids*, U.S. Department of Health and Human Services, Office of Child Support Enforcement, Revised May 1986, p. 1.
3. Ibid., p. 5.
4. Ibid., p. 10.

23: Modification
1. *Ewing v. May*, 705 S.W.2d 910 (Kentucky 1986).
2. *Noddin v. Noddin*, 455 A.2d 1051 (New Hampshire 1983).

3. *In re Marriage of Vetternack*, 334 N.W.2d 761 (Iowa 1983).
4. "Family Law in the Fifty States," *Family Law Quarterly*, ABA Section of Family Law, Chicago, Illinois, vol. 20, p. 559. *Gerber v. Gerber*, 476 N.E.2d 30 (Indiana App. 1986).
5. Ibid., p. 558. *In re Marriage of Steele*, 714 P.2d 497 (Colorado App. 1985).
6. Ibid., p. 559. *Halum v. Halum*, 492 N.E.2d 30 (Indiana App. 1986).

INDEX

affidavits (declarations), 134–35
agency bonds, 74
Agriculture Department, U.S. (USDA), 62
Aid to Families with Dependent Children (AFDC), 22, 37, 44, 104, 154, 159, 163, 178
alimony, taxes on, 100–101
American Academy of Matrimonial Lawyers (AAML), 86
amnesty programs, 155
Appendix A Information Sheet, 60
Appert v. Appert, 127
Application for Order and Supporting Declaration, 224, 240–41
Arizona Bar Journal, 17
arrearage, 115, 156
    collection of, 166, 173–74
    laches and, 175–76
    modification and, 193
    repayment of, 138–39
assets, financial, *see* financial assets
attorney-client relationship, 21–22, 93–106
    chemistry of, 92
    communication in, 95, 106
    documentation of, 102
    emotional support and, 93–94
    phone calls as element of, 94–95

    professional nature of, 21–22, 93, 95
    sexual relations in, 95–97
    time demands in, 93–94
"Attorney Guide," 85
attorneys:
    assets discussed with, 98
    avoiding stand-ins for, 91–92
    bankruptcy problems and, 177, 178, 179
    collection, 172–73
    confidence in, 92
    evaluation of, 86, 89–91
    fees of, 88–90, 101–2, 140, 147–148, 171
    first business conference with, 37, 97–98
    living expenses discussed with, 98
    necessity of, 34, 177, 178, 179
    negotiation skills sought in, 91
    prioritizing issues with, 98–99
    replacement of, 83
    spouse's financial responsibility discussed with, 78
attorney selection, 21, 83–92
    cost factors in, 87–89
    courtroom observation in, 86
    family law background sought in, 83, 86
    initial meeting in, 90–92
    negotiation skills sought in, 91

275

INDEX

attorney selection (*cont.*)
  questions to ask in, 84, 85, 90–91
  referral sources used in, 84–86
automatic support increases, 63
automobiles as asset, 35

bankruptcy forms, 181–87
  Complaint to Determine Dischargeability of a Debt, 179, 184–85
  Motion for Relief from Automatic Stay, 178, 179, 181–183
  Stipulation for Entry of Judgment of Nondischargeability, 179, 186–87
bankruptcy of spouse, 23, 177–87
  child support obligations in, 177, 178–79
  custodial parent as creditor in, 179
  existing support orders and, 178
  legal counsel needed in, 177, 178, 179
  modification of child support and, 179
  non-dischargeable debts in, 177–79
  state and federal claims in, 178
  state vs. federal courts and, 179
  support enforcement and, 23, 177–80
  wage collection and, 179
bank statements, 35
bank trust accounts, 74
Biamby v. Biamby, 127–28
birth records, 201
brokerage firms, 36
Brouder, Kathleen, 71
Bureau of Labor Statistics, 61–62
Bureau of National Affairs, 170

California All Consumer Price Index, 60

California Commission for Economic Development, 53
California family law forms, 224–43
California Lawyer, 96
California State Bar, Board of Legal Specialization of, 86
Carter, Jimmy, 170
Carter v. Morrow, 156
case numbers, 108
Census Bureau, U.S., 18, 19, 53, 65
certificates of deposit (CDs), 73, 75
children, 128–29
  expenses of, 14, 20–21, 29, 40–48, 59–63, 61–63, 118
child support:
  child's age and, 60–63, 61, 62
  confrontations over, 123–24
  control of custodial parent through, 124
  cost of living index and, 60, 63
  creditor obligation and, 146
  determination of, 14
  direct court payment of, 80, 103–4
  emotional attachment in, 124
  enforcement of, *see* enforcement
  failure to pay, *see* noncompliance
  federal employees and, 23, 170–71
  federal government mandates and, 17
  financial inventory for, 31–36
  inflation and, 59–63
  insurance needs and, 64–69
  intimidation and, 22, 122–23
  laches and, 175–76
  majority and, 52–53
  manner of payment and, 78–80, 103–4
  modification of, 23, 191–97
  need for institutional changes in, 15

rationalizations for nonpayment of, 22, 121–22, 198
responsibility of custodial parent for, 17, 19, 106
schedule for, 116–17
spouse's ability to pay and, 30, 103, 137
state formulas for, 31, 154
studies and reports on, 222–23
taxes on, 100–101
visitation and, 79, 126, 127–28
voluntary wage assignment and, 78–79, 104
welfare and, 153–54
child support advocacy groups:
  list of, 203–10
  as referral sources, 84
child support enforcement agencies, 22, 152–58
  attorneys compared with, 152, 157–58
  civil vs. criminal trials and, 152
  first hearing and, 157
  free services of, 157
  jurisdiction of, 155
  legislation and, 153–54
  remedies and, 157
  tax refund interception and, 158
  time factor and, 156, 158
  wage garnishment and, 157
  working with, 156–59
Child Support Enforcement Program, 154, 155
Child Support in America (Lieberman), 19, 146
"Child Support Problem" (Gottsfield), 17, 148–49
"Civil Versus Criminal Contempt" (Vogt), 127
Clements v. Young, 65
collection action, 135, 150–51, 176
collection attorneys:
  arrearage and, 173
  basis of fees for, 172–73
  domestic relations attorneys compared with, 172
collection devices, 23, 172–76

College Board, tuition survey by, 69–71
college education:
  child support provisions for, 52–54
  tuition costs of, 69–71
college savings, 69–75
  basic issues in, 71
  investment options for, 72–75
  professional advice for, 73, 75
College Scholarship Services (CSS), 71
Colorado, University of, 69, 70
community support groups, 84
confrontation, avoidance of, 123–24
Connin v. Bailey, 174
Consumer Price Index Percentage Chart, 29, 59
contempt, 136–39
  inability to pay and, 137–38
  incarceration for, 148–49, 150
  prerequisites for proof of, 136
  previous citations for, 138, 141
  sentencing procedures for, 138
contempt proceedings, 22, 133–51, 172
  burden of proof in, 137, 145–46
  child support payments schedule and, 135
  continuance in, 142–44
  custodial parent's court presence for, 136
  declaration for, 134–35
  delay tactics in, 142, 147
  depositions in, 144–45
  effective handling of, 149–50
  example of, 134
  filing of, 135
  financial responsibility for, 140
  format of, 133
  gathering information for, 144, 145, 146
  hiring attorney for, 139
  information needed for, 134
  interrogatories and, 144
  last minute support payments and, 141

contempt proceedings (*cont.*)
  without legal counsel, 149
  leniency of courts and, 150
  minute orders and, 136–37
  negotiations in, 143–44
  Orders to Show Cause and, 134, 224, 237
  previous contempt citations and, 138, 141
  recording of arrearage in, 136
  recovering legal fees for, 140, 147–48
  refiling of, 141, 151
  repayment of arrearage and, 138–39
  serving of papers for, 135–36
  spouse's appearance in, 141–42
  subpoenas and, 144
  time limit for, 135, 150–51
  "trailing" and, 146–47
  wage garnishment and, 165
continuances, 142–44
corporate records, 35, 195
Costs of Children (Olson), 29
county recorder's office, 34, 194
court appearances, 107–13
  calendar calls and, 110
  case numbers for, 108
  communication with attorney in, 110–11
  continuances and, 142–44
  conversation with opposing counsel in, 109–10
  dressing for, 109
  final support orders and, 108, 113
  financial declarations and, 111
  late arrival of attorney for, 110
  orders for child support and, 108
  preparing for, 22, 107–13
  procedures at, 87, 107–8
  Stipulation to Establish Child Support and, 111–13, 224, 234
  temporary support orders and, 109, 113

Creighton Law Review, 137
CSS (College Scholarship Services), 71

Dearborn, Earl J., 193
debtor's examination, 170, 173, 174
declarations, contempt, 134–35
declarations, financial, *see* financial declarations
defendant (respondent), 108
Delaware Child Support Calculation, 154, 244, 245–52
depositions, legal, 88–89, 144–45
"Development of Guidelines for Establishing and Updating Child Support Orders" (Williams), 63
diaries, 22, 114–18, 161
  arrearage and, 115, 136–37
  child's expenses and, 118
  contempt hearings and, 136–37
  court orders and, 116
  enforcement proceedings and, 115
  modification of court order and, 115
  spouse's financial information and, 117–18
  structuring of, 117
  support payments and, 114–15, 116–17
divorce:
  economic effects of, 13, 14, 18
  emotional stress of, 13, 27–28
  obtaining records of, 202
  statistics on, 13, 153

education, *see* college education; college savings
endowment policies, 72
enforcement:
  child support enforcement agencies and, 115, 133
  contempt proceedings and, 133–51
  documents for, 115
  fees for, 105

improvement of, 19, 199
methods of, 115
options available for, 105
retaining an attorney for, 115, 133
self-initiated action for, 115
Espenshade, Thomas J., 29, 62
Ewing v. May, 191–92
Ex Parte Application for Wage Assignment for Child Support, 224, 242–43
expenses, *see* children, expenses of; monthly expenses

family law forms, California, 224–43
Family Law Quarterly, The, 54
Family Law Reporter, 170
Family Support Act (1988), 154
Fannie Maes, 74
Federal Child Support Enforcement Act (1975), 159, 163
Federal Deposit Insurance Corporation (FDIC), 74
federal employees, 23, 170–71
federal government mandates, 17
Federal Savings and Loan Insurance Corporation (FSLIC), 74
final support order, 108, 113
financial assets, 30–36
  attorney's review of, 98
  communal vs. individual, 30, 34
  inventory of, 20, 31–36
  other than salary, 34–35, 192–94
  recording of, 31–32, 77, 97
  undervaluing or omitting of, 30
financial declarations, 37–49
  deductions and, 40
  defense of, 111
  gross monthly income and, 37–40
  modified, 111
  monthly expenses and, 41–49
  spouse's circumstances and, 111
  see also Income and Expense Declaration
financial instruments, comparative yields of, 75

financial responsibility, 76–78, 106
Ford, Gerald, 153
Foretich, Eric, 127
forms and records:
  birth, 201
  court, 201
  divorce, 202
  local variations of, 23
  marriage records, 202
Fossum v. Fossum, 63
Freddie Macs, 74
FSLIC (Federal Savings and Loan Insurance Corporation), 74

Gerber v. Gerber, 194
Ginny Maes, 74
Gottsfield, Robert L., 17, 19, 148, 150, 153
Guaranteed Student Loans, 53

Halum v. Halum, 196–97
Harvard University, 69, 70
Health, Education, and Welfare Department, U.S., 159
Health and Human Services Department, U.S., 153, 154, 155
health care, 50–51
Henderson, Faye, 127

income, outside sources of, 36
Income and Expense Declaration, 224, 229–32
income deduction, *see* wage assignment
income tax returns, 32, 33, 158, 195–96
inflation, 59–63
  children and, 59–63
  impact of, 21, 59–60
  payment modification and, 60, 63
In re Marriage of Plummer, 54
insurance, *see* life insurance; medical insurance
Internal Revenue Service (IRS), 101, 192
interrogatories, 144

intimidation:
    confrontation and, 123
    non-payment of child support and, 22, 122–23
    types of, 122–23
inventory, financial, 20, 31–36
    advantages of, 32–33
    items in, 31–32
    preparation of, 31–36
Investing in Children (Espenshade), 29
IV-D agency, 158

Jackman v. Jackman, 57
Jasper v. Carter, 175
John Hancock Flexible Life Insurance, 72
Johns Hopkins University, 69, 70

laches, 175–76
Legal Aid Society, 86
legal costs, 88–90
    depositions and, 88–89, 145
legal fees, 87–90
    attorney selection and, 88
    consultation and, 90
    hourly, 89
    obtaining estimate of, 89
    recovery of, 89–90, 101–2, 140, 147–48, 171
    responsibility for, 89–90
    retainers and, 101
    set, 87–88
    for simple divorce, 88
legal preparation, importance of, 19–20, 115, 118, 145, 146, 161, 194
Lieberman, Joseph I., 19, 146
life insurance, 65, 67–68
    accidental death and, 67–68
    children as beneficiaries of, 66–67
    as guarantee of child support payments, 65
    as investment, 72–73
    natural death and, 67–68
    sample rates for, 67
    spouse's inability to accommodate, 67
Life Insurance Marketing and Research Association, 69
Lincoln Savings and Loan, 74
Los Angeles County amnesty program, 155
Los Angeles Daily Journal, 96
Los Angeles Times, 96

majority, age of, 52–53
marriage records, 202
Martin v. Martin, 54
medical expenses, "reasonableness" of, 65
medical insurance, 21, 103
    billing procedures for, 64
    lack of provisions for, 65, 66
    state requirements for, 64–65
Mentell, Carol, 155
Minimum Child Support Worksheet, 44, 224, 233
minute orders, 136–37
Mnookin, Robert H., 148
modification, child support, 23, 191–97
    arrearage and, 193
    assets vs. loss of income and, 192, 193
    California Appendix A Information Sheet and, 60
    change in financial circumstances and, 191, 192, 193, 196
    confirmation of spouse's financial declaration and, 192
    definition of earnings for, 192
    downward, 191–92, 193, 196
    fairness as basis of, 192, 197
    inadequate support order and, 192
    increased child's needs and, 192
    increased payment ability of spouse and, 192
    parental right to, 191, 196
    prior agreements and, 196–97
    real property and, 192–94
    research for, 194–96

upward, 57–60, 192
voluntary unemployment and, 194
money market accounts, 75
monthly expenses, 41–49
  automobile, 47–48
  child care, 46
  clothing, 45–46
  education, 46–47
  entertainment, 47
  financial declaration form for, 41–42
  food and household supplies, 44
  incidentals, 48
  installment payments, 48
  insurance, 46
  laundry and cleaning, 45
  maintenance, 43–44
  medical and dental, 46
  mortgage payments, 40–41
  other, 48
  prior marriages and, 46
  property insurance, 43
  property taxes, 43
  rent, 40
  telephone, 45
  transportation, 47
  utilities, 45
Morgan, Elizabeth, 127
municipal bonds, 74

New York Times, 69
Niemyjski v. Niemyjski, 137
Noddin v. Noddin, 192–93
noncompliance:
  contempt proceedings and, 133
  inability to pay and, 137
  intimidation and, 22, 122–23
  legislation and, 153–54
  planning for, 79, 104–5
  rationalization of, 22, 121–22
  spouse's income level and, 18, 137–38
  statistical frequency of, 17–18, 79, 104, 133, 152, 153, 156–157

visitation and, 79, 126, 127–28
welfare and, 154
Northwestern University, 54
Notice of Motion, 224, 235–36
Notice of Request to Change Support Order, 224, 238–39

Office of Personal Management, U.S., 170, 171
Olson, Lawrence, 29, 62
Order to Show Cause, 134, 224, 237

Parent Locator Service, 23, 159
Pennsylvania, University of, 69, 70
Petition for Disolution of Marriage, 224, 225–27
phantom tax, 73
plaintiff (petitioner), 108
PLS (Parent Locator Service), 23, 159
post-hearing evaluations, 22, 119–20
preparation, legal, 19–20, 115, 118, 145, 146, 161, 194
property, 35, 192
  arrearage collection and, 174
  communally owned, 34
  modification and, 192–94
  solely owned, 34
public records, obtaining copies of, 34–35

rationalization:
  examples of, 121–22
  nonpayment of child support and, 22, 121–22, 198
"reasonableness," in court orders, 65
Registry of Foreign Support Orders, 163
Replogle, John, 178, 179, 183, 185, 186
respondent (defendant), 108
Response, 224, 228
Rowan, Roger, 166
Roybal-Allard, Lucille, 97

savings accounts, 74–75
self-esteem, 198–99
  enforcing support orders and, 198–99
  rationalizing neglect and, 198
  responsibility and, 199
settlement agreements, 98
  specificity of, 99–100
Smith v. Smith, 175
Social Security, 37
Social Security Act (1935), 17, 153, 154, 156, 177–78
Social Security numbers, 35
special needs, 21
  child's majority and, 53, 57
  determination of, 52, 53
  education, 51–54
  extended support for, 52–54, 57–58
  health care, 50, 57
  medical incapacity and, 53, 57
  modification for, 55, 56–57
  prioritizing of, 54–55
spouse, evaluation of, 21, 76–80, 106
state bar associations, 85
state child enforcement offices, 211–21
state laws, variations in, 24
state supported groups, 203–10
Stipulation to Establish Child Support, 111–13
Stipulation to Establish or Modify Child or Family Support and Order, 112, 224, 234
Stipulation to Modify Child or Family Support Order, 111–13
"Student Loans: Are They Overburdening a Generation?," 53
subpoenas, 144
support agreements:
  enforcement of, *see* enforcement
  making provisions for, 100
  spouse's failure to comply with, 104–5
  structuring of, 100

support orders:
  final, 108, 113
  temporary, 109, 113

taxes:
  child support and, 100–101
  dependent children and, 101
  intercepting refunds of, 159
tax returns, 32, 33, 158, 195–96
tax rolls, 35, 194
T-bills, 75
T-bonds, 74
temporary support order (TSO), 109, 113
T-notes, 74
"trailing," 146–47
Tulane University, 69, 70

Uniform Commercial Code, modification research and, 195
Uniform Reciprocal Enforcement of Support Act (URESA), 23, 160
URESA petitions, 160–64
  criminal enforcement procedures and, 163–64
  expense of, 162
  extradition and, 164
  filing support orders and, 163
  jurisdiction and, 162
  out-of-state hearings and, 160, 163
  procedural guidelines of, 161
  time factor and, 162–63
  visitation rights and, 161–62
Utah State Department of Social Services v. Toledo, 136

visitation, 22, 125–29
  child's right to, 126
  custodial parent's responsibility for, 126
  noncompliance and, 79, 126, 127–28
  noncustodial parent's environment and, 128
  noncustodial parent's right to, 126–27, 129

safety of child and, 127–28
scheduling of, 125
structuring of, 126
supervision vs. denial of, 128
withholding of, 126–28, 129
Vogt, Diane J., 127, 137
voluntary wage assignment, 78–79, 104

wage assignment, 78–79, 80
   independent contractors and, 169–70
   original support order and, 169
   procedure for, 169–70
   recoverability of fees and, 171
   state variations in, 166–68, 169
   voluntary, 78–79, 104
   wage garnishment compared with, 165–66
wage deduction, 23
   cost of, 165, 171
   without court hearing, 165
   see also wage assignment; wage garnishment
wage garnishment, 165, 173
   arrearage collection and, 166
   contempt hearings and, 165
   enforcement agencies and, 157
   federal employees and, 23, 170–71
   independent contractors and, 169
   wage assignment compared with, 165–66
Wall Street Journal Guide to Understanding Money & Markets, 59
Weitzman, Lenore, 13, 15
Williams, Robert G., 63
Wisconsin Child Support Formula, 154, 244, 253
writs of attachment, 157

zero-coupon bonds, 73

About the Author

UPON GRADUATING from Friends School in her hometown of Wilmington, Delaware, Carole Chambers attended the Fontainebleau Conservatory in France. After studying music and drama in New York, she married and raised five children while working in the film industry on the West Coast. She is the coauthor of the software program, Letterform1000™, and currently lives in picturesque Laurel Canyon in Los Angeles.